THE FAMILY WELCOME ACCOMMODATION GUIDE 1992

Jill Foster was a professional actress until her retirement at the age of 17. She has been a literary agent for over 20 years and has run her own agency for most of that time. In 1970 she married Malcolm Hamer and they have a daughter, Polly.

Malcolm Hamer was educated at Shrewsbury School and Trinity College, Cambridge. He worked in marketing for various multi-national companies and then formed his own agency to represent sportsmen and television journalists. He is now a full-time writer and his second novel has just been published.

THE FAMILY WELCOME ACCOMMODATION GUIDE 1992

JILL FOSTER & MALCOLM HAMER

Macdonald
Queen Anne Press

A QUEEN ANNE PRESS BOOK

© Hamer Books Ltd 1992

First published in Great Britain in 1992 by
Queen Anne Press, a division of
Macdonald & Co (Publishers) Ltd
165 Great Dover Street
London SE1 4YA

Cover illustration by Andrew Bylo

All rights reserved. No part of this publication may be reproduced, stored in a retrieval system, or transmitted, in any form or by any means, without the prior permission in writing of the publisher, nor be otherwise circulated in any form of binding or cover other than that in which it is published and without a similar condition including this condition being imposed on the subsequent purchaser.

A CIP catalogue record for this book
is available from the British Library

ISBN 0-356-20284-4

Typeset by Tradespools Limited, Frome, Somerset
Printed and bound in Great Britain by BPCC Hazell   Ltd,
Aylesbury, Bucks (Member of BPCC Ltd)

Our special thanks to our Northern editor, Tony Halstead, and his wife, Heather; and also to June Bamford, Cyril and Rita Carter, Jean Howat, Ann Pollard, Carol Quinn, Jenny Parkhouse, Valerie Rahtz, Julia Shuff, and Veronica and John Smart for all their help.

Our thanks also to our very efficient typist, Adrienne Fell of Lynn Associates.

And our love to Polly.

CONTENTS

INTRODUCTION	ix
GUIDE, A–Z	1
MAPS	255
READERS' COMMENTS FORMS	267

INTRODUCTION

In this edition of the Family Welcome Accommodation Guide you will find around 250 establishments. A significant change is that about a quarter of these are self-catering complexes. We have noticed the rapid growth in the availability of self-catering holidays in Britain and the excellence, even sophistication, of the amenities provided. We believe that self-catering holidays offer the flexibility and freedom which families on holiday relish, and self-catering is often cheaper for a holiday than staying in a hotel.

The self-catering establishments which we have included are usually the larger ones, with several cottages or apartments for hire. This gives families more choice of accommodation; and these larger complexes often have the extra facilities which families need: large gardens, play areas, swimming pools, barbecues, tennis or badminton courts, even, in one case, a golf driving range and nine-hole golf course.

As in previous years we have been appalled at the prices demanded by hotels, especially the larger ones, for an often sub-standard room. Many of them have been excluded on these grounds alone. We recognise that many of the 'chain' hotels are solely concerned with business travellers and, to some extent, foreign tourists. And, my goodness, how they fleece them.

We are still able to recommend an eclectic choice of farmhouses, guest houses, hotels both large and small, pubs and restaurants with rooms and country houses where you stay as a paying guest of the owners. As before they must be able to provide a cot, a high chair and an evening meal. The great majority of them also offer a free baby listening service.

In the case of smaller establishments, such as farmhouses, the baby listening is informal: everyone can hear if a baby is crying. You may also find, at these smaller places, that a member of the family will "baby listen" for you if you want to go out for a drink.

What all these different places have in common is that they offer a real welcome to families and make them feel relaxed and "at home". There is no place in the Guide for establishments which merely pay lip-service to the needs of families.

THE ENTRIES

We have stuck to basic simple information, given in the following order and avoiding confusing codes or symbols:

- Name of the town or village and its county or region.
- Name of the establishment.
- Directions.
- Description: we try to give you an impression of what the place is like

INTRODUCTION

and why we have included it – because it's on or near a main tourist route; in an area of exceptional beauty; or has exceptional facilities.

• Nearby: this section is designed to tell you about the various amenities and attractions within a reasonable distance of the hotel. We mention beaches and other water sports facilities, golf courses, leisure centres, fishing facilities, stately homes, museums, theme parks, country parks and zoos and wildlife parks. Lots more information on this topic is contained in the Family Welcome Leisure Guide.

HOTELS

• Food: we give you the serving times, and an idea of the price range and (if possible) type of food on offer. For restaurant meals (as opposed to bar snacks) we quote the price of a three-course meal and an extract from a typical menu. Since prices are hard to forecast we have quoted to the nearest £, and have rounded figures upward. We tell you whether special menus, high teas, etc are available for children.

• Price of rooms: we've given two sets of information; first we've taken the lowest price for bed and breakfast for two people for one night and graded it thus:

£ **low** = up to £40
£ **medium** = from £41 to £60
£ **high** = over £60

• Best Bargain Break: every hotel offers bargain breaks, especially at weekends, and we have given these prices when they are available. There are great advantages in hunting these breaks out, since they really are bargains, especially out of season.

• Children: we give you the terms for children and these are always on the basis that a child is sharing a room with its parents.

• Facilities: we tell you how many cots and high chairs are available, and to what extent a baby listening service is offered.

• Number of rooms: we give the total number of rooms in hotels, and the number of family rooms (i.e. which can sleep at least three people). We also mention suites, and interconnecting rooms. Apart from these, most hotels have other rooms which will take cots and/or extra beds.

• Credit Cards: we have listed the four major cards: Access, American Express, Diners Club and Visa.

• Ale means real ale and we name the brands available.

• Parking: very important to know what is available especially with children, luggage, pots and pushchairs in tow.

• Music: we tell you which places do not inflict music on their customers. We are amazed at how the music industry has conned hoteliers, publicans and restaurant owners into installing expensive sound systems which hardly anyone wants. It seems to us that the music is often played solely for the benefit of the staff.

INTRODUCTION

SELF-CATERING

These are marked SC in the text and ▲ on the maps. When an establishment is marked H/SC in the text it designates a hotel which also has some self-catering properties to offer. The basic information differs from that given for hotels and is as follows:

- Units: we tell you how many houses, cottages or apartments make up the complex.
- Rent: we quote the lowest and highest rent charged per week, and mention short breaks if they are available.
- Other Costs: some places include everything in the rental charges, but others charge extra for linen or electricity. You should always study the establishment's own brochure before you book a holiday.
- Heating: how are the homes heated.
- Cots & High Chairs: how many are available.

Most of the self-catering places are open all year and offer short breaks during the winter. These are often extremely good value, especially for families.

We thank all those people who wrote in to us with recommendations and with comments about places already in the Guide. These are invaluable; and we take your comments very seriously. Many establishments have been excluded, and many added as a result. Please keep writing to us (the forms are at the back of the Guide) and we are particularly interested in your recommendations of self-catering places.

A–Z Guide

Aberdovey, Gwynedd map 5

ABERDOVEY HILLSIDE VILLAGE – ☎ *Aberdovey (0654) 767 522.*

SC *Close to the centre of Aberdovey.*

The village is spread over thirty acres of hillside above the charming resort of Aberdovey, and faces south to the beach and the sea. The three houses, three bungalows and twelve apartments have been designed in a most attractive way and they all have those wonderful panoramic views of the estuary and the harbour with its array of boats. Every house and apartment has a balcony or a terrace so that you can sit and enjoy the views.

The properties are smartly maintained, with comfortable furniture, agreeable decoration and excellent carpeting. The kitchens are well-equipped and include microwave ovens as well as conventional cookers. Most of the properties can accommodate either eight or six people, while four of them can sleep four people. Many of them have an extra bed settee.

The village has a central lounge and sun terrace and a good selection of books, board games and puzzles is laid on. The beautifully kept grounds contain picnic and barbecue areas; and there is a games room with table tennis, and a play area; and the huge sandy beach lies only a few hundred yards away with the Snowdonia National Park behind the village.

On a practical note there is a well-equipped launderette in the village.

Nearby: Aberdovey is a delightful resort which has managed to retain its charm. It has its own beach and many other delightful ones nearby. All sorts of water sports can be arranged including fishing, sailing, sailboarding and water skiing. The resort has a wonderful golf course, too. Railway buffs can take a trip on the Talyllyn or the Vale of Rheidol railways. The whole of the Snowdonia National Park is there to be explored, and the Centre for Alternative Technology is a fascinating place to visit.

Units: 18
Rent: £180 to £550 a week; winter breaks also available
Other costs: electricity on meters
Heating: central or night storage
Plenty of cots and high chairs
Open all year

ABERDOVEY

BODFOR HOTEL – ☎ *Aberdovey (0654) 767 475.*

On the sea front.

This tall, double-fronted hotel has a lovely position overlooking the sea front of this attractive and relatively unspoilt seaside resort. The owners have undertaken an exhaustive refurbishment programme, which is now complete. Most of the bedrooms have their own bathrooms and there are three family rooms.

The hotel offers excellent accommodation for families at a reasonable price – a very good reason for recommending it.

Nearby: Like the other hotels which we recommend in Aberdovey, the Bodfor can secure concessionary rates for its guests at the golf course. Several water sports can be done from the beach including wind surfing and sailing, and there are sandy beaches all along this coast. Railway buffs should be in their element with the Talyllyn, Fairbourne and Vale of Rheidol all within easy reach. The Coed-y-Brenin Forest has several waymarked trails to walk, and you can visit the Llanfair Slate Caverns, and the Maes Artro Tourist Village. Portmeirion is a little further north.

✗ DINNER (7–9pm) £14: avocado & orange salad, roast loin of pork, pudding
Children: own menu, half portions
£ medium
Best Bargain Break £59 per person, 2 nights – dinner, b & b
Children: £9 when sharing with 2 adults
Facilities: 3 cots and 2 high chairs; baby listening to every room
16 rooms, 3 family   Open all year
P – street & car park opposite   Access/Visa

HARBOUR HOTEL – ☎ *Aberdovey (0654) 767 250.*

On the sea front.

Here is a hotel which makes a special effort to make all members of the family feel at home. It is a charming Victorian property which has been restored in a stylish and comfortable way. Amongst the twelve rooms are four smart and comfortable family suites, which comprise two separate bedrooms and a bathroom. These are quiet, since they are at the back of the hotel.

Their family restaurant, Rumbles, is open all day from mid-morning and offers a good range of food including vegetarian dishes at reasonable prices. The hotel dining room is reserved for the adults in the evenings, and the basement wine bar offers an excellent choice of food, wines and beers.

Nearby: There are five miles of sand on the doorstep, and a public play area a hundred yards away. There are many other excellent beaches nearby, and that

ABERDOVEY

lovely golf course just up the road, with concessionary rates for guests. There are many attractions within reach including the Centre for Alternative Technology, the Coed-y-Brenin Forest, the Llanfair Slate Caverns, the Maes Artro Tourist Village, steam railways at Talyllyn, Fairbourne and the Vale of Rheidol, and Portmeirion to the north.

RUMBLES (11am–10pm) £2–8: plaice & chips, seafood platter, spicy vegetable chilli, lamb cutlets, steak;
DINNER (from 7pm) £14: oriental prawns, Purbeck pork, pudding or cheese
Children: own menu, half portions
£ medium
Best Bargain Break 10% discount for 3 or more nights
Children: £5 under 3 years; £12.50 from 4 to 9; £17.50 from 10 to 15
Facilities: 4 cots and 3 high chairs; a baby listening system to all rooms
12 rooms, 4 family   Open all year
P – public car park opposite hotel   Access/AmEx/Diners/Visa

ABERDOVEY

TREFEDDIAN HOTEL – ☏ *Aberdovey (0654) 767 213.*

H/SC   *On the A493 west of the village.*

This appealing hotel has an enviable position just outside Aberdovey and it overlooks the lovely Aberdovey golf course, a great favourite of Bernard Darwin, who wrote: "about this one course in the world I am a hopeless and shameful sentimentalist and I glory in my shame." The hotel naturally offers its guests concessionary rates there. Beyond the links you can see the sandy sweep of Cardigan Bay.

Apart from the golf, a vast expanse of beach, and the sea, there is plenty more at the hotel: a large and well-designed indoor heated pool with a separate paddling pool for children (the area is surveyed by closed circuit television); an all-weather tennis court; table tennis and pool in the games room; and a snooker table. The hotel also has its own speed boat, and water skiing can be arranged.

There is a play area for children up above the hotel and alongside the tennis court. It has a large wooden climbing frame and a safe surface underfoot.

There is a stretch of garden in front of the hotel, and a putting green. It's a lovely place to sit on a summer's day and look across the links below to the vast expanse of sea.

It is an excellent hotel in a very pleasant seaside resort.

Nearby: There are long stretches of beach on which to laze, and a wide choice of watersports: sailing and canoeing, wind surfing and water skiing. Railway enthusiasts have plenty to see: the Vale of Rheidol, Fairbourne and Talyllyn railways. Castle Nant Eos is worth a look, as is the Corris Craft Centre. Pony trekking can be done in the vicinity, and river, sea and lake fishing are available.

LUNCH (12.45–1.45pm) £8: hors d'oeuvres or soup, cold buffet or a hot dish of the day, pudding or cheese;
DINNER (7.15–8.45pm) £15: tuna mousse, cannelloni Mornay, roast leg of lamb, pudding and cheese
Children: high teas, half portions
£ medium
Best Bargain Break £78 per person, 2 nights – dinner, b & b
Children – cots £9; extra bed £21 (includes breakfast and high tea or dinner)
Facilities: 6 cots and 6 high chairs, and baby listening
46 rooms, 4 family, 3 sets interconnecting
Closed January to mid March   Access/Visa
No smoking in dining room   No music
P – own car park

SELF-CATERING

The hotel has a house which overlooks the golf course and the dunes.

With four bedrooms (including bunk beds for children) it can sleep up to ten people and the price includes linen, heating and electricity. The bungalow, which is also in the hotel grounds, has three bedrooms and can sleep up to seven people. The hotel also has a flat in Aberdovey itself and it sleeps up to four people. All the hotel facilities can be used and the rents are between £240 and £500 per week.

Abergavenny, Gwent   map 2

LLANWENARTH ARMS HOTEL – ☎ Abergavenny (0873) 810 550.

On the A40 towards Brecon.

The hotel is more or less halfway between Abergavenny and Crickhowell, and sits in a splendid position above the River Usk. It is a large roadside inn and hotel which has its origins in the 16th century but has been substantially altered and extended in the last two decades.

This is a hotel which has excellent facilities for families, who will find a spacious restaurant alongside the bar, and there are several high chairs available. Down a few stairs there is a sizeable conservatory where they are also welcome to settle. It is appropriately furnished with cane furniture and from here you have a lovely view of the river below – down a steep bank which is crowded

ABERGAVENNY

with bushes and small trees. On warmer days you can sit on the paved terrace which has the same views of the Usk Valley. The hotel has two stretches of salmon and trout fishing which are available to guests.

Nearby: This is a lovely part of Wales and you could do no better for scenery than to follow the Usk south. There are a great number of castles to see. The ruined one at Abergavenny has a museum on site; Tretower Castle; Raglan; and the three castles of Gwent which form a triangle – Grosmont, Skenfrith and the White Castle. The area is a splendid one for walkers, golfers, fishermen and horse riders, and plenty of other sports are available.

BAR SNACKS (12–2pm & 6–10pm) £3–13: vegetable curry, fillet steak, Tandoori chicken, salmon & prawn bake, medallions of venison;
DINNER (6–10pm) £18: French onion soup, rack of Welsh lamb, pudding or cheese
Children: own menu
£ medium
Best Bargain Break £50 per person, 2 nights – b & b
Children: half price
Facilities: 2 cots and 4 high chairs; no baby listening
18 rooms   Open all year
Access/AmEx/Diners/Visa   • Ale – Bass, Wadworth's
P – own car park

Also recommended in the Family Welcome Pub & Restaurant Guide.

WERNDDU FARM COTTAGES – ☎ *Abergavenny (0873) 5289.*

SC   *Off the B4521 east of Abergavenny.*

If you crave some peace and quiet, head for Wernddu, situated in the rolling countryside just outside the fine old town of Abergavenny. There has been a building on the site of Wernddu since the 12th century but the present farmhouse was mainly built during the 17th and 18th centuries.

Opposite the house several farm buildings have been converted to make six stone cottages and form an open square around a gravelled courtyard. The cottages provide a range of accommodation: Bramble Cottage has one bedroom, Beech Cottage has three and the rest have two bedrooms and would suit up to four people.

We looked in detail at one of them, Fern Cottage, which has a spacious and comfortably furnished living room, with a door to a little patio and a small enclosed garden. Beyond, there is farmland and then the hills. There is a spacious and well-equipped kitchen and a twin-bedded room on the same floor. Up above is a pleasant double bedroom.

Enthusiastic golfers will also find this to be a real haven since the owners have constructed a good-sized driving range on their land and by now a nine hole golf course should also have been opened.

It is also good to report that there are no hidden extras; central heating, electricity, linen, towels, etc are all supplied within the rental.

Nearby: Abergavenny is an interesting town, with a ruined castle, and is surrounded by delightful countryside. There is no shortage of other castles to see including Grosmont, Raglan, the White Castle and Tretower Court and Castle. Across the border into Powys you can explore the Brecon Beacons and the Mountain Centre is a starting point for a number of walks.

Units: 6
Rent: from £110 to £250 per week
Other costs: none
Central heating: provided
Cots and high chairs available
Open all year

Aldeburgh, Suffolk map 4

WENTWORTH HOTEL, Wentworth Road – ☎ *Aldeburgh (0728) 452 312.*

Next to the beach, near the town centre.

We felt we should recommend a hotel in this part of the country and this quiet hotel in a well-known resort fits the bill. The lounges and dining room face a pebbled beach, where the fishermen sell their catch in the morning. The interior of the hotel is particularly appealing, light and bright, and well-furnished. There is a terrace on one side and a small garden on the other.

Although there are no permanent family rooms here, fourteen of the bedrooms can be set up to take two adults and a child.

Nearby: Although the beach is shingle Aldeburgh lies on the Suffolk coastal path which runs from Felixstowe to Lowestoft. Just to the north you can visit Minsmere Nature Reserve and the interesting village of Dunwich with its museum. The music festival is held every June at Snape Maltings and there are castles at Orford and Framlingham. Adults with an interest in wine might try visits to Brandeston Priory and Bruisyard Wines.

BAR LUNCH (12–2.30pm) £1–5: plaice & chips, omelettes, fisherman's pie, grilled lambs liver;
LUNCH (12–2pm) £13: egg mayonnaise, roast rib of beef, pudding or cheese;
DINNER (7–9pm) £16: seafood hors d'oeuvres, roast leg of lamb, pudding or cheese
Children: high teas, half portions
£ high
Best Bargain Break £96 per person, 2 nights – dinner, b & b

AMBLESIDE

Children: free to age 2, £7.50 thereafter
Facilities: 2 cots and a high chair; baby listening on four lines
31 rooms   Access/AmEx/Diners/Visa
Closed 2 weeks after Xmas   No music
🅿 – own car park & on street   • Ale – Adnams

Ambleside, Cumbria   map 9

ROTHAY MANOR HOTEL – ☎ Ambleside (05394) 33605.

In the town where the A593 and A591 meet. The entrance is clearly signposted.

This elegant regency style hotel was once the home of a prosperous Liverpool merchant and has an air of quiet sophistication. The first floor veranda with its cast iron railings is a notable feature and it overlooks the manicured lawns. Every care is taken to ensure the comfort of visitors, from the fresh flowers and open fires to the doggie trail in the garden.

The hotel has been in the care of the same family since 1967 and many antiques have been collected during that time to adorn the main rooms. The restaurant is non-smoking and so is one of the lounges.

There are 15 bedrooms all individually furnished to a high standard. Three suites are available in the grounds of the hotel, two of which are ideal for families, both with double and twin bedrooms and two with an additional single.

Residents have free use of a nearby leisure club with swimming pool, sauna, steam room and jacuzzi. Squash is also available. During the winter the hotel *offers music, bridge and cookery courses.*

The hotel has an excellent reputation for its food which is freshly cooked from local produce.

Nearby: The hotel is situated in the heart of the Lake District with all its attractions. Fishing, golf, riding and watersports are readily available. Brockhole Visitor Centre, the Steam Boat Museum, Sizergh Castle, Levens Hall, Brantwood, the Beatrix Potter Exhibition, Fell Foot Park, Grizedale Forest Centre and the Ravenglass and Eskdale Railway (the 'Ratty') are all within easy reach.

DINNER (8–9pm) £21: scallops & scampi, beef lacey, raspberry pavlova
Children: high teas, half portions
£ high
Best Bargain Break 5% discount for stays of 4 nights or more
Children: cot free; extra bed £10
Facilities: 3 cots and 2 high chairs; portable baby alarms
15 rooms, 5 family, 3 suites   Open February to December
Access/AmEx/Diners/Visa   No music
No smoking in dining room and one lounge
P – own car park

Appleby, Cumbria   map 9
APPLEBY MANOR HOTEL (Best Western) – ☎ (07683) 51571.

Off the A66. Follow the signs to the hotel.

ASHBY ST LEDGERS

This imposing manor house, made of rose coloured Westmorland stone, overlooks the village of Appleby and the castle. The hotel was extended a few years back and is an excellent mix of old and new, and there is a notable pitch-pine staircase in the hall. The new conservatory lounge with its pine furniture is peaceful and relaxing and the games room has pool and table tennis. The leisure club has a small pool, sauna, jacuzzi and steam room.

With several family rooms and a good supply of cots and high chairs, this is an excellent family hotel and a good base for exploring this part of England.

Nearby: There is superb countryside all around, a great area for walking, fishing and riding. Appleby is a delightful town and the children will enjoy a visit to the conservation centre based at the castle. Lowther Park is close and it is easy to reach all the attractions of the Lakes and of the Yorkshire Dales.

✗ DINNER (7–9pm) £15: smoked mackerel paté, Westmorland lamb cutlets, pudding or cheese
Children: own menu, half portions
£ high
Best Bargain Break £50 per person per night – dinner, b & b
Children – free to age 15
Facilities: 5 cots and 3 high chairs; and a baby listening system
30 rooms, 8 family   Access/AmEx/Diners/Visa
Open all year   No smoking in restaurant
P – own car park

Ashby St Ledgers, Northants   map 7
OLDE COACH HOUSE INN – ☎ *Rugby (0788) 890 349.*

Off the A361 north of Daventry, and close to Junction 18 of the M1.

This is a delightful village of stone houses with thatched roofs and it has its place in history because Robert Catesby hatched the Gunpowder Plot in Ashby Manor, an elegant building next to the church of St. Leodegarius.

When Sir Edwin Lutyens restyled the village a stone Victorian facade was added to a farmhouse of an older vintage to make a pub for the villagers, and it was originally called the Coach and Horses. It's a lovely old pub with various rooms and alcoves where you can settle and these include a couple of rooms, away from the bar, where you can take the children. Real ale fans will find a good choice here, including Marston's. The rooms have a good quota of heavy wooden beams, excellent wooden furniture and panelled walls, and several fireplaces which are in use during the winter months.

On summer days the garden is wonderfully inviting. The patio is shady under its trailing plants and there are plenty of bench tables on the spacious lawn plus a slide, and you can enjoy a barbecue in the garden (weekends during the summer).

AUCHTERHOUSE

Nearby: It is a very pleasant part of the world with many attractions within easy reach: country parks at Draycote Water and Daventry, Guilsborough Wildlife Park, Althorp with its magnificent paintings, Coton Manor, Holdenby House, and further afield Canons Ashby.

BAR SNACKS (12–2pm & 6–9.30pm, not Sun pm) £2–12: devilled beef, lemon sole, maigret duck, tournedos;
DINNER (7.30–9.30pm) £14: whitebait, chicken supreme, pudding or cheese
Children: own menu, half portions
£ medium
Children: free up to 5 years
Facilities: 2 cots and 2 high chairs; no baby listening
6 rooms, 2 family   Open all year
• Ale – Everard, Flowers, Marston's   Access/Visa
P – own car park

Also recommended in the Family Welcome Pub & Restaurant Guide.

Auchterhouse, by Dundee, Tayside   map 11
THE OLD MANSION HOUSE – ☎ *Auchterhouse (082 626) 366.*

Follow the hotel sign from the B954 north of Muirhead.

This stylish and immaculately maintained 16th century baronial house has beautiful gardens, and a courtyard where visitors and guests may eat outside one of the two bars. The interior is superb with its stone walls and floors, antique furniture, huge open fires and a marvellous Jacobean vaulted ceiling. The house has been owned by some notable families including the Strathmores and the Earls of Buchan, and William Wallace is said to have stayed in the house. Hence the tower to the east is named "Wallace's Tower".

Facilities include a squash court, grass tennis court, heated outdoor swimming pool and a croquet lawn. The eleven acres of garden comprise a series of secluded lawns and flower beds with sheltering yew hedges, huge trees, and woodland to explore.

The bar serves food morning and evenings. The chef will cook 'whatever they want' for the children or they can eat at half price from the à la carte menu.

This lovely hotel adds up to an exceptional place to go to – whether for a quick drink and a meal or a longer stay.

Nearby: Fishing and shooting can be arranged via the hotel and there are some great golf courses within reach – Carnoustie, St Andrews, Rosemount and Gleneagles for example. You are well placed for sightseeing with Camperdown Wildlife Centre on the doorstep and easy access to the McManus Galleries in Dundee, Glamis Castle, Scone Palace, and J.M. Barrie's birthplace.

BALA

🍴 BAR SNACKS (12–2pm & 7–9.30pm) £2–12: smoked salmon mousse, cold buffet, steaks, fried fillets of sole;
LUNCH (12–2pm) £14: Stilton & chive mousse, poached salmon, apple crumble;
DINNER (7–9.30pm) £24: fresh asparagus, medallions of venison, crème brulée
Children: half portions
£ high
No Bargain Breaks
Children: free to age 12
Facilities: 2 cots and 2 high chairs; 3 baby listening lines
6 rooms, 2 suites   Access/AmEx/Diners/Visa
Closed first week in Jan   No music
🅿 – own car park   No smoking in restaurant

Bala, Gwynedd   map 5

ERW FEURIG FARM, Cefnddwysarn – ☎ Llandderfel (067 83) 262.

Just off the A494 north east of Bala. The turning is close to the village of Cefnddwysarn.

The farm is in a lovely spot, with wonderful views of the Berwyn Mountains and with Bala Lake quite close. The farmhouse has been enlarged to provide accommodation and guests are housed in a comfortable modern extension with light and airy, well-furnished rooms. The four double rooms have the great merit of being large enough to accommodate both bunk beds and a cot. Alternatively a set of bunk beds can be put into the one single room with parents in an adjoining double room.

There is plenty of space around the farm for children to play – in the lawned gardens or in the adjoining fields. The farm also has its own private lake where guests can fish, or they can head for Bala Lake, where there is also a sailing club.

Nearby: There are excellent walks amid delightful countryside, with many other attractions within reach: the Bala Lake Railway is nearby; Coed-y-Brenin Forest offers good walking amid varied wildlife; and Meirion Mill, the railways at Fairbourne and Talyllyn, Llanfair Quarry and Portmeirion are all within easy reach.

🍴 DINNER by arrangement
£ low
Children: half price up to 9 years; three quarters from 9 to 12
Facilities: 2 cots and a high chair
5 rooms, 2 family   Open March to December

No credit cards   Unlicensed
🅿 – plenty   No smoking in dining room

FRONDDERW PRIVATE HOTEL – ☎ Bala (0678) 520 301.

On the outskirts of the town, near the golf course.

The house is situated on a hill and overlooks the town with splendid views of the Berwyn Mountains and the famous Bala Lake. It is a handsome late 17th century country house with a rather imposing entrance hall and comfortable rooms with plenty of space. There are books in the main lounge and a separate television lounge and dining room. The three family rooms include a two bedroomed suite with its own bathroom.

The house is encircled by a large garden which includes lawns and a wooded area and there are swings for the children.

Nearby: Golfers will be glad to hear that there is a nine-hole course next door, and water sports enthusiasts need look no further than Bala Lake where you can sail and fish, or simply have a picnic by the water. Railway buffs have the Bala Lake Railway at hand, or, further afield, the Talyllyn and Fairbourne railways. It is a beautiful part of Wales, with lovely walks and magnificent scenery; the Coed-y-Brenin forest lies to the west and Lake Vyrnwy to the east, for example, and the great waterfall of Pistyll Rhaeadr is not far away.

✘ DINNER (7pm) £8: leek soup, pork chop with apple sauce, fresh fruit salad
Children: small portions
£ low
Best Bargain Break £119 per person per week – dinner, b & b
Children: cot £2; £5.50 up to 5 years; £8.50 from 6 to 16
Facilities: 3 cots and 2 high chairs; baby listening by arrangement
8 rooms, 3 family   Open March to November
No credit cards accepted   No smoking in dining room
🅿 – own car park   No music

Ballachulish, Highland   map 12

BALLACHULISH HOTEL – ☎ Ballachulish (08552) 606.

On the A828 on the south side of Ballachulish Bridge.

The hotel has a superb position alongside Loch Linnhe and is overlooked by the hills of Ben a' Bheithir. It is a grand building in the Scottish baronial style with curved Gothic windows and pointed gables. The interior is just as stylish with high ceilings, deep leather armchairs, groups of comfortable sofas and some interesting oil paintings.

BALLACHULISH

Local produce forms the basis of the food served here, and the adults can enjoy a good range of malt whiskies. After a good meal and a glass of malt you can take your ease in one of those armchairs in front of a log fire.

There is a garden with a lawn and it contains a little slide for younger children. You can enjoy the magnificent views and plan your next walk.

Nearby: This is an unrivalled area for walking, and the hotel can advise you on the various routes. Fishermen have a choice of loch, sea or river, and all sorts of water sports can be arranged. Hill climbing, pony trekking and golf are all available and the leisure centre at Fort William has a swimming pool, squash and tennis. Glencoe and Ben Nevis are close, and the children will enjoy a visit to the Sea Life Centre north of Oban. In the winter the area is a popular ski centre.

BAR MEALS (12–9.30pm) £2–7: smoked Loch Leven salmon, haddock & chips, tortellini, game pie;
DINNER (7–9.30pm) £18: mushroom provencale, supreme of Loch Linnhe salmon, pudding or cheese
Children: own menu, half portions
£ medium
Best Bargain Break £70 per person, 2 nights – dinner, b & b
Children: free up to 16 years
Facilities: 2 cots and 2 high chairs; and 4 lines for baby listening
30 rooms, 3 family   Open all year
Access/Visa   • Ale – Arrol's
P – own car park

ISLES OF GLENCOE HOTEL – ☎ *Ballachulish (08552) 603.*

Close to the A82, about a mile west of the village of Glencoe.
This is certainly the newest hotel ever listed in the Guide, since its official opening date is March, 1992.
It is under the same ownership as the Ballachulish and has its own distinctive style, built with a definite Scandinavian look. It has an unrivalled situation, right on the shore of Loch Leven with the dramatic pass of Glencoe behind. There are two loch-side harbours and nearly two miles of water frontage, with an abundance of water sports available.
Each bedroom has spectacular views, either of the mountains or the loch, views which are shared by the restaurant.
The hotel is set in forty acres of parkland, which the whole family can enjoy and there is a leisure centre with a swimming pool, sauna and steam room.

Similar times, prices and menus to those at the Ballachulish Hotel
Children: own menu, half portions
£ high

Best Bargain Break £65 per person, 2 nights – dinner, b & b
Children: cot £6, extra bed £16
Facilities: 2 cots and 2 high chairs; baby listening system
39 rooms, 4 family   Open all year
Access/Visa   P – own car park

Bantham, Devon   map 1

SLOOP INN – ☎ Kingsbridge (0548) 560 489.

H/SC   *West of Kingsbridge off the A379/B3197.*

Bantham is a pretty village in one of the loveliest parts of South Devon and the Sloop Inn suits it well, a 16th century building which was once owned by a notorious smuggler and wrecker called John Widdon. It is a spacious pub with a separate family room where adults and children can eat and drink together, and on warmer days you can head for the patio. Food is available every day and includes a good choice of local fish; and there is a choice of real ale too, including Bass.

There are two family bedrooms, which have their own bathrooms, and include a double and a single bed.

Nearby: There is an excellent stretch of sandy beach a few hundred yards from the inn, which is patrolled by lifeguards during the summer because of the currents, but is safe as long as the warning notices are heeded. It is also a marvellous beach for surfing and there are other pleasant beaches nearby including Thurlestone. If you prefer dry land the South Devon Coast path goes from Bantham towards Hope Cove and offers a walk with some spectacular views. There are two golf courses, at Bigbury and Thurlestone, and there is plenty of sea and river fishing to be had, plus water sports of all kinds. There are many other attractions within reach: the National Shire Horse Centre and the Dartmoor Wildlife Park, the Torbay Aircraft Museum, Buckfast Abbey and the Dart Valley Railway.

✗ (12–2pm & 7–10pm) £2–8: turkey broth, local smoked mackerel, plaice & chips, steaks, fresh crab salad
Children: half portions
£ medium
Children: cot £2; half price thereafter up to 11 years
Facilities: 3 cots and 2 high chairs
5 rooms, 2 family   Open all year
• Ale – Bass, Boddington's, Usher's   P – own car park

Also recommended in the Family Welcome Pub & Restaurant Guide.

SELF-CATERING
There are three flats at the back of the pub. They each have two

bedrooms, a double and a twin; a sofa bed can also be utilised. The flats are equipped to a high standard with fridge/freezers, microwave ovens, dishwashers and utility rooms with washing machines and driers. Central heating is provided. There are lovely views of the bay and of Burgh Island.

The rents range from £180 to £500 a week.

Barnham Broom, Nr Norwich, Norfolk   map 8

BARNHAM BROOM HOTEL, GOLF & COUNTRY CLUB – ☎ *Barnham Broom (060 545) 393.*

About eight miles west of Norwich between the B1108 and the A47. Barnham Broom is signposted from both roads.

A great array of sporting facilities awaits you here: two 18-hole golf courses; four squash courts; three hard tennis courts; an indoor swimming pool; and other sports can be arranged nearby including water-skiing, wind surfing, archery and clay-pigeon shooting, trout fishing and horse riding. Improvements are always being planned. The Bothways Bar, open from 9.30 in the morning to 11 at night, has a snooker table, and provides hot and cold snacks.

It's a pleasant, well-designed hotel with masses of activities for all the family. There are also sixteen time-share apartments here, and they are connected to the baby listening system.

Nearby: Norwich is the hub of the county with roads radiating out from its centre and it is quite easy to reach most areas. Even the north Norfolk coast is not difficult, where you could visit the Norfolk Shire Horse Centre, Felbrigg Hall and have a ride on the North Norfolk Railway. The Norfolk Wildlife Park is closer, as is Thrigby Hall Wildlife Garden. The Broads can also be reached with ease.

BOTHWAYS BAR (9.30am–9.30pm) £1–10: salads, gammon, burger, fried scampi, rump steak;
LUNCH (12.30–2pm) £9: 3-course carvery;
DINNER (7.30–9.30pm) £14: seafood mousse, roast leg of pork, pudding or cheese
Children: own menu, half portions
£ high
Best Bargain Break £100 per person, 2 nights – dinner, b & b
Children – free to age 16
Facilities: 5 cots and 2 high chairs; 5 baby listening lines
52 rooms, 8 family   Access/AmEx/Diners/Visa
Open all year   P – own car park

Bassenthwaite, Nr Keswick, Cumbria   map 9
ARMATHWAITE HALL HOTEL – ☎ *Bassenthwaite Lake (07687) 76551.*

Off the A591 – don't go to Bassenthwaite village but follow the signs for the Lake. Turn off at the Castle Inn.

This is a splendid 18th century stone building very much in the "Baronial" style, and set in 450 acres of parkland; its lawns flow down to Bassenthwaite Lake, where guests can fish.

Sir Hugh Walpole wrote of it:

'Speaking of Romance, is there anything more romantic than Armathwaite Hall. With the trees that guard it and the history that inhabits it, it is a house of perfect and irresistible atmosphere.'

There are some wonderful rooms here including a huge lounge with a grand marble fireplace, wood-panelled ceiling and walls and leaded windows – all glassily surveyed by the stags' heads on the walls.

In addition to its beautiful situation, there are good facilities within the hotel: a leisure centre with indoor heated swimming pool, gymnasium, a hard tennis court, a pitch and putt course, and a large indoor games area – one room with table tennis, space invaders and a children's library and another with a pool table. A snooker table (for over-16's) is in a remarkable panelled room with walls covered with scores of original Punch cartoons.

The hotel has acquired more land, over 300 acres, and has opened a riding centre with fully qualified instructors.

The hotel is expensive but certainly offers value for money.

Nearby: From this base you can reach any part of the Lakes with ease, including Grasmere, Hardknott Roman fort, Brantwood, the Lake District headquarters at Brockhole. The children will no doubt vote for Fell Foot Park which has facilities for all types of water sports, or the Grizedale Forest Visitor Centre. Railway buffs have several choices including the famous Ravenglass and Eskdale, known as "Ratty", and all the family will love a trip on it.

LEISURE CLUB (12–5.30pm & 6.30–10pm) £2–9: garlic mushrooms, spaghetti Napoli, chicken curry, sirloin steak;

LUNCH (12.30–1.45pm) £14: mushrooms with garlic mayonnaise, roast beef with Yorkshire pudding, lemon cheese cake;

DINNER (7.30–9.30pm) £30: Mediterranean prawns, breast of guinea fowl en croute, pudding or cheese

Children: own menu

£ high

Best Bargain Break £128 per person, 2 nights – dinner, b & b

Children: cots £5; extra bed £15

Facilities: 6 cots and 6 high chairs, and a baby listening system for each room

42 rooms, 4 family, 5 sets interconnecting

Access/AmEx/Diners/Visa   🅿 – own car park

Beauworth, Nr Alresford, Hants   map 3

THE MILBURY'S – ☎ Bramdean (0962) 771 248.

About two miles south of the A272, and one mile beyond the hamlet of Beauworth.

Standing alone on top of the hill, the 17th century pub is built in soft warm Hampshire brick with hung tiles, flint walls and dormer windows set in a many angled roof line. Much renovation has been done, and it is good to report that families are welcome in various areas, so that adults can still enjoy the real ales which are available and the excellent range of food. A notable feature of the pub is the well in the bar. It is three hundred feet deep and an ice cube, dropped from the safety grid, takes eight seconds to hit the water. There is also a huge treadmill to be seen.

A new family room has been built in a converted barn, where dark wooden settles and chairs are set around half a dozen tables. The dark beams of the ceiling contrast with the white-washed walls. This is a peaceful spot and the bedrooms, attractively decorated and with beamed ceilings, are in character with the rest of the pub. There is also a family suite with a bedroom and a sitting room.

There is a delightful garden with superb views of the wide open countryside. There are plenty of picnic tables and barbecues are held during summer weekends. Two swings and a see saw make up a play area in a corner of the garden.

Nearby: You are quite close to the splendid city of Winchester with its castle, cathedral and museum. Marwell Zoo is also nearby, as is Paulton's Park, Broadlands, Farley Mount Country Park and Mottisfont Abbey. The Mid-Hants Railway runs down the "Watercress Line" from Alton to Alresford.

BAR SNACKS (12–2pm & 7–10.30pm) £1–10: smoked salmon, cod fillet Mornay, steaks, plaice, chilli con carne;
DINNER (7–10pm) £17: moules à l'ail, lamb fillet, pudding or cheese
Children: own menu, half portions
£ low
Children: cot free; extra bed £7.50
Facilities: 1 cot and 1 high chair; no baby listening
4 rooms, 1 family   Open all year
• Ale – Courage, John Smith's   Access/AmEx/Visa
P – own car park

Also recommended in the Family Welcome Pub & Restaurant Guide.

If you wish to recommend an establishment to the Guide please write to us – report forms are at the back of the book. We need your help to extend and improve the guide.

Bellingham, Nr Hexham, Northumberland   map 9
RIVERDALE HALL HOTEL – ☎ Hexham (0434) 220 254.

On a minor road just west of Bellingham on the north bank of the River Tyne. Bellingham is on the B6320, 16 miles north of Hexham.

The core of the hotel is a Victorian country house which overlooks the North Tyne River. It is the nearest hotel to Kielder Water and has recently undergone a major programme of refurbishment. It is a friendly, family-run place with good facilities including an indoor swimming pool and a games room.

The owner is a cricket enthusiast and has his own cricket field which also doubles for other sports. There is a putting green; you can fish in the adjoining river and the golf course lies opposite. So sports fans are well catered for. Alternatively you can simply relax in the five acres of garden.

Nearby: Kielder Water, with its wide variety of water sports, can be enjoyed by the whole family; and the castle is the starting point for many walks and nature trails through the Kielder Forest. To the south you can follow the line of Hadrian's Wall with its chain of forts. Within easy reach you will find Belsay Hall, Wallington House, Cragside House and the ruins of Brinkburn Priory.

✗ BAR SNACKS (12–2pm & 6.45–9.30pm) £1–9: garlic prawns, steaks, stir fried dishes, sole meunière, mixed grill;
DINNER (6.45–9.30pm) £16: marinated herring, soup, sole duglére, pudding or cheese
Children: own menu, half portions
£ medium
Best Bargain Break £78 per person 2 nights – dinner, b & b
Children: free up to 3 years; one third of adult rate from 3 to 8; two thirds from 9 to 14
Facilities: 3 cots and 2 high chairs; baby listening system
20 rooms, 5 family   Access/AmEx/Diners/Visa
• Ale – Ind Coope Burton   Open all year
🅿 – own car park

Berea, Nr St David's, Dyfed   map 5
CWMWDIG WATER GUEST HOUSE – ☎ Groesgoch (03483) 434.

Off the A487 a few miles north east of St David's.

The house is less than a mile from the Pembrokeshire coastal path, and guests are therefore well set for excellent walks in the area. The guest house was converted from a 17th century farmhouse and its adjacent barns, and offers very comfortable accommodation in rooms which mostly have views towards Abereiddy Bay.

BEREA

The useful facility of a small kitchen is provided so that you can make snacks and drinks there, and there are two sitting rooms: a large one with a beamed ceiling and an open fire and a good selection of books, and a smaller television room. There is a separate dining room and a small bar. We stayed here last year and were impressed by the excellent value offered; the food was particularly good, cooked with skill and generously served.

Nearby: Pembrokeshire has so much to offer the holiday maker and the lovely town of St David's is just five miles away. There are many good beaches along the coast; Abereiddy Bay and Whitesand Bay are close, and the latter is particularly good for surfing. Children will no doubt be keen to visit the Wildlife Park at Cardigan, and there is a Marine Life Centre and a butterfly farm near St David's. There is quite a choice of museums and castles: at Scolton Manor, Haverfordwest, Pembroke, Manorbier, Tenby and so on.

BAR MEALS (7–10pm) £1–5: gammon & chips, local trout, plaice, lasagne verdi;
DINNER (from 7pm) £9: pear & cheese salad, steak paprika, pudding and cheese
Children: half portions
£ low
Children: babies free; £3.50 from 2 to 5 years; £7 from 5 to 7; £10.50 from 8 to 12
Facilities: 2 cots and 2 high chairs; baby listening system
11 rooms, 2 family   Open all year except Xmas
Access/AmEx/Diners/Visa   No music
No smoking in dining room   **P** – ample

Please let us have reports – good or bad – on any establishments listed in the Guide as soon as possible after your visit.

Betws-y-Coed, Gwynedd   map 5

TY GWYN HOTEL – ☎ Betws-y-Coed (069 02) 383.

On the A5 just south of Waterloo Bridge.

This handsome stone hotel, partly built in the 17th century, was one of our earliest finds for the Family Welcome Guide and remains a firm favourite. It has a stylish interior with antique furniture scattered about, comfortable armchairs, highly polished oak furniture and old prints on the walls. The bar too is most appealing with its low-beamed ceiling, iron stove and antique bric-a-brac.

There is a continuous programme of improvements here; for example a delightful suite, with a four-poster bed, lounge and own balcony was completed a year or two ago. In contrast, there is a dormitory bunkhouse available, which is split into two sections, housing ten people. This costs just £7.50 per person per night.

You will find some excellent food here, both in the bar and the restaurant – and some real ale, too. It is owned and run by the Ratcliffe family, who always extend a friendly welcome.

Nearby: Four main valleys converge at this town, which is the gateway to the beauties of the Snowdonia National Park. The great mountain is not far away and you can travel close to its summit on the mountain railway, which starts at Llanberis. Enthusiasts can also sample the Ffestiniog Railway. There are many attractions within easy reach, including Gwydyr Forest and the Cwm Idwal nature trail, the slate caverns at Blaenau and Portmeirion. The north coast can be reached quickly, where there are many sandy beaches; at Llandudno, for example, a traditional seaside resort with a pier, donkey rides, Punch and Judy shows, etc., plus the Great Orme Country Park.

BAR SNACKS (12–2pm & 7–9.30pm) £2–9: seafood gratin, fresh Conwy salmon, steaks, chicken tikka, braised pheasant;
DINNER (7–9.30pm) £14: local smoked trout, roulade of Welsh lamb, pudding or cheese
Children: own menu, half portions
£ low
Best Bargain Break £70 per person, 2 nights – dinner, b & b
Children: free up to 3 years; 75% off from 4 to 6; 50% from 7 to 12; 25% from 13 to 16 years
Facilities: 2 cots and 2 high chairs; baby listening system
13 rooms, 2 family   Access/Visa
Open all year   • Ale – McEwan's
P – own car park

Blackawton, Devon   map 1

NORMANDY ARMS – ☎ *Blackawton (080 421) 315.*

Take a minor road from the B3207 – it's not far, though some of the lanes are single track. Use the church tower as a guide – the pub is only a little way from there.

This pub was renamed the "Normandy Arms" in honour of the Normandy landings of the Second World War since many of the troops were trained on nearby beaches. Helmets and berets on the walls of the charming bar, and some caricatures of WW2 leaders, commemorate this.

There's a good atmosphere in this pub and a pleasant children's room upstairs, where there are tables and chairs and lots of toys and games. It is nice to report that there are no gaming machines nor pool tables.

There's one high chair in the restaurant, but book if you want to eat there at the weekend. There is a very good choice of food all of which is freshly prepared on the premises; and small portions of most dishes can be served up for children. The traditional Sunday lunch at around £7 is good value.

Nearby: All along the nearby coast there are excellent beaches – from near Plymouth, via Bantham and Broadsands to the various Torquay beaches. There is lots of entertainment for all the family, including the National Shire Horse Centre and Dartmoor Wild Life Park, Buckfast Abbey, the Dart Valley Railway, and the castles of Compton and Totnes.

BAR SNACKS (12–2pm & 7–10pm, not Sun pm in winter) £2–6: plaice & chips, chicken & ham pie, vegetable pancake, steak sandwich;
DINNER (7–10pm) £14: avocado & crab, gamekeepers casserole, old English apple pie
Children: own menu, half portions
£ low
Children: £5 up to 5 years; £10 thereafter
Facilities: 1 cot and 1 high chair
4 rooms, 1 family   Open all year
• Ale – Bass, Blackawton, Ruddles   Access/Visa
P – own car park

Also recommended in the Family Welcome Pub & Restaurant Guide.

Hotels were asked to quote 1992 prices, but not all were able to give an accurate forecast. Make sure that you check tariffs when you book.

Blair Atholl, Tayside — map 12

THE FIRS, St Andrew's Crescent – ☎ Blair Atholl (079 681) 256.

In the centre of the village.

The house was built around the turn of the century, and was recently modernised. It looks smart in its coat of white paint, and the rooms are cheerfully decorated with flowered prints. It is a friendly place, run by a family, and there are two family rooms available, both with a double and a single bed.

A feature of the house is a particularly attractive garden with a large lawn, herbaceous borders, a rockery, and a children's play area with swings and climbing nets, a sand pit, a tree house and various toys for young children. Bicycles can also be provided for most sizes of guests.

Nearby: The village is famous for the remarkable Blair Castle, which certainly demands a visit, and the attractive town of Pitlochry with its well-known festival theatre is just down the road. Other attractions for holiday makers include the Hydro dam, Castle Menzies and Glengoulandie Deer Park. A little further on is Loch Rannoch with its many water sports; and this is wonderful country for the walker, rider, golfer and fisherman.

✕ DINNER (7.30pm) £8
Children: own menu, half portions
£ low
Children: free up to 2 years; £5 from 2 to 5; £7.50 from 5 to 14

BLAKENEY

Facilities: 2 cots and 1 high chair, and a baby alarm
4 rooms, 2 family   Open March to October
No credit cards   Unlicensed
No smoking in dining room and bedrooms   No music
P – own car park

Blakeney, Norfolk   map 8
BLAKENEY HOTEL, The Quay – ☎ *Cley (0263) 740 797.*

Just off the A149 between Cromer and Wells.
A fine building of flint and brick in a marvellous situation overlooking the harbour, which is owned by the National Trust. It is now for small craft only, but in medieval times was a noted port. The area is a paradise for naturalists and ornithologists; and for golfers too, with Hunstanton, Brancaster and Sheringham close by.
There is a large lawned garden, beautifully kept and shaded by tall trees, and it has some swings for the children. The games room has a pool table and table tennis and darts, and there is a heated indoor swimming pool and a sauna.
One of our readers, from Aberdeen, wrote to commend the hotel and described it as 'superb all round'. We agree with that judgement.
Nearby: Blakeney Point is an area of outstanding natural beauty, over 1000 acres of it, and has a great wealth of bird life. There are two observation hides and a nature trail for children. Holkham Hall, the Norfolk Shire Horse Centre, Felbrigg Hall and the North Norfolk Railway are all within easy reach.

✕ LIGHT LUNCH (12–2pm) £2–7: seafood pancake, Norfolk trout, lasagne verdi, cold buffet;
DINNER (7–9.30pm) £14: grilled local herring, casserole of beef, pudding or cheese
Children: own menu, half portions
£ high
Best Bargain Break £55 per person per night – dinner, b & b
Children: £6 up to 12 years
Facilities: 8 cots and 4 high chairs and a baby listening system
50 rooms, 3 family   Access/AmEx/Diners/Visa
Open all year   • Ale – Greene King
P – own car park

To qualify for inclusion in the Guide hotels must offer the basic facilities of a cot, a family room and an evening meal. Self-catering establishments must provide cots and high chairs..

Bleadon, Nr Weston-super-Mare, Avon   map 2
PURN HOUSE FARM – ☎ *Weston-super-Mare (0934) 812 324.*

Off the A370 south of Weston-super-Mare.

Sound advice from the owners is to leave the M5 at junction 22 rather than endure the heavy traffic around Weston-super-Mare. But you will find peace and quiet at this handsome 17th century farmhouse, which is situated at the foot of Purn Hill at the western end of the Mendips. There are splendid views of the surrounding countryside and across to the Bristol Channel.

There are excellent facilities for families, including four family sized rooms; a high chair and a cot. Much of the food served by the friendly owner is grown on the farm's 400 acres, and visitors are welcome to walk around and watch the various farming activities. Children must of course be supervised. There is a games room with snooker, table tennis, darts and board games; and there are plenty of books available.

The large lawn is encircled by a drive and there is a rockery and a small garden pond. You can sit in the sun in a secluded walled area and even have a picnic there.

Nearby: There is plenty to do and see in the area. Guests can fish in the River Axe which flows through the grounds of the farm and trout fishing can be had at Chew Valley and Blagdon Lakes; riding and pony trekking can be arranged at local riding schools. Nearby attractions include Cheddar Gorge, Wookey Hole Caves, Wells and Glastonbury, and the East Somerset Railway near Shepton Mallet. There are plenty of sandy beaches within easy reach: at Uphill, Burnham and Berrow for example.

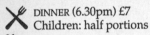
DINNER (6.30pm) £7
Children: half portions
£ low
Children: half price under 3 years; two thirds price from 3 to 11
Facilities: 1 cot and 1 high chair; and a baby listening system
6 rooms, 4 family   Open February to October
No smoking in dining room and bedrooms
Unlicensed   No credit cards
🅿 – loads

Blockley, Nr Moreton-in-Marsh, Glos   map 2
LOWER FARM COTTAGES – ☎ *Blockley (0386) 700 237.*

SC   *In the village, which is off the A44 west of Moreton-in-Marsh.*

Lower Farm Cottages are situated in a delightful Cotswold village, and the conversion, from a huge old barn with mellow stone walls, has been done with great style and charm. The main building, with its two roof to floor pillared windows, resembles a small manor house.

The cottages can accommodate between four and six people, with the exception of Ratty's Retreat, which is a little retreat for two people only. It has a galleried bedroom with a Victorian half-tester bed.

We were very impressed with the excellent design of the cottages we saw, and in particular the feeling of space. Some of the entrance halls go up to the rafters and most of the rooms have lovely vaulted ceilings. Clever use has been made of floor to ceiling windows, which give lovely views of the gardens; there is some splendid antique furniture, complemented by old wooden doors; and two of the cottages have spiral staircases.

The kitchens are extremely well equipped and have everything a cook would need. There is a laundry room and you will find comprehensive information here also about the surrounding area.

The three acres of garden comprise immaculately kept lawns, which are bounded by a cheerful brook. Swings and a tree fort are provided for the children, plus footballs and toys. All the family can play croquet or table tennis and make friends with the ducks and the chickens. Herons and kingfishers also visit the garden.

These are exceptional and well-organised properties in a delightful spot.

Nearby: Katie Batchelor, who runs Lower Farm, gave us a huge information pack (it is supplied to every cottage) and this tells you of the array of things to see and do in the locality. Batsford Arboretum is on the doorstep; and Sezincote, Snowshill Manor, Hidcote Manor Garden and Sudeley Castle are close. The children will want to see the waterfowl at Folly Farm and the Cotswold

Farm Park; Bourton on the Water has a model village, a motor museum and Birdland; and the Cotswold Wildlife Park and Blenheim Palace are a short drive away.

Units: 6
Rent: £170 to £500. Special breaks also available
Other costs: none
Central heating: provided
3 cots and 3 high chairs
Open all year

Bolton Abbey, Nr Skipton, North Yorks map 9

DEVONSHIRE ARMS COUNTRY HOUSE HOTEL (Best Western) – ☎ Bolton Abbey (075 671) 441.

On the A59 at the junction with the B6160.

Set in wonderful countryside, this stylish hotel was extended some years ago and the new building at the rear blends in well with the old stone coaching inn on the roadside.

Many of the rooms have splendid views across the river, and a night here is an excellent way to round off an energetic day in the Yorkshire Dales, Harrogate or the beautiful countryside around Bolton Abbey. The public rooms and the bedrooms are beautifully furnished and there are some fine oil paintings to be seen. The open fire in the entrance hall is delightfully evocative, especially on a cool day.

Apart from fishing on the Wharfe, the hotel has no specific facilities for families. They are hardly needed because within easy reach there is a mass of interesting things to do and see. It is of course expensive, but it is a lovely spot.

Nearby: The hotel has several miles of trout fishing on the Wharfe, and golf can be arranged at Skipton. Special breaks at the hotel also include clay pigeon shooting, vintage car excursions, and even hot air ballooning. There are lovely walks through Upper Wharfedale and these are waymarked from Bolton Abbey. Malham Cove, Skipton Castle, Fountains Abbey, Stump Cross Caverns, Ripley Castle and the lovely town of Harrogate are all close.

BAR SNACKS (12–2pm & 6.30–9.30pm) £1–4: soup, meat & potato pie, salads, lasagne, daily special;
LUNCH (12–2pm) £15: avocado mousse, lambs' kidneys, pudding or cheese;
DINNER (7–9.30pm) £24: Ogen melon, soup, noisette of beef, pudding or cheese
Children: own menu, half portions
£ high
Best Bargain Break £115 per person 2 nights – dinner, b & b

Children: cots £5.50, extra bed £10
Facilities: plenty of cots and high chairs; baby listening on six lines
40 rooms   Access/AmEx/Diners/Visa
Open all year   No music
• Ale – choice of two always on tap   P – own car park

Boncath, Pembrokeshire, Dyfed map 5
FRON FAWR – ☎ *Boncath (0239) 841 285.*

SC *Off the A478 south of Cardigan.*

The first thing you will notice at Fron Fawr is the tranquillity of the place, and then the spectacular views.

The three cottages were converted by Mr and Mrs Cori from a huge barn and each contains three bedrooms (a double and two singles), an open plan living area, a kitchen and bathroom. The bald description does no justice to the excellent design of the cottages, into which much has been packed without any hint of strain.

The furnishings are stylish and comfortable and are nicely in harmony with the decorations. As well as easy chairs you will find pine tables and the occasional rocker. There are cushions in plenty, interesting water colours on the walls and bright flowers on the tables. It seems like home, not rented holiday accommodation.

The kitchens are superbly equipped with all a cook would need, down to a food mixer and a microwave oven. The same goes for the rest of the rooms with nothing forgotten: even first aid kits are supplied.

The sloping ceilings of the bedrooms on the upper floor are particularly attractive, and each cottage has its own patio.

Fron Fawr has sixty-five acres of land and this includes seventeen acres of woodland. There is a beautiful lawned garden which the whole family can enjoy and some children's swings are set up here. You can gaze up the slope, past an old barn, to the wood beyond. It is a great haven for wildlife of all kinds including badgers and buzzards (Boncath is Welsh for buzzard). If you have an interest in the natural world this is a great spot to be.

On a more practical level you will find a bottle of wine and a meal waiting for you when you arrive, and there are no hidden extras in the price. You can even have your clothes laundered (£1 per load).

When you want a change from cooking, Mrs Cori has a most impressive list of frozen meals, all home cooked from fresh local ingredients.

Nearby: This is wonderful walking country and you can start nearly two hundred miles of the Pembrokeshire coastal path at nearby Cemaes Head. Sailing and pony trekking are available, and a good choice of fishing either in the sea or on the River Teifi. The sea is not foo far; Poppit Sands is only a few miles and the lovely bay at Mwnt is an alternative. The children will no doubt urge a visit to the wildlife park at Cardigan; there are the falls to see at Cenarth and the ruins of Cilgerran Castle.

Units: 3
Rent: £150 to £450 per week
Other costs: electricity is metered
Central heating: provided
A cot and a high chair for each cottage
Open all year

Borrowdale, Cumbria

STAKIS LODORE SWISS – ☎ *Keswick (07687) 77285.*

On the B5289, south of Keswick.

Many of our readers have praised this hotel, which "nestles close to the shores of Derwentwater and is shadowed by beautiful waterfalls". These are the words of the manager, and we endorse his excellent description.

It is indeed a splendid hotel: a traditional-looking Cumbrian slate facade gives way to an interior which is modern and very comfortable. The list of facilities on offer for families would be hard to surpass – even by the grandest hotel.

There's an indoor pool, sauna and solarium, and an outdoor one; the priceless bonus of a supervised nursery with trained nannies from 8am to 6pm each day (and where children's meals are served); a fully-equipped games room; outdoor play areas with a sandpit and a bouncy castle; and tennis and squash courts.

The hotel actually stands in forty acres of grounds, which include the famous falls, and there are a couple of acres of lawned garden, where several thousand geraniums are planted each year.

The fine, and difficult, balance is struck here between the needs of children, and the comfort and relaxation of adults. For example, children under six are not welcome in the dining room at night, when the adults want to enjoy themselves. They have, by the way, a choice of three menus.

To quote one of our readers: "extremely comfortable, wonderful food, and very friendly staff." It is a marvellous place to stay.

Nearby: A short drive will take you to the heart of the Lake District – to Grasmere, the Hardknott Roman Fort and the Ravenglass and Eskdale Railway; to Windermere and the Lake District headquarters at Brockhole, where the children can see, amongst many other things, a Beatrix Potter exhibition. Fell Foot Park has all sorts of water sports (as have the other lakes) and the Grizedale Forest Centre is the starting point for many interesting walks.

BAR SNACKS (12–2pm) £1–9: smoked salmon, fillet of plaice, rump steak, medallions of pork;
LUNCH (12.30–2pm) £13: Lodore terrine, avocado platter, pudding;
DINNER (7.30–9.45pm) £23: crudités, brill mornay, beef Stroganoff, pudding or cheese
Children: own menu, half portions
£ high
Best Bargain Break £60 per person per night – dinner, b & b
Children: from £12.50 to £39 depending on age
Facilities: 8 cots and 7 high chairs; and baby listening to every room
70 rooms, 8 family   Access/AmEx/Diners/Visa
P – own car park   No music

Bournemouth, Dorset   map 2

HINTON FIRS HOTEL, Manor Road, East Cliff – ☎ Bournemouth (0202) 555 409.

Follow the signs for East Cliff.

Like many of its neighbours this agreeable hotel has a mansard roof. It occupies a corner site in the heart of the hotel area of the town, and is just a hundred yards or so from the cliff top. Lifts and paths go down to the beach.

This is very much a family hotel, with a good number of family rooms which are all quite spacious and are furnished and decorated in a light and airy style. There are plenty of cots and high chairs available (in the words of the manager "as many as are required"), and a baby listening service, and all the bedrooms

BOURNEMOUTH

have bathrooms attached. In addition an annexe contains six rooms, two of which are family rooms.

The facilities are excellent here. There is a heated outdoor pool with a children's play pool in a sheltered spot in the attractive lawned garden, which has some fine trees and rhododendron bushes. This pool is a great asset, for all the guests, and especially for families and you can have a buffet lunch alongside. An indoor pool has also been built, and there is a games room with table tennis and pool.

This hotel offers excellent value in a popular holiday area.

Nearby: Apart from the many attractions of Bournemouth itself you have easy access to the rest of Dorset: to Corfe Castle, the Swanage Railway and Durlston Country Park; to Brownsea Island and Merley Bird Gardens, and to Kingston Lacy and Wimborne Minster.

BAR LUNCH (12.30–2pm) £3–6: fried scampi, omelettes, chicken Kiev, ploughman's;
LUNCH (1–1.45pm) £7: soup, grilled bream, pudding;
DINNER (7.15–8.30pm) £11: egg mayonnaise, soup, roast leg of pork, pudding & cheese
Children: own menu
£ high
Best Bargain Break £33 per person per night – dinner, b & b
Children: babies free; one third up to 5 years; half price from 5 to 11; two thirds over 11
Facilities: plenty of cots and high chairs, and a baby listening system
52 rooms, 14 family   Open all year

No smoking in dining room & one lounge   Access/Visa
P – own car park

Nr Bradford-on-Avon, Wilts   map 2
WOOLLEY GRANGE – ☎ Bradford-on-Avon (02216) 4705.

At Woolley Green, off the B3105 north east of Bradford-on-Avon.
This 17th century manor house is an engaging sight, built as it is from a warm-looking limestone and with its pointed gables and tall chimneys.

It was a family home for several hundred years until Mr and Mrs Chapman adapted it a couple of years back as a country house hotel. They have done it in a most appealing style, and style is the keynote from the moment you step into the wood-panelled hall with its patterned plaster ceiling and comfortable chairs and sofas.

The original style is maintained in the sitting rooms and the attractive dining room; and the Long Room, which is part library, part television room and part games room is a delight. So are the bedrooms which are all differently furnished and decorated but in every case reflect the owners' wishes to provide their guests with comfortable and elegant surroundings.

The huge Victorian conservatory, with its excellent cane furniture, is a lovely place to sit over coffee or something stronger. Outside there are stretches of garden and a stone paved terrace where you can have al fresco meals. Through a gate you will find a heated swimming pool, a croquet lawn in an enclosed

Nr BRADFORD-ON-AVON

area, two grass tennis courts and an all-weather court, and a badminton court. There are fourteen acres of garden in which to relax, and an adventure playground has now been built. As well as the Moulton bicycles provided at the hotel, guests can try an authentic Indian trishaw.

Amid all these comforts and excellent facilities it has been remembered that many adults have children who also have to be cared for. This is done with a will, too. There are plenty of cots and high chairs and certain rooms are interconnecting and can form family suites.

Woolley Bear's Den occupies a large barn and it is packed with toys and games for younger children; and there is a pool table, table tennis and table football for older children. A nanny is in attendance every day (from 10am to 6pm) and the children can be fed in the nursery off the play room; lunch is at noon and tea at 5 o'clock.

What a boon for parents, who can enjoy their food in peace. The hotel has a notably good chef and the same attention to detail goes into the buying of the raw ingredients for the dining room. The hotel also has a two acre kitchen garden which provides the fruit and the vegetables.

This is a really splendid hotel which provides marvellous facilities, and a proper welcome, for all the family.

Nearby: If you can tear yourself away from the comforts of Woolley Grange there is a range of places to visit. The beautiful city of Bath is very close, as are Corsham Court, Sheldon Manor, Lacock Abbey and Bowood House, which has a wonderful adventure playground. Longleat Safari Park is also within reach, with Stourhead a little further south. Riding and clay pigeon shooting can be arranged and the hotel provides bicycles and local maps to guide you. The route along the Kennet and Avon canal is recommended.

LIGHT LUNCH (12–2pm) £3–10: fresh goat cheese salad, smoked salmon & scrambled eggs, fillet of salmon, Bayonne ham & salad;

DINNER (7.30–10pm) £25: smoked duck, beans & cabbage salad, darne of cod, farmhouse cheese, warm chocolate tart

Children: own menu

£ high

Best Bargain Break £180 per person, 2 nights – dinner, b & b

Children: free

Facilities: 10 cots and 6 high chairs; a baby listening system; and a nursery with a nanny

20 rooms, 8 family, 2 suites   Open all year

Access/AmEx/Diners/Visa   No music

P – own car park

If you wish to recommend an establishment to the Guide please write to us – report forms are at the back of the book. We need your help to extend and improve the guide.

Braithwaite, Nr Keswick, Cumbria — map 9

COLEDALE INN – ☎ *Braithwaite (07687) 78272.*

Just off the A66 at the top of Braithwaite village.

Set snugly up a small hill, towards the top of this picturesque village, you will find the Coledale Inn which is a small country hotel and pub. It was built in the early 19th century as a woollen mill, became a pencil mill and was then converted to an inn. The building commands superb views of Skiddaw at the front while to the rear, the panoramic Grisdale Pike rises steeply into the sky.

The number of bedrooms has been increased and they are all very well furnished indeed with the sort of facilities you would normally associate with more pretentious establishments. Scattered through the hotel you will find plenty of Victorian prints, furnishings and antiques.

Apart from the other normal hotel facilities, guests also have the bonus of two convivial bars at their disposal which serve real ale and a good range of meals and bar snacks. There is also a children's menu.

There is an attractive garden with colourful shrubberies and lawns and bench seats and tables where you can take your ease in fine weather. If you fancy more active pursuits, the proprietor can offer membership of the nearby tennis and bowls club.

Nearby: The wonderful Lakes scenery is all around you and Keswick is well worth a visit for its interesting shops and other attractions. The birthplace of William Wordsworth is very close and the many sights of the Lake District lie to the south: Grasmere and Windermere, the Grizedale Forest, Fell Foot Park,

Brantwood and so on.

✘ BAR SNACKS (12–2pm & 6.30–9pm) £1–7: filled baked potatoes, Cumberland sausage, scampi, chilli con carne;
DINNER (6.30–9pm) £9: smoked mackerel, sirloin steak, pudding or cheese
Children: own menu
£ medium
Best Bargain Break: 3 nights for the price of two (midweek only during winter)
Children: under 4's £5; half price thereafter
Facilities: 1 cot and 1 high chair
11 rooms, 5 family   Open all year
No smoking in residents' dining room   Access/Visa
P – own car park   • Ale – Yates, Younger's

Branscombe, Nr Seaton, Devon   map 2
THE BULSTONE, Higher Bulstone – ☎ *(029 780) 446.*

Off the A3052. Turn at the junction called Branscombe Cross. It is signposted to Bulstone.

We continue to receive highly favourable reports of this hotel, which is run specifically for families by the charming and indefatigable Mr and Mrs Freeman. When we called in recently the hotel looked in pristine condition.

The hotel has been extended and the new stone walls fit in very well with the rest of the building, part of which dates back to the 16th century. The delightful sitting room with its fine fireplace testifies to the age of the original building and this is the only room which is for adults only.

The children have a large play room of their own and it is very well provided with toys and games including a very snazzy (and robust) Lego table. The garden has loads of space for children to play and they can help to look after the chickens, the cats and Barney the rabbit. A large grassy play area contains slides, climbing frames, a sandpit, a football net, and a tree house, but the layout will gradually change as a nature garden is made in the paddock and part of the orchard. This is a long term project to attract the local wildlife into the grounds.

There is a pleasant conservatory in which to sit and parents on holiday will be glad of the laundry room and the well-equipped kitchen in which they can prepare drinks or snacks. Glad, too, of the way the family rooms are designed with separate bedrooms for the children.

Everything at this hotel is geared to the needs of families on holiday and this includes the provision of a cot for every room in the hotel and as many high chairs as could be required. It's a superb family hotel, which offers remarkable value, and makes you realise how poorly equipped are most other hotels to cope with the needs of families.

The food here is always made from fresh, local produce; and artificial flavourings and colourings are avoided. The children have their high teas between 4.45 and 5.30pm, so that the adults can enjoy their meals together later.

Nearby: The sea is very close with pleasant beaches, although some have pebbles under foot. There is, however, a sandy beach at Sidmouth. It is a delightful part of the world with many benefits for holiday makers: the Donkey Sanctuary near Sidmouth, the Farway Country Park, Bicton Park, Pecorama and Crealy Working Farm are all an easy drive away.

DINNER (7.45–8.30pm) £14: haddock & egg mornay, spicy lamb, pudding and cheese
Children: own menu
£ low
Best Bargain Break £60 per person, 2 nights – dinner, b & b
Children: free up to 5 years; 40% of adult rate from 5 to 7; 60% from 7 to 12
Facilities: loads of cots and high chairs; a baby listening system
12 rooms, 10 family   Closed Dec and Jan
No credit cards accepted   No music
No smoking in whole house, except lounge
P – own car park   • Ale – Newquay Steam

Bridestowe, Nr Okehampton, Devon   map 1

KNOLE FARM – ☎ *Okehampton (0837) 86241.*

Off the A30 south-west of Okehampton.

The farmhouse is a delightful place, built towards the end of the last century. It is a charming building on two storeys, with a couple of tall chimneys, and a well-maintained garden with plenty of grassy spaces for children to play on. Guests are also welcome to walk the farm, where safety permits, and there are lovely views of Dartmoor.

There is a very pleasant family atmosphere here, and the owners offer an enthusiastic welcome to their guests, and clearly like to share their home with their visitors. There is a very comfortable and well-furnished lounge; and the traditional home cooking with fresh local produce is served in generous portions. Guests receive remarkably good value at Knole Farm.

Nearby: This is an ideal base from which to explore Devon, and Dartmoor stretches away to the south and east of the farm in all its splendour. There are delightful villages to see, and many pubs which welcome all the family. There are excellent walks, good fishing and golf, water sports, horse and pony riding,

and much else besides: Lydford Gorge, Becky Falls with its nature trail, the Parke Rare Breeds Farm and the remarkable Castle Drogo. Morwellham Quay is also a reasonable drive away.

DINNER (6.30pm) £7
Children: half portions
£ low
Children: cot £1.50; from £4 to £14 thereafter for b & b and an evening meal
Facilities: 1 cot and 1 high chair; and baby listening by arrangement
4 rooms, 2 family   Open Easter to November
No credit cards   Unlicensed
P – own car park   No music

Brighton, East Sussex   map 3

OLD SHIP HOTEL (Best Western), King's Road – ☎ Brighton (0273) 29001.

A building with a long history which is now a large and bustling hotel and where the staff are at great pains to welcome families, who come to enjoy the busy charms of this interesting seaside town. The building was first bought in 1651 on the proceeds of a reward paid by Charles II to Nicholas Tettersell, who helped the king to escape to France. The Old Ship Royal Escape Yacht Race is held every May to commemorate this event.

A great feature is made of their weekend breaks or "weekend cruises" as they term it. A nanny is available on Friday and Saturday evenings and at Sunday lunchtime and she presides over the spacious playroom with plenty of toys.

BROAD HAVEN

During the summer, trips are organised to nearby attractions.

Each family suite in the hotel has a sofa bed and they are spacious enough to accommodate a family of two adults and two children without any strain. One of our readers, Anne Douglas from London, told us that the hotel offers "unbeatable value", that the food was delicious and that her children loved the hotel.

Nearby: The town itself is full of interest, from the famous Lanes with their antique shops to the Brighton Pavilion and the Marina. Volk's electric railway, built in 1883, still runs between the Palace Pier and the Marina. Further afield you can visit castles at Lewes and Arundel, Drusillas zoo and adventure park, the Seven Sisters country park and the Bentley Wildfowl and Motor Museum.

LUNCH (12.30–2.30pm) £12, 2 courses: smoked poultry, whole plaice;
DINNER (7–9.30pm) £17: seafood cocktail, soup, roast guinea fowl, pudding or cheese
Children: own menu, half portions
£ high
Best Bargain Break £98 per person, 2 nights – dinner, b & b
Children: free up to age 16
Facilities: 7 cots and 8 high chairs; a baby listening system
152 rooms, 19 family, 6 sets interconnecting
Open all year   Access/AmEx/Diners/Visa
• Ale – Ruddles   No music
P – own car park (£6 per day)

Broad Haven, Pembrokeshire, Dyfed   map 5

MILLMOOR FARM COTTAGES and ROCKSDRIFT APARTMENTS –
☎ *Broad Haven (0437) 781 507.*

SC   *In the centre of Broad Haven.*

Helen and Eric Mock have quite an array of cottages and apartments to offer in the seaside village of Broad Haven, which is made so appealing by its large stretch of sandy beach.

Alongside the post office (also owned by Mr and Mrs Mock) and facing directly on to the beach, though there is a road in between, are the Rocksdrift Apartments. There are two spacious flats in a large Victorian house and each of them has three bedrooms – a triple, a double and a twin. Behind the house you will find the old stone coach house and this has been converted to provide nine apartments: the ground floor ones have two bedrooms each and the upper floor flats have three. All the ground floor apartments are suitable for guests in wheelchairs.

The apartments are well-designed and offer their guests plenty of space. They are centrally heated and the kitchens contain everything required, down to full-size cookers, food blenders and microwave ovens.

A few hundred yards away, Millmoor Farm Cottages have been converted from an 18th century farmhouse and the adjoining stone farm buildings. The house has been divided into two large cottages which can each accommodate a family of eight. Again the units are well-designed and equipped and there is plenty of space. The seven cottages in the adjoining courtyard can sleep between four and eight people, some of them on the ground floor and some in loft bedrooms. Two of the cottages can accommodate guests in wheelchairs.

There is plenty of room at the back of the cottages for the children to play. There are some swings and a rope climber and another good stretch of lawn to one side of the house. The beach is only a few hundred yards away and from the garden you can take in the full sweep of the bay of Broad Haven itself.

Nearby: As well as Broad Haven there are many other lovely sandy beaches and the whole of the Pembrokeshire countryside to explore – great fun if you like to walk, ride a horse or a pony, go fishing or golfing, or simply sit in the fresh air and relax. St David's, with its famous cathedral, is close and there is a Marine Life Centre and a butterfly farm in its vicinity. If you enjoy castles there are plenty: Pembroke, Carew, Manorbier and Tenby, for example.

Units: 20
Rent: £140 to £600
Other costs: none
Central heating: provided
Cots and high chairs available
Open all year

Brockenhurst, Hants   map 3

WATERSPLASH HOTEL – ☎ *Brockenhurst (0590) 22344.*

On the B3055.

This hotel is situated in a quiet road, and the various extensions do not entirely hide the original Victorian building with its high roofs and dormer windows. The dining room overlooks the garden, whilst the functional but comfortable lounges are in the older part of the house.

The family bedrooms are at the top of the house on the second floor, large and airy with sloping ceilings and dormer windows, and they have been recently refurbished. A family who have been coming here for many years praised the English cooking and friendly atmosphere.

The large gardens are sheltered by trees and are beautifully kept. There is also a vegetable garden, and the resulting produce helps to feed the guests. Other facilities include a fair-sized heated outdoor swimming pool, and a snooker table; and a cards and board games area available for guests.

BROSELEY

Nearby: This is the heart of the New Forest with beautiful countryside and pleasant villages all around; a lovely place to walk and browse. There are many places to visit within easy reach: the famous motor museum and stately home at Beaulieu, the Bucklers Hard Maritime Museum, the New Forest Butterfly Farm, the Bolderwood Arboretum with its delightful walks, Paultons Park which offers splendid entertainment for families, and Broadlands, the home of Palmerston and later of Lord Mountbatten. In addition there are some excellent sandy beaches less than half an hour's drive away.

BAR SNACKS (12–2pm) £1–4: scampi & chips, chicken & chips, ploughman's, filled baked potatoes;
DINNER (7.30–8.30pm) £14: game paté, fillet of plaice, pudding and cheese
Children: high teas, half portions
£ medium
Best Bargain Break £75 per person 2 nights – dinner, b & b
Children: cots free; one third of adult rate from 4–10 years; half the adult rate from 10–16 years
Facilities: 3 cots and 3 high chairs; baby listening to all rooms
23 rooms, 6 family   Access/Visa
Open all year • Ale – Eldridge Pope
P – own car park

Broseley, Shropshire   map 6
CUMBERLAND HOTEL, Jackson Avenue – ☎ *Telford (0952) 882 301.*

On the B4373 - look for the sign to the hotel.
You would be hard pushed to find two more charming examples of 18th century architecture than the two buildings which comprise the Cumberland Hotel. It is a pleasant shock to find them – just off a main road through the town – and realise just how peaceful the hotel is.

The main building was extended in Victorian times and has a couple of bars on the ground floor, where you will always find a good choice of real ales. The dining room is attractively decorated and is notable for its collection of Coalport china. At the front there is a large lawned garden, a peaceful place with lots of flowers.

The annexe is another superb Georgian building which has a direct connection with the Industrial Revolution. It was at a meeting here in 1775 that the decision was taken to build the famous Iron Bridge. It also has a delightful and tranquil garden.

The bedrooms are comfortable and quiet and very nicely decorated, and most of them overlook the various gardens. This is a really excellent hotel which offers value for money to families.

Nearby: It is a good spot if you wish to visit Ironbridge, which has a marvellous

BROSELEY

museum. *The exhibits are spread over six sites, including the Museum of Iron, the Coalport China Museum, the Jackfield Tile Museum, and so on. South Shropshire is a delightful area, and there are many other attractions including the Midland Motor Museum, the Severn Valley Railway, Carding Mill Valley and Wilderhope Manor.*

BAR MEALS (11am–3pm & 7–10.30pm) £1–4: lentil pie, vegetable Stroganoff, lemon sole, mixed grill, smoked haddock pasta; DINNER (7–10.30pm) £10: grilled prawns, game pie, pudding or cheese
Children: own menu, half portions
£ low
No Bargain Breaks
Children: £5 approx.
Facilities: 3 cots and 2 high chairs; baby listening system
17 rooms, 5 family   Diners/Visa
• Ale – Ansell's, Ruddles, Webster's   Open all year
P – own car park

To qualify for inclusion in the Guide hotels must offer the basic facilities of a cot, a family room and an evening meal. Self-catering establishments must provide cots and high chairs.

Bude, Cornwall   map 1

CLIFF HOTEL, Maer Down – ☎ Bude (0288) 353 110.

Near Crooklets Beach, which is well signposted.

This small family hotel is situated at the top of a cul-de-sac in five acres of grounds. It is very safe for children, and offers excellent facilities. A sandy beach lies only two hundred yards away.

The garden has extensive lawns and paddocks, and a special play area for children with swings, slides, a see-saw and a sand pit. For the adults and the older children there is a hard tennis court and a putting green; and everyone can enjoy the sizeable indoor swimming pool. There is also a spa bath in a separate building and darts and a pool table in the games room. Alternatively, you can just relax in a comfortable chair on the patio.

The hotel has several public rooms: a bar and a lounge, a separate wine bar, and a sun lounge cum writing room, which has fine views of the cliff top and the sea. The food is freshly cooked and will always include a good choice of fish, and the roast of the day will be carved for you at your table.

This is a friendly seaside hotel in a pleasant setting, and the owner can offer very special discounts to families in the off-season periods: April to the middle of May, but not Easter, and mid-September to October. Give Mr Sibley a call.

Nearby: Bude is well-known as a surfing resort, and there are other excellent beaches nearby including Sandy Mouth, Widemouth Sand and Crackington Haven. Further afield you can visit the Tamar Otter Park near Launceston, which has a famous castle, and nearby is the starting point for the Launceston Steam Railway.

DINNER (6.30pm) £6: paté, local salmon, profiteroles
Children: own menu, half portions
£ low
Children: 25% reduction up to 12 years
Facilities: 2 cots and 2 high chairs; baby listening by arrangement
15 rooms, 14 family   Open Easter to October
P – own car park   No credit cards

Nr Bude, Cornwall   map 1

HOUNDAPITT FARM COTTAGES – ☎ Bude (0288) 355 455.

SC   *North of Bude, off the A39. The brochure has clear directions.*

The cottages have the great advantage of being less than a mile from Sandymouth, a sandy beach where you can swim or surf, or just laze about. Lifeguards patrol the beach.

The cottages were converted from old farm buildings, of traditional stone and slate construction, and form a courtyard. The whole area is enlivened by the tubs and baskets of flowers which are scattered about. There is a bright and welcoming look to the cottages, with their white walls and pine fittings, and the original wooden beams have been used to good effect in the bedrooms. Fitted carpets are in place and the open plan kitchens cum dining rooms are well-equipped and include microwave ovens as well as electric cookers.

The cottages vary in size: there is a one-bedroomed cottage, three which can sleep four people, four which can sleep six, while the Grenville Farmhouse can accommodate nine people.

A converted barn houses a games room where there are two table tennis tables, a pool table, a playpen with plenty of toys and a selection of books. Outside you will find a sizeable, grassy play area for the children with a swing and a slide. There are picnic tables here and a barbecue, a nice spot to be on a summer day.

Guests are welcome to walk the 150 acres of farmland and there is a well-stocked fishing lake which guests can enjoy. Each week, the owner, Mr Heard, supervises a clay pigeon shoot.

All the elements necessary for a relaxing family holiday are present at Houndapitt, and you will be in the care of the charming Heard family.

Nearby: Sandy beaches abound on the north Cornish coast and it is a notable area for surfing, and all the other water sports can be arranged. Bude has a golf course, squash and tennis courts and a leisure pool. There are splendid walks in the vicinity of Houndapitt and the views from the coastal path are truly magnificent. The farm has its own riding stables near Bude and guests can take advantage of reduced rates. Bude has an interesting museum and the Tamar Otter Park, Bodmin Moor, Pencarrow House, Wesley's Cottage and the nature reserve at Braunton Burrows are within reach.

Units: 9
Rent: £110 to £455 a week; short breaks available
Other costs: none
Heating: central heating
Several cots and high chairs available
Open 5 January to 14 December

Bulwick, Nr Corby, Northants   map 7

BULWICK PARK COTTAGES – ☎ *Bulwick (078 085) 245.*

SC   *Off the A43 north east of Corby.*

The six cottages are situated on the Bulwick Park estate which runs for several miles between the two villages of Bulwick and Harringworth.

An elegant stone country house, part 17th and part 18th century, lies at the heart of the estate and it is encircled by fifty acres of parkland with a river on one side, where guests can fish.

Two of the cottages adjoin the hall. Garden Cottage is a delightful 17th century limestone building of three storeys. It is spacious, with three double bedrooms, and has a splendid walled garden. On the other side it overlooks a huge vegetable garden. The Coach House, another 17th century building, overlooks parkland and has recently been converted to provide four double bedrooms and spacious living areas including a sitting room and a dining room. It has its own enclosed lawned garden.

On the other side of the park and close to the village, Thatch Cottage and Pheasant Cottage are adjoining stone cottages and look so attractive under their thatched roofs. Both have their own enclosed gardens, very pretty with an array of flowers and bushes. Each cottage has two double bedrooms.

The four cottages are within an easy stroll of the village of Bulwick which has several shops, a post office and a pub.

The other two properties are in Harringworth, which also has a pub, a post office and shops. Lavender Cottage is another attractive stone cottage with a tile roof and has a lovely enclosed garden. The house looks on to meadowland and has two double bedrooms. Meadow Cottage is built of limestone under a tile roof and has the village church in the background. There is a large lawned garden and for keen riders, there is a riding stable next door.

We were very impressed by the high standards of all these properties; lovely cottages in peaceful surroundings in the rolling countryside. The rents are very reasonable indeed.

Nearby: Rutland Water, with its array of water sports, is a short drive away in one direction while Wicksteed Leisure Park lies in the other direction. Bulwick is ringed by fascinating places: Burghley House, Kirby Hall, the ancient Rockingham Castle, Boughton House, Rushton Triangular Lodge and Southwick Hall. Further afield you can visit Belvoir Castle and the children will certainly vote for a visit to Lilford Park with its farm, adventure playground and aviary.

Units: 6
Rent: £75 to £250 a week
Other costs: £5 per person for linen; heating fuel is metered
Heating: central heating provided
Cots and high chairs provided
Open all year

Burneside, Nr Kendal, Cumbria map 9

GARNETT HOUSE FARM – ☎ *Kendal (0539) 724 542.*

Half a mile off the A591 – follow signs to Burneside.

This delightful 15th century farmhouse once belonged to the family of Catherine Parr – one of Henry VIII's six wives – and the Parr family also owned Kendal Castle. With its four-foot thick walls, beamed ceilings and oak panelled lounge, the farmhouse retains its great character.

Garnett House is a working farm of nearly 300 acres, with sheep and dairy cattle and families are welcome to see around the farm and take an interest in what is going on: the cows are milked morning and evening; it is lambing time in March and April; sheep shearing in June and July; and so on.

You will receive a warm welcome from the Beaty family, and the food is freshly cooked from local ingredients, including the farm's own lamb and beef. The five rooms include two family rooms and there is a cot and a high chair available. The front rooms have splendid views of Howgill Fells, and those at the side look out to Potter Fell.

Nearby: It is a charming place for a holiday, and as well as the local walks there is plenty to do and see in the vicinity, since you are in the heart of the Lake District. Kendal itself is well worth a look, and Levens Hall is nearby, as is Holker Hall with its motor museum. The children will probably be interested in Fell Foot Park and the Grizedale Forest Centre; and steam enthusiasts will head for the Lakeside Railway, the Steamboat Museum at Windermere, or further afield, the famous "Ratty" railway.

DINNER (6.30pm) £6
Children: small portions
£ low
Children: reductions depending on age
Facilities: 1 cot and 1 high chair; baby listening by arrangement
Open all year except Xmas and New Year
5 rooms, 2 family   No credit cards
No music   Unlicensed   P – ample

Caernarfon, Gwynedd   map 5

GORFFWYSFA, St David's Road – ☎ *Caernarfon (0286) 2647.*

Just off the A487.

The house was built in the late 19th century, and has an imposing look to it as you would expect of a former rectory. The owners have retained many of the original features such as the fireplaces, stained glass windows and pine staircase. They offer good facilities and a real welcome to families, and the three spacious family rooms have views of the sea. Very useful for families is the suite which comprises a double room, an adjoining room with bunk beds and space for a folding bed, and a bathroom. They are also willing to arrange baby listening and sitting, and high teas are included in the reduced price for children, if parents are having dinner. It is good to know that vegetarian meals can also be provided, if you let the owners know in advance.

The house is built on three storeys and you enter into a spacious tiled hall and reception area with lovely leaded light windows. Toys and books are made available in the guests' lounge, and there is a pool table. Children can play in the rear garden which has a swing and a paddling pool in the summer. The large front garden overlooks the Menai Strait, and Anglesey.

CAERNARFON

A great advantage of the house is that it is situated in a quiet residential area, and yet is within walking distance of the centre of the town.

Nearby: Caernarfon is not a "bucket and spade" town, but there are excellent beaches nearby: Llanddwyn, with its adjoining nature reserves, on Anglesey; and further south Traeth Penllech and Porthoer. Dinas Dinlle, an EC safe beach, is only a couple of miles away. This is also the land of castles, in Caernarfon itself, Dolbadarn, and Penrhyn. The many attractions of Snowdonia lie close at hand, as do Llyn Padarn Country Park, the Cwm Idwal Nature Trail, and Gwydir Forest with its many walks.

BAR SNACKS (12–10pm) £1–3: baked potatoes, burgers, salads, omelettes;
DINNER (7pm) £7: soup, roast beef & Yorkshire pudding, fruit crumble
Children: own menu, half portions
£ low
Children: free up to 2 years; half price from 2 to 12
Facilities: 2 cots and 2 high chairs; baby listening system
8 rooms, 3 family   Open all year
No credit cards   No smoking in dining room
P – own car park and on street

Nr Canterbury, Kent map 4

SPRING GROVE FARM, Wye – ☎ Wye (0233) 812 425.

SC *Off the A28 south of Canterbury.*

These unusual properties have been converted from an old oast house and are situated on a farm of around a hundred acres in delightful countryside. Spring Grove Farm is within walking distance of the village of Wye in the Great Stour Valley.

The apartments have been converted with imagination and style and take full advantage of the charm of the oast house. One of the great bonuses for guests is the view over the surrounding countryside. The properties are notable for the excellent furniture; pine tables and chairs and comfortable easy chairs. The kitchens are equipped with everything a cook might need. There is a laundry room, an extra bed for each apartment, and as many cots and high chairs as necessary.

Four of the properties sleep up to six people; Brambling sleeps four; Brewers Gold can accommodate up to eight. All of them share the same front entrance, except Pride of Kent which has its own front door.

The facilities at Spring Grove are exceptional, and especially so for families. The landscaped gardens, with their lawns and well-kept flower beds, contain a tennis court and a heated outdoor swimming pool. In addition the games room has table tennis and darts.

Guests are very welcome to walk the farm, and four acres of land by the river have been set aside as a wetland conservation area where many geese, swans, ducks and wading birds can be seen.

This is a lovely spot where families are particularly well cared for.

Nearby: Walkers can follow the North Downs Way and there is a nature trail on the farm. Guests can fish the Stour and riding can easily be arranged with nearby stables. Golfers are within easy reach of a number of fine courses including Deal and Royal St Georges. The children will certainly vote for a trip to Howletts Zoo Park or Port Lympne Zoo; and there are castles to see at Deal, Dover and Walmer as well as the enchanting Leeds Castle. A journey on the Kent and East Sussex Railway or the Romsey and Hythe Railway will appeal to many. Above all, Canterbury, with its many treasures, merits a visit.

Units: 6
Rent: £220 to £625 a week (winter breaks available)
Other costs: electricity
Heating: night storage
Cots and high chairs provided
Open all year

Cawsand, Cornwall   map 1
WRINGFORD DOWN – ☎ Plymouth (0752) 822 287.

From the B3247 south of Torpoint, follow the signs for Cawsand. The hotel's brochure gives detailed directions.

Harvey and Andrea Jay have a very clear view of who their customers are; they are families with very young children. Their brochure states that they "try very hard to dissuade people without children from staying here. Everything is geared to help you look after your babies and toddlers as you would at home." Needless to say that there are plenty of cots and high chairs and an efficient baby listening service.

This unusual hotel is housed in a nice old stone house, the main part of which is 18th century, and has been extended over the years. The facilities include a small bar with a conservatory, a pool table in an adjoining room, and a restaurant. There is a spacious lounge with an open fire, and a quiet play room with a piano and plenty of books.

The enterprising owners provide loads of amusements both indoors and out for children. There is a spacious playroom with a rocking horse, building bricks and all sorts of toys. Alongside is a huge play barn which would keep the children amused for days. It has an aviary, a huge and very practical padded playpen, a sandpit, a trampoline and climbing ropes on a special safety surface, ride-on toys, and a small swimming pool.

Move outdoors and you can enjoy a large garden with lovely views over the surrounding countryside with a church spire on the horizon. There are plenty of bench tables for the adults; and swings, a slide and a climbing frame for the children plus geese, ducks, chickens, goats and sheep for them to make friends with. Donkey rides are also organised.

This hotel has splendid facilities for families and represents outstanding value. The owners have an unusual and very enterprising approach to family holidays and it is a real haven for parents and children alike.

Nearby: There are many sandy and safe beaches and many other attractions within easy reach: Mount Edgcumbe Country Park is just up the road; there is a monkey sanctuary near Looe, the Shire Horse Centre east of Plymouth and Dartmoor Wildlife Park; Morwellham Quay, Cotehele House, Dobwalls Theme Park, Lanhydrock, and Restormel Castle.

DINNER (7pm): smoked mackerel, lamb in apricot sauce, apple crumble
Children: high teas, small portions
£ low
Bargain Breaks available in Spring and Autumn
Children: free up to 5 years; half price from 5 to 10
Facilities: 20 cots and 20 high chairs; baby listening system to every room

13 rooms, all family, 6 sets interconnecting
Open all year except Xmas
P – own car park

Chagford, Devon   map 1
MILL END HOTEL – ☎ Chagford (0647) 432 282.

On the A382 – not in Chagford.

This lovely hotel was once a flour mill and the wheel still turns in the courtyard. You are well shielded by walls in the gardens, and it is very peaceful in the back garden, shaded by enormous trees.

Children are accommodated free to a ripe old age, and in fact a third person sharing a room with two others does not pay extra – an enlightened policy which more British hoteliers ought to follow.

The charming and hospitable owners now welcome children of all ages into the restaurant in the evenings, provided that reasonable standards of behaviour are met. High teas are still available at 6pm.

It's a lovely part of the country – on the edge of Dartmoor – and another claim to fame is that Evelyn Waugh wrote Brideshead Revisited while staying in the village in 1944.

Nearby: Fishermen are well catered for here. They can fish for salmon and trout in the Upper Teign River which flows past the hotel, and also in some nearby reservoirs. Further stretches of the river are also available. There is a golf course about five miles away, and this is a lovely part of the world for walking and riding. The remarkable Castle Drogo is next door and you can quickly reach Killerton House, Powderham Castle, Becky Falls, Parke Rare Breeds Farm and the nature reserve at Dawlish Warren.

✗ LIGHT LUNCH (12.30–2pm) £2–8: soup, ploughman's, salads;
DINNER (7.30–9pm) £25: Scotch smoked salmon, roast Guinea fowl, pudding, cheese
Children: high teas, half portions
£ high
Best Bargain Break £107 per person, 2 nights – dinner, b & b
Children: free to any age
Facilities: 3 cots and 2 high chairs; a baby listening system to all rooms
Open all year
17 rooms, 2 family   Access/AmEx/Diners/Visa
• Ale – Wadworth's   No music
P – own car park

Nr Chagford, Devon   map 1
THORNWORTHY HOUSE – ☎ *Chagford (0647) 433 297.*

South west of Chagford on the minor roads. From Chagford follow signs to Fernworthy, and then signs for Thornworthy.

If you like peace and quiet and simple relaxations, such as walking or riding or the odd game of tennis, or simply doing nothing much, this is the place to go. It is out on Dartmoor, three miles on narrow roads from lovely Chagford, and is a delightful Victorian stone house with rambling outbuildings. A working farm is next door and all around are the many natural pleasures of Dartmoor. The hotel garden is delightful too, with plenty of lawn, superb rhododendrons, a duck pond, a swing, and a hard tennis court.

The owners run the place not as an hotel but as their own family house with guests to stay; since they have several children and many pets there is an informal air to the whole place; and this extends to the baby listening, which is done almost on a "co-operative" basis. The food will always be fresh (from local suppliers such as the farmer next door). Younger children are not encouraged in the dining room at night, when the adults want to play.

There is also a self-catering cottage, Barn Cottage, attached to the hotel which has three double bedrooms, a patio and a garden. The rent is £375 a week.

Nearby: You can enjoy the beauties of Dartmoor where there are facilities for riding and trout fishing (at Fernworthy Reservoir); and the extraordinary Castle Drogo is on the doorstep. Becky Falls, the Parke Rare Breeds Farm and the many museums of Exeter are quite close. For the beaches you must head for the coast between Dawlish Warren and Torquay where there are several sandy coves.

DINNER (8pm onwards) £18: Caesar salad, grilled lemon sole, strawberry tarlets, cheese
Children: high teas
£ high
Children: cot £7.50
Facilities: 1 cot and 1 high chair
6 rooms, 1 cottage   No credit cards accepted
🅿 – own car park   No music

If you wish to recommend an establishment to the Guide please write to us – report forms are at the back of the book. We need your help to extend and improve the guide.

Chale, Isle of Wight   map 3

CLARENDON HOTEL & WIGHT MOUSE INN – ☎ *Isle of Wight (0983) 730 431.*

Just off the A3055 in the south of the island.
The hotel began life as a coaching inn in the 17th century and the stone building, with its dormer windows, is full of character.

The owners, John and Jean Bradshaw, have extended the hotel over the years and offer an excellent array of facilities for families. There are eight family-sized rooms (including an attractive family suite) and they are comfortable, spacious and well-furnished. There are always half a dozen cots and high chairs available for very young children.

The new dining room is nicely furnished with whicker backed chairs and the hanging plants give it a relaxing look. Large windows give wonderful views out to sea.

The hotel has its own pub, the Wight Mouse Inn, which is also geared up for families with several areas where they can sit together. The family rooms are full of character with an eclectic collection of musical instruments, antique bottles, prints, maps and pictures. The pub is open all day and has an extensive menu and a good choice of real ales. The list of whiskies, a different brand for every day of the year, is amazing.

Outside you will find a large and grassy garden which looks out to sea. There

CHAPEL AMBLE

are plenty of tables and chairs and a separate play area for children with swings, slides, climbing frames, a petanque pitch and a pets corner with rabbits, chickens and lambs.

The hotel offers splendid facilities (including live entertainment each evening in the inn) for families and is run in an enterprising and well-organised manner.

Nearby: Sandy beaches are easy to find on the island and there are lovely walks close to the hotel. There is a great deal to see and do and none of the attractions are difficult to reach. The nearest to the hotel is Blackgang Chine, a theme park which is recommended in the Family Welcome Leisure Guide. Yafford Mill, Carisbrooke Castle, Arreton Manor, Haseley Manor, the Needles Pleasure Park, Robin Hill Park and Flamingo Park are all within easy reach. Golf, fishing and horse riding can all be arranged.

BAR MEALS (11am–10pm, Mon to Sat; 12–2.30pm & 7–9.30pm Sun) £1–9: gravadlax, steaks, crab & prawn mornay, burgers, pizzas

DINNER (7pm onwards) £10: quiche Lorraine, grilled lemon sole, fresh fruit meringue and cheese

Children: own menu, half portions

£ medium

Children: £2 up to 2 years; £4 from 3 to 5; half price from 6 to 12; two thirds from 13 to 16

Facilities: 6 cots and 6 high chairs; portable baby alarms

15 rooms, 8 family, 1 suite   Open all year

• Ale – Boddington's, Burt's, Marston's, Wadworth's

P – own car park   Access/Visa

The Wight Mouse Inn is recommended in the Family Welcome Pub & Restaurant Guide.

Chapel Amble, Nr Wadebridge, Cornwall   map 1

THE OLDE HOUSE – ☎ *Wadebridge (0208) 813 219.*

SC *The village is off the B3314 north of Wadebridge and The Olde House is close to the village pub, the Maltsters Arms.*

There are 30 cottages from which to choose at this enterprising holiday centre and farm. It all began in 1978 when Andrew and Janice Hawkey converted a couple of their old farm buildings, and the venture has grown every year. The latest additions to the list were five new cottages, finished in 1989, but made of Cornish stone and with slate roofs.

The other cottages are all built from the old stone outbuildings and every effort has been made to insert all the comforts which families on holiday require while retaining the character of the buildings. They mostly accommodate four to six people, although Wheel Cottage sleeps only two and three other cottages can take up to eight.

The cottages have been made from a barn, a mill, a stable and a cow house and grain store, but they have one thing in common: they have been converted with style and good taste, and are well-furnished and well-equipped.

One of the great advantages of staying here is the presence of an excellent, purpose-built leisure centre. It has a sizeable swimming pool, a children's pool, jacuzzi, sauna and solarium, and a snooker table. It has its own lounge area and a babies' playpen. Outside, there is an adventure playground, swings and a climbing frame, and an all-weather tennis court.

The Olde House is at the centre of a working farm of 500 acres and the guests are welcome to join in; and the farm animals are particularly appealing to the children. This is a marvellous place for a family holiday.

Nearby: There is no shortage of safe and sandy beaches in the area, and Daymer and Polzeath offer surfing and swimming, while Rock has sailing, wind surfing and water skiing. You can follow the coastal footpath and there are plenty of stables from which to go riding. Fishermen and golfers are well catered for. If you like to see the sights you can head for Pencarrow House, Lanhydrock House, Dobwalls Theme Park, Trerice and the Lappa Valley Railway. The children will enjoy a visit to Newquay Zoo and the Tropical Bird Gardens at Padstow.

Units: 30
Rent: £120 to £750 a week
Other costs: linen at £2.50 a person; electricity is on a meter
Heating: central heating
As many cots and high chairs as required
Open all year

Chew Magna, Nr Bristol, Avon   map 2

CHEW HILL FARM – ☎ *Bristol (0272) 332 496.*

SC *Off the B3130 south of Bristol.*

Chew Hill Farm has an unrivalled location nearly 500 feet above the village on the south slopes of Dundry Hill. From there you have wonderful views over the Chew Valley and to the Mendips beyond.

There are three properties on the farm and they have one very important characteristic in common, especially for a family on holiday – plenty of space. West Lodge is an agreeable Victorian lodge with three bedrooms and it has its own lawned garden and a garage. East Lodge was built in 1963 and has three bedrooms, a spacious lawned garden and a garage. Finally, the Bailiff's House, built in 1955, provides the same facilities as East Lodge but with a smaller garden.

CHIDDINGLY

Each house is comfortably furnished and carpeted and has a well-equipped kitchen. Above all, it is the peace and tranquillity of the place and the wonderful views which will appeal to the holiday maker. So will the rental charges, which are reasonable.

Nearby: Chew Hill is an excellent base for a holiday with so much to see and do in the vicinity. Bristol and Bath, and Wells with its magnificent cathedral are close. Fishermen are well looked after, with trout to catch at Blagdon Lake and Chew Valley Lake and the latter is also a nature reserve. If you head south to the Mendips you can visit Wookey Hole Caves, Cheddar Gorge and Ebbor Gorge; and a little further afield Nunney Castle, Montacute House, the Fleet Air Museum, Ham Hill Country Park and the wildlife park at Cricket St Thomas.

Units: 3
Rent: £200 to £260 a week
Other costs: electricity on a meter
Heating: night storage heaters
2 cots and 1 high chair available
Open all year

Chiddingly, Nr Hailsham, East Sussex　　　　　　　　　　map 4

PEKES – ☎ *(for bookings) Mrs Eva Morris 071–352 8088.*

SC　*Off the A22 north of Hailsham.*

If you hanker for a bit of style, try Pekes, a Tudor manor house with grounds covering nearly thirty acres. It is a quiet and secluded spot and comprises four properties for letting.

The Wing, as the name suggests, is attached to the main house. It started life as a cowshed and was converted just after the turn of the century to serve as a drawing room and library for the main house. It is a most attractive building, long and low, with a large bay window. The main L shaped room is very large and serves as both a living area and dining room. The one bedroom adjoins this, but there are two divans in the main room. A family of four could be accommodated here.

Tudor View looks like a cottage but is actually a bungalow. It was built in the late 'thirties but fits into the general scheme of things very well. There are two bedrooms, a double and a twin, a sitting room and a dining room. It is the nearest property to the swimming pool and has its own little fenced garden.

The Gate Cottage is a delightful tile-hung cottage on two floors and was originally built (in 1911) for the coachman. There are two bedrooms, a living room and a dining room.

The Oast House is a most appealing building, its focal point being the two large round towers which were once used for drying hops. It was converted in 1911 and there are two circular bedrooms upstairs and two large reception rooms below. A further two bedrooms (one double and one single) have been built. A family of eight can easily be accommodated.

In addition to the lovely and peaceful grounds, parts of which can be used by guests, there are other excellent facilities, including a tennis court and new covered swimming pool. A sauna, solarium, spa bath and some exercise equipment is also available (50p meter). A badminton net is also provided.

The properties are all well-equipped and have central heating. The only extra is the hire of linen; and Tudor View has a meter for its electricity.

Nearby: Apart from the appealing countryside of Sussex there is no lack of things to do and see in the vicinity. Mitchelham Priory, Firle Place and Herstmonceux Castle are close; while the children will no doubt beat a path to Drusillas and the Seven Sisters Country Park, which has a Living World exhibition. There are leisure centres at nearby Hailsham and at Eastbourne.

Units: 4
Rent: from £140 to £800 per week
Other costs: linen; and electricity at Tudor View and the Oast House
Central heating: provided
Two cots and two high chairs; baby sitting by arrangement
Open all year

Chollerford, Nr Hexham, Northumberland   map 9
GEORGE HOTEL (Swallow) – ☎ Humshaugh (0434) 681 611.

On the B6318.

If you follow the magnificent Roman road, arrow-like alongside Hadrian's Wall, you will find this nice old stone hotel on the bank of the North Tyne, where guests can fish. The gardens running along the river are a mass of flowers in summer, and at the end of the garden is an excellent indoor heated swimming pool with an exercise area and a sun patio. There is a very large grassy play area here, with swings, a slide, seesaw, a putting green and a golf net.

This is a very pleasant hotel with excellent facilities, and it is deservedly popular with families.

Nearby: The B6318 follows the line of Hadrian's Wall and you can visit several of the forts, the Roman Army Museum and the Roman site near Corbridge. There are many other attractions within reach including Belsay Hall, Wallington House and the Beamish Open Air Museum. Kielder Water has an array of water sports and Kielder Castle is the starting point for walks through the surrounding forest.

LUNCH (12–2pm) £13: soup, cold buffet, pudding or cheese;
DINNER (7–9.45pm) £17: vegetable terrine, soup, haddock fillet, pudding or cheese

Children: own menu, half portions
£ high
Best Bargain Break £117 per person 2 nights – dinner, b & b and one lunch
Children: free up to 14 years
Facilities: 5 cots and 4 high chairs; and a baby listening system
50 rooms, 6 family   Access/AmEx/Diners/Visa
Open all year   **P** – own car park

Cholmondeley, Nr Malpas, Cheshire   map 6
CHOLMONDELEY ARMS – ☎ Cholmondeley (0829) 720 300.

On the A49 five miles north of Whitchurch.

The Harrison family used to own the excellent Crown at Hopton Wafers, which has been listed by us for many years. Together with Guy and Carolyn Ross-Lowe they have now converted this Victorian school (it was the local school until 1982) and have made a really splendid job of it.

The original building has not been altered, but the interior has been opened into three sections; in the centre is a bar and there are two areas, away from the bar, which are intended mainly for food and where families can settle.

The high schoolhouse windows are curtained from top to bottom, and there is a mixture of oak and pine furniture: oblong and round tables, settles, bucket and cane chairs, standard lamps in the corners, and china plates and prints scattered on the walls. It all hangs together very well.

There is a huge lawned garden with plenty of bench tables, and a children's play area with swings and a large wooden climbing frame.

Nearby: You are close both to the Shropshire and the Welsh borders, with lovely countryside within reach. There are many interesting castles on the borders: Erddig and Chirk for example; and you can see the lovely Dee Valley by taking the Llangollen steam railway. The fascinating town of Chester is not too far away, while Bridgemere Wildlife Park and Stapeley Water Gardens are close at hand.

(12–2.15pm & 6.30–10pm) £1–10: saffron prawns, blinis with smoked salmon, chicken piri piri, Madras beef curry, salmon fishcake
Children: own menu
£ low
Children: £5 for cot or extra bed
Facilities: cots must be ordered when booking; 6 high chairs
4 rooms, 1 family   Open all year
• Ale – Boddington's, Marston's and guests

Access/Visa P – own car park

Also recommended in the Family Welcome Pub & Restaurant Guide.

Churchstoke, Montgomery, Powys   map 6
DREWIN FARM – ☎ *Churchstoke (0588) 620 325.*

Off the B4385, just south of Churchstoke.
Be sure to get directions from Mrs Richards, because the farm is not easy to find – but well worth the effort. The Offa's Dyke footpath runs through the farm, which is a mixed one, where sheep and cattle are reared and corn is grown. After a long day of tramping along the Dyke, or other parts of the lovely countryside, you will be glad of the comforts which are offered here.

The farm has been in the same family for six generations, and the farmhouse is a lovely 17th century, stone building with a handsome interior of oak beams, and comfortable furniture; and there is an inglenook fireplace. The separate sitting room has a piano and an electric organ. The family rooms have a double bed and a single and can also accommodate a cot, and one of them has its own bathroom.

There is plenty of lawned garden at the side of the house, and guests can walk the farm, if they wish. Children must of course be supervised. The old granary has been converted to a games room and houses a snooker table, table tennis table and a darts board.

Nearby: The surrounding countryside is a delight to walk through, and there is also good fishing to be had, and pony trekking can be organised. There are *many border castles to be seen – at Powis, Clun and Montgomery for example – and South Shropshire is a lovely spot especially round Clun, Ludlow and Church Stretton. The Welshpool and Llanfair Light Railway is not far away, nor is the Offa's Dyke Heritage Centre.*

✕ DINNER (6–7.30pm) £7
Children: half portions
£ low
Children: half price under 10 years
Facilities: 1 cot and 1 high chair; baby listening/sitting by arrangement
2 rooms, 2 family   Open April to November
No credit cards   No music
No smoking in bedrooms   Unlicensed   🅿 – own car park

Clifton Dykes, Nr Penrith, Cumbria   map 9
WETHERIGGS POTTERY – ☎ *Penrith (0768) 62946.*

Off the A6 four miles south of Penrith. There is a sign to the Pottery.

This is a splendid little complex based around a working pottery which has been going since 1855. Today it comprises an excellent and well stocked pottery shop, gallery, museum, restaurant and tearoom. The tables set up in the gallery look over the pottery workshops and this is an interesting place to sit.

All the food is home-made with a strong vegetarian theme although one of the specialities is an American Sunday brunch – ham and eggs etc for around £5. All the food is cooked with fresh ingredients.

You can get light snacks all day and there are daily specials at lunchtimes, all made from fresh ingredients.

Children are very well looked after. Outside in the garden there are picnic tables and a playground but the owners also encourage their young visitors to try their hand on the potter's wheel. It is refreshing to find a place which is a little bit different and where the owners give families such a good welcome.

This is an interesting and relaxing place to stay and there are four comfortable and functional bedrooms to let, including a family room. The price for bed and a substantial breakfast is very reasonable, as are the prices for food.

Nearby: Ullswater, with its many water sports, is just down the road, as is Lowther Park, where you can picnic amongst the herds of red deer. There are many nature trails, plus an adventure playground for the children. To the south you can quickly reach all the well-known attractions of the Lake District: Grasmere, Windermere, Brantwood, the Grizedale Forest Centre. Or you can simply enjoy the peace and quiet of the countryside around Penrith.

✕ £1–5: pizzas, moussaka, mushroom & yoghurt quiche, home-made soup & bread, American Sunday Brunch

Children: own menu, half portions
£ low
Children: half price
Facilities: 1 cot and 1 high chair
4 rooms, 1 family   Open all year
Access/Visa   No smoking
P – own car park

Also recommended in the Family Welcome Pub & Restaurant Guide.

Colaton Raleigh, Nr Sidmouth, Devon   map 2
DRUPE FARM – ☎ *Colaton Raleigh (0395) 68838.*

SC   *On the B3178 west of Sidmouth.*

The conversion of old farm buildings was carried out in 1976 with great success. The smart cottages, some built from the local pink-tinged stone and others painted white, form a natural courtyard around a lawned garden with lots of cheerful flowers and shrubs.

Drupe Farm is just off the main street of the attractive village, and the shops and a smart-looking pub ('The Otter') are within a short stroll.

Most of the fourteen cottages sleep up to four people, while two can sleep six and two others can sleep up to seven people. There are plenty of high chairs and cots available. The properties have plenty of space and they are comfortably and unfussily furnished. Many of them, such as Bulverton Cottage, have open plan living areas and we noticed how the old beams of the original buildings had been retained and used to good effect. One of the great bonuses of staying at Drupe Farm is the lovely views from the cottages.

The facilities here are excellent and include a laundry; a very well-equipped games room with table football, table tennis, pool table, a dart board and some amusement machines; and a very safe and well-kept play area with swings, a see saw, wooden climbing frames, a sandpit, and an old tractor on which children can play. There are bench tables here and a barbecue; it's a lovely spot to have an al fresco meal while the children amuse themselves.

One of the cottages overlooks the picnic cum play area and its semi-circular living room is an unusual and charming conversion. With fourteen cottages to look after, refurbishment is a continual process here and the manager told us that many of the kitchens are going to be updated in the near future.

Nearby: East Devon is a beautiful part of the country and Drupe Farm sits in an area of outstanding natural beauty. The countryside offers much to walkers, or you can enjoy it all from horseback. Fishermen have a good choice of river or sea fishing and there are golf courses within a few miles. There are many beaches including Budleigh Salterton, Sidmouth and Branscombe and the attendant water sports. There are plenty of interesting places to see: Bicton

Park, the donkey sanctuary near Sidmouth, the Farway Park, the Maritime Museum in Exeter, Killerton House, Powderham Castle and the nature reserve at Dawlish Warren.

Units: 14
Rent: £125 to £375 a week (short breaks also available in winter)
Other costs : none
Heating: gas central heating
Plenty of cots and high chairs
Open all year

Colmonell, Girvan, Ayrshire, Strathclyde   map 11
BURNFOOT FARM – ☎ *Colmonell (046 588) 220.*

Off the A765 and close to the village of Colmonell.

This traditional Scottish farmhouse, long and low and built of stone which is now painted white, has a lovely situation on the south side of the Stinchar valley. The house is ringed by gentle hills and the green acres of the farm itself.

You will receive a warm and friendly welcome from the owner and the accommodation is especially suitable for families. One bedroom has a double and a single bed; and the family suite comprises two adjoining rooms, one with a double and a single bed and the other with two single beds – ideal for a large family. Colour televisions and tea and coffee making facilities are provided.

There is a very comfortable and warm sitting room with several easy chairs and a dining room of pleasant proportions. It is good to report that many of the vegetables and fruit are grown in the large garden alongside the farmhouse.

Nearby: Whatever your interests you will find plenty to do and see in this part of Scotland. Visitors are welcome to join in the activities of the farm, which has 150-odd acres for sheep and cattle, and the children will no doubt make friends with the farm's Highland pony. There are sandy beaches nearby at Ballantrae, Girvan, Lendalfoot and Ayr, while the golfer has a multitude of fine courses to play. The river Stinchar offers excellent salmon fishing, and the locality offers lovely walks; Culzean Castle and Country Park is close, as is the Burns Museum and the bird sanctuary on Ailsa Craig.

DINNER (6.30pm) £6
Children: half portions
£ low
Children: £5.50 up to 6 years; £7.50 from 6 to 12
Facilities: 1 cot and 1 high chair
2 rooms, both family   Open April to October
No credit cards   Unlicensed
No smoking in dining room and bedrooms   No music   **P** – ample

Cooden, Bexhill-on-Sea, East Sussex   map 4
THE COODEN RESORT HOTEL – ☎ *Cooden (0424) 32281.*

Off the A259 west of Bexhill; follow the sign to the railway station.

In a splendid spot right by a shingle beach, there is an interesting look to this building, long and low and stretching in a semi-circle: it was built in the 'thirties and its wooden verandahs make it look like a vast and eccentric cricket pavilion.

We recommend it for its facilities which include an outdoor heated swimming pool in the big, lawned garden which stretches down to the sea; an indoor pool with some exercise machines alongside; and there is a golf course next door, which offers guests reduced prices.

Nearby: There is lovely countryside inland, and if you fancy seeing the sights you can head for the castles at Hastings, Herstmonceux or Pevensey, while the ruined Battle Abbey is close. The grown-ups might like a tour of the Carr Taylor vineyards; and Drusillas, which has been recommended in the Family Welcome Guide for many years, has something for everyone.

BAR SNACKS (12.30–2pm) £1–5: plaice & chips, lasagne, ploughman's, filled jacket potatoes;
LUNCH (12.30–2pm) £13: mussel salad, liver & bacon, pudding or cheese;
DINNER (7.30–9.30pm) £18: melon & Parma ham, lobster bisque, pork cutlet Normande, pudding or cheese
Children: own menu, half portions
£ high
Best Bargain Break £84 per person 2 nights – dinner, b & b
Children: free to age 12
Facilities: 5 cots and 3 high chairs; baby listening on 10 lines
42 rooms, 9 family   Access/AmEx/Diners/Visa
Open all year   • Ale – Bass, Harvey's
P – own car park

Corney, Nr Bootle Village, Millom, Cumbria   map 9
FOLDGATE FARM – ☎ *Bootle (06578) 660.*

Off the A595 north of Bootle.

The farm covers ninety acres and is situated in delightful countryside and is within relatively easy distance of most of the Lake District amenities.

The farmhouse is built of Lakeland stone and is partly 19th century, and partly of an earlier vintage. It is a comfortable place, with traditional furniture such as an old dresser with china mugs hanging on it, and meat hooks in the ceiling.

COUNTISBURY

The friendly owners have a long experience of looking after holiday makers, and you will get good country cooking, including the farm's own fruit, vegetables and lamb, and free range eggs.

A small garden sits at the back of the farmhouse and you can fish for brown trout in a nearby beck.

Nearby: The Ravenglass and Eskdale railway is close, as is Muncaster Castle with its wonderful rhododendron garden; and it is not too long a drive across to Coniston and Windermere Lakes, to Grasmere and all the other attractions of the Lake District: Brantwood, Belle Isle, the Steamboat Museum at Windermere, Holker Hall and the Lakeside and Haverthwaite Railway. The children will particularly enjoy a visit to Fell Foot Park and the Grizedale Visitor Centre.

DINNER (6pm) £8
Children: half portions
£ low
Children: reductions by age
Facilities: 1 cot and baby sitting by arrangement
2 rooms, 2 family   Open January to November
No credit cards   Unlicensed
P – ample

Countisbury, Devon   map 1

COOMBE FARM – ☎ *Brendon (059 87) 236.*

East of Lynton on the A39 – take the turning for Brendon.

The farmhouse dates back to the middle of the 17th century and is built of local stone, with steep roofs and a front porch. You approach it through the farmyard, with its various barns and outbuildings, including stables for the horses. It is close to the famous Doone Valley and offers guests a very peaceful holiday, with mile upon mile of beautiful countryside in which to walk or ride. The farm itself comprises nearly 400 acres, on which Exmoor Horn sheep, cattle and horses are reared.

The rooms in the farmhouse are cosy and welcoming. The spacious lounge with a wood burning stove, has a selection of books, and plenty of leaflets to tell you about the surrounding area; and in the beamed dining room you will be served food made from the farm's own produce.

Nearby: The coastal footpath runs through the farm, and trout fishing can be arranged on the nearby East Lyn river. There are also riding stables nearby. It's a great area for a holiday, since the coast with its many beaches is very close, as is the wide and beautiful expanse of the Exmoor National Park. The Lyn and Exmoor Museum at Lynton will tell you about the history of the area. There is much else to see and enjoy including Exmoor Bird Gardens, Arling-

ton Court, Watermouth Castle, Dunster Castle, Combe Sydenham Hall and the West Somerset Railway.

✕ (7pm) £10
Children: half portions
£ low
Children: sliding scale up to 11 years
Facilities: 1 cot and 1 high chair; baby listening by arrangement
5 rooms, 2 family   Open April to October
No credit cards   No smoking in dining room
🅿 – ample   No music

Cranford St Andrew, Northants   map 7

DAIRY FARM – ☎ *Cranford (0536) 78273.*

Off the A 604 just east of Kettering.

This thatched manor house, which was built in the early 17th century, is full of character. Underneath its steeply pitched roof, with its dormer windows and tall chimneys, you will find charmingly furnished rooms with their fair share of oak beams and inglenook fireplaces. The family room has a double bed and its own bathroom, and either a cot or a single bed can be set up as well.

There is half an acre or so of attractive garden, with some fine mature trees, and a notable medieval stone dovecote. The grounds are mostly enclosed and children can play in safety, and there is also a swing and a croquet lawn. Guests are welcome to wander around the farm, as long as they stay well clear of any machinery.

Nearby: This is an interesting part of the country and, apart from the pleasant walks which you can enjoy, there are many other diversions. The children will no doubt be keen to see the nearby Wicksteed Leisure Park, while Guilsborough Grange is a bit further away and has a wildlife park. Boughton House, Lamport Hall, Lilford Park, and Rockingham Castle are all within easy reach.

✗ (7.30pm) £10: celery soup, chicken casserole, trifle
Children: half portions
£ low
Children: half price under 10 years
Facilities: 1 cot; baby patrol by arrangement
3 rooms, 1 family   Open all year except Xmas
No credit cards   No music
P – own car park   Unlicensed

Crantock, Newquay, Cornwall   map 1

CRANTOCK BAY HOTEL – ☎ *Newquay (0637) 830 229.*

Off the A3075 south of Newquay.

The hotel is a bit further along the road from Crantock and is probably in West Pentire. But no matter: suffice to say that the hotel has one of the best coastal

CRANTOCK

positions we have seen. Its long grassy gardens, complete with hedges forming wind-breaks and sun-traps, slope down towards the sea and afford you a magnificent view of the lovely Crantock Bay – a good place to swim and loll, but you must be careful at low tide (obey the signs). It is patrolled by life guards during the summer; and is a great spot for surfers too.

The hotel is very much geared up to family holidays with plenty of facilities to keep young and older occupied. The children have an activity area with a very substantial wooden fort, swings and climbing frames; and there is a tennis court, and croquet and putting can be done on the lawns.

Indoors, you can enjoy the swimming pool and there is a toddler's pool alongside. The really energetic can tone up their muscles in the exercise room and then recover in the sauna or the spa bath. The games room has table tennis and skittles and there is a play room for young children.

In the field alongside the hotel there are donkeys, pigs and chickens which belong to the hotel and it is pleasing to report that the owners grow a lot of their own vegetables (as well as providing their own free-range eggs). Children are encouraged to eat smaller versions of the adults' food – mini-dinners are served at 5pm.

This is a delightful place and the prices charged are very reasonable indeed; the hotel represents outstanding value for families on holiday.

Nearby: As well as Crantock Bay there are many good beaches for swimmers and surfers, and deckchair huggers: Porth Joke, owned by the National Trust, is well worth a visit. The Gannel Estuary is a great spot for walking, riding and wind surfing. There are many attractions around Newquay including the zoo, the Lappa Valley Railway, Dairyland Farm Park, St Agnes Leisure Park and the beautiful Elizabethan house of Trerice.

LUNCH (12–2pm) £1–3: soup, cold buffet;
DINNER (7–8.30pm) £13: soup, ravioli parmesan, scampi provencale, pudding or cheese
Children: own menu, half portions
£ medium
Children: free up to 2 years; one third of adult rate from 2–5 years; half from 6–8; threequarters from 9–12 years
Facilities: many cots and high chairs, and baby listening
36 rooms, 4 family   Access/AmEx/Diners/Visa
Closed Dec-Feb
No smoking in the dining room and garden lounge
P – own car park

Please let us have reports – good or bad – on any establishments listed in the Guide as soon as possible after your visit.

Nr Craven Arms, Shropshire   map 6
HALFORD HOLIDAY HOMES – ☎ *Craven Arms (0588) 672 382.*

SC   *Off the B4368 north east of Craven Arms.*

This attractive barn conversion was completed a couple of years ago by Mr and Mrs James and it is situated opposite their farmhouse. An indication of the success of the project is that it has been put into the "Three Key" category by the English Tourist Board.

The five apartments, three of which are constructed on two floors, will accommodate from two to six people. The rooms are clean and bright and well-furnished, as befits units which have so recently been completed, and have well-equipped kitchens, which include microwave, as well as electric, cookers.

You can count on peace and quiet in this attractive area of Shropshire, which is a good base for a relaxing family holiday.

Craven Arms is quite close and there is a shop and a pub less than a mile away. The rental costs, which include heating, light and linen, are very reasonable.

Nearby: Fishing, horse riding and golf can all be arranged locally and it is fine walking country. South Shropshire is particularly attractive and has towns such as Clun and Ludlow (both with castles) and Church Stretton, with the adjacent Carding Mill Valley, to visit. Wilderhope Manor, the Severn Valley Railway, the Ironbridge Gorge Museum, the Aerospace Museum at Cosford and the West Midland Safari Park are all within easy reach.

Units: 5
Rent: £85 to £200 a week
Other costs: none
Heating: night storage heaters
2 cots and 2 high chairs available
Open all year

Criccieth, Gwynedd   map 5
MOELWYN RESTAURANT, Mona Terrace – ☎ *Criccieth (0766) 522 500.*

By the sea front off the A497.

The restaurant is housed in a Victorian building which is framed with creeper. It is bright and welcoming and the restaurant itself is smartly decorated with patterned wallpaper and pink tablecloths. There is an excellent range of food on offer here, including a special menu for children and smaller portions of most dishes.

The restaurant has a lovely situation with splendid views of Cardigan Bay, the hills and in the distance Harlech Castle, and especially so from the small garden, which is a delightful place to sit on a summer's day. A comfortable *lounge with a television is also available to residents.*

Nearby: There is a wealth of things to do and see in this part of Wales. There are good beaches to be found all along the coast line of Cardigan Bay and many other attractions for the holiday maker. The ancient castle of Criccieth is worth a visit simply for the view, while the extraordinary village of Portmeirion is very close. Harlech Castle, the Ffestiniog Railway, the Lloyd George Museum, and the slate caverns at Blaenau are all nearby, and the beauties of Snowdonia are not too far away.

LUNCH (12–2pm) £2–4: crab paté, mushroom & lentil terrine, fried sea clams, grilled Welsh lamb chops;
DINNER (7–9pm) £16: smoked Welsh salmon, noisette of lamb, pudding or cheese
Children: own menu, half portions
£ low
Best Bargain Break £54 per person, 2 nights – dinner, b & b
Children: cot free; £6 thereafter up to 12 years
Facilities: 1 cot and 2 high chairs; baby alarm is provided
5 rooms, 1 family   Open Easter to Christmas
No smoking in dining room   Access/Visa
P – on the street

Also recommended in the Family Welcome Pub & Restaurant Guide.

Crieff, Tayside   map 11
CRIEFF HYDRO HOTEL (Consort) – ☎ Crieff (0764) 2401.

H/SC   *On the hillside above the centre of Crieff – ask directions.*

This vast Victorian building, built of stone with a very slight tinge of pink, is quite a sight in its position high above the town. It has been managed by the same family for well over a hundred years, and is very much a family hotel, with over a quarter of its 200 rooms designated as family rooms.

The public rooms are huge and include a marvellous sun lounge with a splendid balustraded balcony which runs round the front of it and overlooks the lovely gardens.

The facilities are comprehensive and ideal for an active family holiday: there is a heated indoor pool which has recently been upgraded to include jacuzzi, sauna and steam room; snooker, table tennis and pool; a sports hall with badminton, basketball, short tennis, two squash courts, and a small fitness room; five tennis courts, a riding stable, a putting green, paddling pool, a children's playground, a nine-hole golf course and an all weather bowling green.

Parents can enjoy themselves in peace, especially at meal times, since there is a nursery, and children under 10 have their meals there.

Nearby: Apart from the excellent golf and fishing, there are many attractions including Drummond Castle Gardens, Huntingtower Castle, Scone Palace, the Hermitage Woodland Walk and the Loch of the Lowes. The adults will enjoy a visit to the Glenturret Distillery.

LUNCH (1–2pm) £7: vegetable soup, ravioli, pudding;
DINNER: (7–8.30pm) £13: corn on the cob, soup, sirloin of beef, pudding
Children: own menu, half portions
£ medium
Best Bargain Break £59 per person 2 nights – dinner, b & b
Children: from free to £23
Facilities: plenty of cots and high chairs; and a baby listening system
200 rooms, 61 family, 6 sets interconnecting
Open all year   Access/AmEx/Diners/Visa
No smoking areas in the dining room, sports hall and cinema
P – own car park   No music

SELF-CATERING
There are sixteen wooden lodges in the grounds of the hotel. Each has a twin bedroom, a bunk bedroom, and a sofa bed in the living room. The kitchens are well-equipped and everything is included except towels. All the facilities of the hotel can be used by the occupants of the lodges. The rent varies from £240 to £500 a week.

Crostwick, Norfolk   map 8
OLD RECTORY GUEST HOUSE – ☎ *Norwich (0603) 738 513.*

On the B1150 four miles north of Norwich.

The house is smartly painted white and has an unusual double-gabled roof. It was built as a rectory in the early 19th century, and offers good facilities for families. The very large garden has an immaculate lawn and is surrounded by some fine old trees. It has a swimming pool, which is heated during the summer, and a children's play area with swings, a see-saw and a swing-boat. In addition there is a games room in the house with table tennis, bar billiards and snooker, and some exercise equipment, if you are committed to fighting the flab.

It's nice to know that some of the fruit and vegetables grown in the garden will be part of your three-course evening meal.

Nearby: The Broads are quite close, and there are other attractions in the vicinity such as the Norfolk Wildlife Park, Blickling Hall, Wroxham Barns and the whole expanse of the delightfully unspoiled North Norfolk coast. It's a great place for wildlife enthusiasts, especially bird watchers, and for birdie chasers too, since there are some excellent golf courses, including Sheringham. You might also visit the Norfolk Shire Horse Centre and Felbrigg Hall, while train enthusiasts can try the North Norfolk Railway at Sheringham.

✕ DINNER (7pm) £9: soup, roast beef & Yorkshire pudding, home made apple pie
Children: half portions
£ low
Children: half price under 12
Facilities: 2 cots and 2 high chairs; baby listening on three lines
13 rooms, 3 family   Open all year
Access/Visa   P – ample

Nr Cullompton, Devon   map 2
WISHAY FARM, Trinity – ☎ *Cullompton (0884) 33223.*

On minor roads near Cullompton. The farm's brochure has excellent directions.
You will find peace and quiet in abundance at this long and well-proportioned 17th century farmhouse. It is surrounded by rolling countryside, and there is a spacious lawn at the front of the house. The children can play happily here, and there is a swing and a slide for them to use.

Inside you will find sizeable and attractive rooms, and the windows have charming wooden shutters. The sitting room is very comfortable and relaxing, with a large stone fireplace with alcoves at each side, and windows on to the garden. Each of the family rooms, which have plenty of space and are very

nicely furnished, has a double and two single beds, and one of them has an en suite bathroom. The other has a separate bathroom which is shared with the one single room.

The owners also have a play room at the rear of the house and it is packed with toys and games. So if the weather turns nasty the children will have plenty to occupy their day. Not that there is any lack of diversions in this part of the world.

Nearby: Bickleigh Mill and Bickleigh Castle are very close, as is Knightshayes Court and Killerton House. Also within easy reach are the Donkey Sanctuary near Sidmouth, Farway Countryside Park, Bicton Park, Powderham Castle, and Exeter's many museums. A whole line of excellent beaches stretches south to Torquay and includes Dawlish Warren, where there is a splendid nature reserve.

✗ DINNER (6.30pm) £7
Children: half portions
£ low
Children: half price
Facilities: a cot and a high chair; informal baby listening
3 rooms, 2 family   Open February to November
No credit cards   No music
P – ample   Unlicensed

Cupar, Fife   map 11
MOUNTQUHANIE HOLIDAY HOMES – ☎ *Gauldry (082 624) 252.*

SC *Just north of Cupar, off the A914.*

The estate has been in the hands of the family of the present owners, Mr and Mrs Andrew Wedderburn, for over 400 years. An ancestor was lady-in-waiting to Mary Queen of Scots.

The ruins of both Creich Castle and Mountquhanie Castle remain on the estate, but the core of it is Mountquhanie House, an elegant mansion which was built in 1820.

Most of the nineteen properties are scattered throughout the estate and offer peace and seclusion in the wooded grounds. Three of them, which sleep four, six and eight people, are part of the main house; and the others, stone farmhouses and cottages in a variety of interesting styles, can accommodate from four to twelve occupants. Most of them have spacious and well-maintained enclosed gardens (some with sandpits and play areas) and are highly suitable for family holidays. Creich Farmhouse, which sleeps eleven people, stands alongside Creich Castle.

Some of the houses are in, or in the vicinity of, St Andrews and are ideal properties for groups of golfers. The Nydie houses and cottages have superb views over the Eden Valley towards the Tay and the foothills of the Grampians.

Knockhill of Nydie House accommodates up to ten people and has a pleasant enclosed garden.

Our inspectors were very impressed with the quality of all the properties. They are decorated and equipped to an exceptionally high standard, with excellent kitchen and bathroom facilities and attractive furniture and decorations. Each kitchen includes a microwave oven, and there are dishwashers and freezers in the larger properties.

Guests are welcome to wander about the estate. There is a nature trail, a children's play area, burn fishing, a hard tennis court and mown grass areas where golfers can hone their chip and pitch shots.

This is a splendid place for a family holiday in the beautiful kingdom of Fife in the care of the friendly and well-organised Wedderburn family.

Nearby: Golfers have some of the best courses in Scotland to sample (St Andrews, Carnoustie and Gleneagles for a start) and fishermen, apart from the burns on the estate, can buy permits to fish on the estate's stretch of the River Eden at Nydie. Sightseers might start with a browse around St Andrews and there are many other spots within an easy drive: Earlshall Castle, the Hill of Tarvitt, Kellie Castle, Falkland Palace, the gardens at Aberdour Castle, the burgh of Culross and Scone Palace. If you pop south across the Firth of Forth you can visit Hopetoun House and the country parks of Beecraigs and Almondell, while Edinburgh with all its attractions is easily accessible.

Units: 19
Rent: £135 to £555 a week (golf packages can be arranged)
Other costs: electricity is metered; linen £8 a head
Heating: central heating
A dozen cots and high chairs available
Open all year

Dawlish, Devon   map 2

RADFORDS COUNTRY HOTEL, Lower Dawlish Water – ☎ Dawlish (0626) 863 322.

In the countryside near Dawlish – the hotel provides an excellent map.

This hotel, the heart of which is an attractive, pink washed thatched building, has been in the Family Welcome Guide since the first edition many years ago, and we have had nothing but good reports of it ever since. It is everything a family hotel should be and is aimed at parents with young children. One of our readers, Mrs Stepney from Surrey, wrote: 'Ten out of ten for child tolerance. My nine-year-old daughter thought it was wonderful... Excellent value.'

Every room is a family room and there are masses of cots and high chairs available. The owners are punctilious in the way their guests are cared for: for example the indoor pool, with its separate children's pool, is always attended by a *life-guard. Similarly, two of the staff are on duty as baby-sitters every night from 7pm to 11.30pm and will check each child at regular intervals. What a relief for parents who, after all, need a holiday too!*

The facilities are comprehensive: a games room with a pool table, skittles, darts, table tennis, space invaders, etc; a play area with swings, a slide, a roundabout and a climbing frame; a playroom with a selection of toys, an outdoor badminton court; and, of course, the indoor pool. Entertainments for the children are organised almost every day, and they have a chance to learn horse riding. A new wooden fort has recently been added – and it has been approved for safety by the local authority.

Nearby: Guests have the advantage not only of the hotel's spacious grounds but also of the glorious countryside surrounding it. There are many sandy beaches nearby, including Dawlish Warren, which has a nature reserve adjoining it, where a huge variety of birds can be seen. Nature lovers will also be interested in the Parke Rare Breeds Farm, while the Dartmoor Wildlife Park and the Shire Horse Centre are a bit further away (near Plymouth). Other nearby attractions include Powderham Castle, Bicton Park, the remarkable cottage of A La Ronde, Compton Castle and the Dart Valley Railway – plus the busy resort of Torquay.

DINNER (6–7pm): gazpacho, roast venison, summer pudding
Children: own menu, half portions
£ medium
Best Bargain Break £70 per person, 2 nights – dinner, b & b
Children: from no charge to 75% of adult cost, depending on season
Facilities: numerous cots and high chairs; a baby listening system to each room and a baby patrol from 7pm to 11.30pm
37 rooms, all family, 11 sets interconnecting
Closed mid Nov-Mar   Access/Visa

No smoking in dining room • Ale – Courage
P – own car park

Dawlish Warren, Devon map 2
LANGSTONE CLIFF HOTEL (Consort) – ☎ Dawlish (0626) 865 155/6.

Take the signs for Dawlish Warren off the A379.

This is a large and well-organised hotel which is a bit reminiscent of the better Spanish resort hotels: it has very spacious public rooms and many of the bedrooms have balconies, which overlook the grounds of the hotel with their wide lawns and woodland.

The facilities are plentiful with an outdoor and an indoor swimming pool, both with paddling pools, a tennis court and a play area for children in the nineteen acres of gardens. You can also play snooker, table tennis or darts, and there is a golf course next door.

With dozens of high chairs and cots available and over fifty family rooms (including family suites with two bedrooms), the hotel is firmly in the family market and copes with it with skill.

Nearby: Right next door there is the Dawlish Warren Nature Reserve, with a multitude of Brent geese; other wildfowl can be viewed from a hide. There is a host of attractions within reach: Powderham Castle, Castle Drogo, Parke Rare Breeds Farm, Compton Castle, the Dart Valley Railway and Buckfast Abbey. There are many excellent beaches on which to loll, starting with Dawlish Warren, from which dogs are banned, and those around Torquay.

✗ COFFEE SHOP (10am–6.30pm) £1–5: soup, cottage pie, roast of the day, beef curry & rice, plaice & chips;
DINNER (7–9pm) £13: Brixham crab, roast turkey, pudding and cheese
Children: high teas, half portions
£ high
Off-season Bargain Breaks only
Children: free up to 6 years; half price thereafter
Facilities: 20 cots and 20 high chairs; baby listening system to every room
64 rooms, 52 family   Access/AmEx/Diners/Visa
Open all year   **P** – own car park

Hotels were asked to quote 1992 prices, but not all were able to give an accurate forecast. Make sure that you check tariffs when you book.

Dolwyddelan, Gwynedd   map 5

ELEN'S CASTLE HOTEL – ☎ Dolwyddelan (06906) 207.

On the A470 south west of Betwys-y-Coed.

This charming stone hotel, its walls hung with ivy and Virginia creeper, dates back to the 18th century and was once part of the Earl of Ancaster's Welsh estate. It was once a village alehouse and later a coaching inn.

It is a comfortable and relaxing hotel with a pleasant bar, with an open fire, in what was once the kitchen; the game hooks are still in place. The lounges are comfortably furnished, as are the nice unfussy bedrooms.

It is a fine place to relax, especially in the large garden alongside the hotel. It is safely enclosed and rises on three levels, each separated by rambling roses and flower beds. Children can play in an adjoining field, which contains the legendary Roman well, which is reputed to have healing qualities.

Nearby: The hotel is situated in the lovely Lledr Valley in the middle of the Snowdonia National Park. It is a splendid spot for walkers, climbers and fishermen. The hotel is a starting point for many walks, including the popular one to the summit of Moel Siabod. Fishermen can try their luck for trout and salmon in the nearby river, and coarse fishing is also available to hotel guests. Pony trekking can also be arranged locally. Dolwyddelan Castle, built in the 12th century by Llywelyn the Great, is well worth a visit, as are Gwydir Castle, Gwydyr Forest with its many walks and the Cwm Idwal Nature Trail. Bodnant Garden and the Great Orme Country Park are close, and you can easily reach the sandy beaches of the north coast.

BAR SNACKS (12–2pm) £2–7: marinated herring fillets, seafood gratin, lasagne, Bulghur wheat & walnut casserole, sirloin steak; DINNER (8pm onwards) £12: paté, grilled plaice, pudding
Children: own menu, half portions
£ medium
Children: free up to 3 years; half price from 4 to 8; three quarters from 9 to 14
Facilities: 1 cot and 3 high chairs; a baby alarm
10 rooms, 2 family   Open all year
No smoking in dining room   Access/Visa   **P** – own car park

Dorchester, Dorset   map 2

HIGHER WATERSTON FARM – ☎ Puddletown (0305) 848 208.

SC   *On the B3143 north east of Dorchester.*

This is a working sheep farm in the beautiful undulating countryside in the heart of Thomas Hardy country. The brick and flint cottages, converted from a stable yard, are as appealing as any seen by our inspectors.

The four cottages sleep either four or six people and each has its own York stone terrace, well provided with teak furniture. You can sit and admire the views and enjoy a meal or a drink al fresco. Inside you will find open plan living areas, light and airy, and with ancient beams and pillars in place and pine doors and staircases. In the bedrooms, the old beams have been used to remarkable effect to give sloping and eccentric ceiling planes. It is noticeable how much space there is in these cottages.

The furniture is comfortable and the decorations attractive; and the kitchens are particularly well-equipped with microwave as well as conventional cookers, food mixers, washing machines and tumble driers, and dishwashers.

There is plenty of space outside and the large central lawned area is safe for children. An excellent all-weather tennis court will appeal to aspiring tennis champions, and if the weather turns nasty there is a barn with a full sized badminton court and a table tennis table.

Plenty of books and board games are provided, and guests are welcome to wander about the farm. A barbecue is provided beside the lawn.

Higher Waterston Farm is a delightful spot, with splendid dwellings where families will really feel at home.

Nearby: The countryside is beautiful, a delight to see either on foot or on horseback. There is good fishing to be had, and several golf courses to play. The sea is only about ten miles away and you can follow the Dorset Coastal Path. A little further afield Swanage and Studland have excellent sandy beaches. There are many places to visit: Dorchester itself, the Tutankhamun exhibition, Hardy's Cottage, the Tank Museum at Bovington Camp, Corfe Castle, Brownsea Island and the Sea Life Centre at Weymouth.

Units: 4
Rent: £165 to £410 a week (winter breaks available)
Other costs: electricity on meters
Heating: central heating and wood burning stoves
3 cots and 3 high chairs available
Open all year

Dovedale, Nr Ashbourne, Derbyshire   map 7

IZAAK WALTON HOTEL – ☎ *Thorpe Cloud (033 529) 555.*

Off the A515, north of Ashbourne.

Dovedale, in an area of great natural beauty in the Peak District National Park, is thought to be the model for Eagle Valley in George Eliot's Adam Bede. It's a wonderful spot, overseen by the peak of Thorpe Cloud and in great walking and fishing country.

The heart of this comfortable country hotel is a 17th century stone farmhouse and it overlooks Thorpe Cloud and the River Dove. Izaak Walton stayed here regularly to fish and to compile material for "The Compleat Angler".

The interior is nicely furnished while outside there is a pretty garden with a spacious lawn from which you can sit and view the scenic delights around you.

Apart from the normal dinner menu, there is also a buttery bar where you can have a light lunch and obtain snacks at other times of the day.

Nearby: Dove Dale itself provides a variety of walks amid beautiful scenery and the hotel has three miles of fishing on the River Dove (£10 per day). There is a great variety of places to visit within easy reach: Alton Towers, which is far and away the best theme park in Britain; the Heights of Abraham, Gulliver's Kingdom and the Riber Castle Wildlife Park; the National Tramway Museum; Chatsworth House and Haddon Hall; and, a little further away, the American Adventure Theme Park.

BUTTERY BAR (12–2pm & 7–9pm) £2–6: filled baked potatoes, haddock & chips, burgers, chilli con carne, chicken tikka;
DINNER (7–9.15pm) £17: galantine of duck, fillets of sole, pudding or cheese
Children: own menu, half portions
£ high
Best Bargain Break £49 per person per night – dinner, b & b
Children: free to age 15
Facilities: 2 cots and 2 high chairs; a baby listening service
34 rooms, 1 family, 2 sets interconnecting
Open all year   Access/AmEx/Diners/Visa
P – own car park   • Ale – Riding, Old Bailey

Dover, Kent   map 4

TOWER GUEST HOUSE, 98 Priory Hill – ☎ Dover (0304) 208 212.

Near the town centre. The brochure includes a detailed map.

When we last stayed at the Tower Guest House we were delighted with the attractively furnished and comfortable rooms. Delighted, too, by the warm and friendly welcome extended by Mrs Wraight.

Although evening meals are not available, and this would normally preclude the Tower from being recommended in the Guide, Dover is a special case, since many families need accommodation here if they have booked an early ferry. Also there is a very good choice of restaurants nearby in the town. This guest house, situated at the back of the Wraights' own home (the Old Water Tower) and built into a hillside, would suit such travellers very well. The house sits high above Dover and once was a notable landmark, although other houses now surround it. But the views of the town remain.

The family room, which has twin beds and bunk beds, is on the ground floor,

and a kitchen is available to guests where they can heat baby food and make hot drinks and snacks.

Nearby: If you envisage a longer stay in Dover there are many things to do and see: the zoos at Port Lympne and Howlett for example; the theme park at Margate; the castles at Walmer, Deal and Dover itself; and challenging golf at Deal and Sandwich.

£ low
Children: £8 per child
Facilities: 1 cot and 1 high chair
5 rooms, 2 family   Open all year except Xmas
No credit cards   No music
P – garages, and on street   No smoking in dining room

Drumnadrochit, Highland   map 12

POLMAILY HOUSE HOTEL – ☎ *Drumnadrochit (045 62) 343.*

On the A831 just west of Drumnadrochit.
This Edwardian country house faces south from the slopes of Glen Urquhart and is close to the shores of Loch Ness.
You are assured of peace and seclusion here since the hotel is encircled by eighteen acres of garden. Fine beech hedges flank the drive as you approach the hotel; colourful flowers and stately trees complement the spacious lawns, and there is a pond with attendant ducks. A steep wooded hill runs behind the house, an ideal place for the children to play, while the adults relax below. If you feel energetic there is an outdoor swimming pool, a hard tennis court and a croquet lawn.

DULNAIN BRIDGE

Relaxation is the keynote in the hotel, too, with a comfortable lounge with an open fire and plenty of books in evidence, while the dining room is just as attractively laid out and decorated. If children want to watch television or play board games they can do this in a small study.

This is a delightful spot which offers a warm welcome to families.

Nearby: This is an excellent base for outdoor pursuits such as fishing, walking and pony trekking; the beautiful Glen Affric is quite close, for example. Fort George, Culloden Battlefield, Cawdor Castle, the ruins of Urquhart Castle, and Brodie Castle are all within reach; and the children will no doubt be eager to visit the Loch Ness Monster Exhibition, which is on the doorstep.

DINNER (7.30–9.30pm) £20: lettuce & basil soup, roast loin of lamb, pudding or cheese
Children: high teas, half portions
£ high
Best Bargain Break – discounts of 5% and 10%
Children: free up to 14 years
Facilities: 2 cots and a high chair; plug-in baby alarm
9 rooms, 1 family   Open Easter to end October
Access/Visa   No music
No smoking in restaurant   P – own car park

Dulnain Bridge, Grantown-on-Spey, Highland map 12

MUCKRACH LODGE HOTEL – ☎ *Dulnain Bridge (047 985) 257.*

On the A938 half a mile west of Dulnain Bridge.

The large granite house, which was once a shooting lodge, reposes in ten acres of gardens in the Dulnain Valley with a wealth of activities within easy reach. From the house there are splendid views of the Cairngorms and the Cromdale Hills.

It is a bright and comfortable hotel, with spacious and elegant rooms. There are large arrangements of flowers scattered about and they complement the pleasing colour schemes and agreeable furniture. It is a busy and bustling place, where the owners and staff do their utmost to make their guests feel relaxed and at home. For example there is real flexibility about children's food; within reason it can be arranged to suit a child's likes and dislikes.

Nearby: This is a marvellous spot for fishermen with excellent salmon and trout fishing on the Dulnain, Findhorn and Spey rivers; and for golfers, too, with four courses within ten minutes of the hotel. Walking, skating, swimming and pony trekking can all be arranged, and wild life enthusiasts should head for the well-known osprey look-out at Boat of Garten. There are many attractions nearby: Culloden battlefield, the castles of Cawdor and Urquhart, the Loch Ness Monster Exhibition, Landmark Visitor Centre, Highland Wildlife Park, the Glenmore Forest Park and the Rothiemurchus Estate.

DULOE

✘ BAR LUNCHES (12–2pm) £1–5: veal Mexicaine, fresh fillet of codling, substantial sandwiches, omelettes;
LUNCH (12–2pm) £9: smoked mackerel & avocado mousse, chicken Stroganoff, pudding;
DINNER (7.30–9pm) £18: avocado with Stilton, soup, medallions of lamb, pudding and cheese.
Children: half portions, and high teas
£ high
Best Bargain Break £84 per person, 2 nights – dinner, b & b
Children: free in cots, then £5 up to the age of 12
Facilities: 1 cot and 2 high chairs; a baby listening system
12 rooms, 3 family   Access/AmEx/Diners/Visa
Open all year   • Ale – Federation
P – own car park

Duloe, Nr Liskeard, Cornwall   map 1

TREFANNY HILL – ☎ *Lanreath (0503) 220 622.*

SC *Off the B3359 north of Pelynt.*

If you crave peace and quiet in lovely surroundings you should head for Trefanny Hill. It was an abandoned hamlet which Mr and Mrs Slaughter had the courage to take on in the early 'sixties. They have restored the old cottages with great care and style.

As they say in their informative (and accurate) brochure: 'if you are looking for the peace of the countryside and a really lovely cottage, this is what we have to offer you.' Trefanny Hill is situated on the side of a hill and is backed by farmland and hills. Down below is the West Looe Valley.

There are fifteen cottages of varying sizes and they range from very small ones for two people up to three bedroomed ones for six, with room for a cot. What every cottage has in common is comfort and an agreeable style, even though they have all been furnished and decorated in different ways. They have thick stone walls, ancient oak beams and most have open fires. The furniture is excellent and varied, so that you feel at home.

Every cottage has a fully equipped kitchen with all the items any cook needs. Each has its own private garden where you can relax and perhaps use the barbecue during those long summer evenings. On a practical level the cottages have dishwashers, irons and ironing boards; the larger ones also have washing machines and driers and the mini cottages have shared use of the communal machines.

You will also enjoy the thirty-five acres of garden, which has the added attraction of a heated swimming pool. There is a grass badminton court and the shuttlecocks and racquets are provided. Golfers will be pleased to hear that there is a golf practice net.

No one wants to cook every meal on holiday and there is a pleasant little inn, for residents only, where you can have a meal and a drink; the Sunday lunches are especially popular. In addition you can order pre-cooked dishes which are delivered to your door. There is a good choice of meals and the prices are very reasonable.

This is a delightful spot for a family holiday.

Nearby: This is a wonderful place for peaceful walks in the countryside and on the coastal pathway and there is an excellent choice of quiet and sandy coves: Lantic Bay and Lantivet Bay for example. Horse riding, tennis, water sports and golf (reduced green fees at the local club) are all easily arranged. If you have some sightseeing in mind there is plenty of choice: Dobwalls Theme Park, Lanhydrock House, the ruined Restormel Castle, Pencarrow House, Dairyland Farm Park, Trerice House and Newquay Zoo can all be reached with ease.

Units: 15
Rent: £130 to £500; short breaks are available
Other costs: electricity on a meter
Heating: night storage
Plenty of cots and high chairs
Open all year

Dunbar, Lothian   map 11

SPRINGFIELD GUEST HOUSE, *Belhaven Road* – ☎ *Dunbar (0368) 62502.*

About half a mile from the High Street, and near Belhaven Parish Church.

A warm welcome awaits families at this pleasant and comfortable Victorian villa, which sits in its own grounds not far from the centre of the town. The owner has three children of her own and understands the needs of families. She was a dietician and can allow for special diets; since she grows many of her own vegetables and herbs you can be sure that the food will be cooked from fresh ingredients.

Guests can take their ease in the spacious back garden which is totally enclosed and safe from the road. There are many apple trees here, and flowers encircle the lawn. Children will find a selection of toys here and there are toys indoors too and various board games. It is a comfortable house with a pleasant atmosphere, and offers excellent value.

Nearby: Dunbar has some good beaches nearby, especially Coldingham and Pease Sands, although the latter is ringed by a caravan site. A new leisure complex has recently opened in the town. Like most parts of Scotland there are many excellent golf courses, including North Berwick; and if you are interested in castles Tantallon, Dirleton and Hailes are nearby. The Myreton Motor Museum and the Museum of Flight are also close, and Edinburgh itself is a short drive.

DINNER (6pm) £9: turkey broth, steak pie, chocolate mousse, cheese
Children: half portions
£ low
Children: babies free; £9 from 2 to 5 years; £13 from 5 to 12; £17 over 12 (includes meals)
Facilities: 2 cots and 2 high chairs and a baby listening system
5 rooms, 2 family   Open March to October
Access/Visa   No music
P – own car park

Dunoon, Strathclyde   map 11
ENMORE HOTEL, Marine Parade – ☎ Dunoon (0369) 2230.

On the A815 just north of Dunoon.

The Enmore is an attractive whitewashed hotel standing on the Clyde Estuary where it has a small beach. There are two squash courts at the hotel and many other activities can be arranged in and around the local lochs and mountains – sailing, fishing, walking and island-hopping as well as tennis, golf, swimming, etc. The hotel has attractive terraced gardens.

Not surprisingly the five-course dinner menu includes Loch Fyne fish and

Nr DUNSTER

another speciality is the children's cocktails. Children are, however, discouraged from the dining room in the evenings, since high teas are provided.

Nearby: Dunoon is an attractive resort with the advantage of the many water sports which can be done locally. If you are in the mood for sightseeing you can reach Inveraray Castle, the Younger Botanic Garden and the Kilmun Arboretum with ease. If you cross the ferry to Gourock you can reach the many fine museums and other attractions of Glasgow with ease.

BAR SNACKS (10am–10pm) £2–10: whole prawns in garlic butter, Loch Fyne herring, vegetable casserole, sirloin steak;
DINNER (7.30–9pm) £19: smoked goose breast, soup, local roast venison, pudding and cheese
Children: own menu
£ high
Best Bargain Break £147 per person, 3 nights – dinner, b & b
Children: babies free; £5 from 1 to 7 years; half price from 7 to 15
Facilities: 1 cot and 1 high chair; 2 baby listening lines
11 rooms, 1 family   Access/Visa
Open all year   P – own car park

Nr Dunster, Somerset   map 2
DUDDINGS COUNTRY HOLIDAYS – ☎ Timberscombe (0643) 841 252 or 841 536.

SC   *On the A396 on the Dunster side of the village.*

Duddings has an enviable location alongside the valley created by the River Avill; from the cottages you have a delightful view of the gentle wooded hills and scattered fields.

The cottages have been built from the old barns, whose walls were made from the attractive local stone, which is reddish-brown in colour. The smallest pro-

perties can accommodate two people and the largest seven, with half a dozen cottages able to sleep between four and six people.

We were impressed with the care which has clearly been exercised in converting the buildings. The original features, the ancient beams and stone walls, have been retained and enhanced by the provision of comfortable and stylish furniture and excellent decorations. There are fitted carpets throughout the cottages and the kitchens have everything a cook would need, including microwave ovens. The proprietors are on the spot to ensure that the guests are well looked after.

The cottages have the great advantage of a lovely setting, and there are little picnic areas with bench tables, set amongst the trees in the immaculately maintained gardens. The cottages also have their own little patios where you can have a quiet drink or an al fresco meal.

The other facilities are excellent, too. There is loads of space for the children to play in the paddock and in the fields and alongside the river; and Duddings has the bonus of a hard tennis court, an indoor heated swimming pool, which is four feet in depth and suitable for most members of a family, a putting green, pool room and a table tennis table. There are many pets with whom the children can make friends: dogs, kittens, ducks and peacocks. This is a marvellous spot for a family holiday in an area which has so much to offer.

Nearby: Fishermen are well catered for on the local rivers, the Exe and the Barle, and there are brown trout in the Avill, which flows through the Duddings' grounds. It is a superb part of the world to see from the back of a horse or pony and there are several riding centres in the vicinity. The beaches of the North Somerset Coast are close and a new leisure pool has been built in Minehead. There are many attractions to see: Dunster Castle, Combe Sydenham Hall, the West Somerset Railway, the Exmoor National Park Centre, Fyne Court, Poundisford Park, while Cricket St Thomas Wildlife Park is just a little further afield.

Units: 11
Rent: £100 to £500 a week (off peak breaks available – a minimum of 3 nights)
Other costs: electricity (at cost)
Heating: convector heaters in all rooms
4 cots and 4 high chairs
Open: end of February to early January

Dunsyre, Strathclyde map 11

DUNSYRE MAINS – ☎ *Dunsyre (089 981) 251.*

Off the A702 north of Biggar.
When you leave the main road at Dolphinton follow the B & B signs to the

farmhouse. As you drive along the tree lined road, past the sheep, horses and cattle, beware of the occasional pheasant or sheep dog.

This is a working farm which rears a large flock of Scottish black face sheep and a big herd of beef cows. It has a lovely position on the edge of the Pentland Hills and is bordered by the Medwin River. The house itself was built in the 17th century, and the attached farm buildings form a courtyard, where there are masses of colourful geraniums, lobelia and begonias on show in pots and painted barrows.

The walled gardens, with stretches of lawn and flower beds, are spacious, and you will find the house comfortable and inviting. The family room has a double and a single bed. The lounge has a television and various board games for families, and there are some toys for the children.

Nearby: Although Dunsyre is in the Strathclyde region it is close to the Borders and is only twenty or so miles from Edinburgh which has so many places of interest. It is a most attractive area, with much to interest the holiday maker: the John Buchan centre at Broughton, Neidpath Castle and Kailzie Gardens at Peebles, Dawyck Botanic Garden and Traquair Castle are all in the near vicinity.

DINNER (7pm) £9
Children: half portions
£ low
Children: various reductions according to age
Facilities: a cot and a high chair; baby listening by arrangement
3 rooms, 1 family   Open all year
No credit cards   Unlicensed
No smoking in dining room and bedrooms   No music
P – ample

Dymchurch, Kent   map 4
CHANTRY HOTEL, 21 Sycamore Gardens – ☎ *(0303) 873 137.*

Close to the centre of the village.

The hotel has a secluded position at the end of a minor road and has the great bonus for families that it sits alongside a safe and sandy beach.

The building dates from the 19th century, is half timbered with weather boarding over the brick, and has some dormer windows. The rooms are spacious and the hotel has a bar and a lounge where board games are made available.

The garden is spacious too, with plenty of lawn and with roses and borders of flowers, and some swings for the children. You can sit at your ease there or on the small terrace. A little bridge leads to the beach across a promenade, which is free of cars and therefore safe for children.

This friendly and comfortable hotel is well organised to look after families.

EAST HADDON

Nearby: Apart from the beaches which stretch along this part of the coast there is an array of things to do and see. Golfers have many fine courses within reach including those at Deal and Sandwich; wildlife enthusiasts can head for Port Lympne and Howletts zoo parks; there are castles to see at Dover, Deal and Walmer; and railway buffs can travel on the Romney, Hythe and Dymchurch and the Kent and East Sussex railways. Canterbury, with its famous cathedral, is not too far away.

DINNER (6.30–8pm) £14: mushrooms in garlic, lamb Shrewsbury, pudding and cheese
Children: own menu, half portions
£ low
Best Bargain Break £40 per person, 2 nights – dinner, b & b
Children: half price up to 12 years
Facilities: 2 cots and 2 high chairs; baby listening by arrangement
6 rooms, 5 family   Open all year
No smoking in dining room   Access/AmEx/Visa
P – own car park

East Haddon, Northants   map 7

RYE HILL FARM COTTAGES – ☎ *Northampton (0604) 770 990.*

SC *Off the A428 north west of Northampton.*

The farm sits in delightful rolling countryside; you really can see for miles and miles and the views from the windows of the cottages give you a great sense of peace and relaxation.

The five cottages are grouped around a gravelled courtyard and were made from old barns and stables. The conversions have been done with imagination and style; the original features have been retained wherever possible and used to good effect. There are some fine old wooden beams holding up the ceilings, whose slopes and angles are particularly attractive. The use of spiral staircases in three of the cottages is a very successful feature.

Two of the cottages can sleep up to six people and two can sleep four. There is also one small single storey cottage for two people and it is suitable for disabled guests.

The cottages are very comfortably furnished and some of them contain bunk beds for children. We were impressed by the high standard of the decorations and furnishings; guests are made to feel at home, and all the equipment any cook might need is present in the kitchens, including microwave ovens and dishwashers.

There is plenty of space for children to play in the two and a half acres which surround the smallholding and they can make friends with the many animals:

goats, a pig, sheep, ducks, chickens and geese. There is a badminton net on one of the lawns, boule, a playground with swings and a climbing frame, a duck pond, a sandpit and bicycles to borrow.

In addition there is a playroom with plenty of toys and games, a mini snooker table, subbuteo and a rebounder (a small version of a trampoline). On a practical note there is a very well-equipped laundry room, with four washing machines, tumble driers and ironing facilities.

Mrs Widdowson provides really excellent self-catering accommodation, where families are very well cared for; the rental costs are very reasonable.

Nearby: The charming village has an excellent pub, and it is a delightful part of the world in which to browse. There are good facilities for fishermen and golfers, and plenty of stables from where you can ride out. Althorp, the house owned by Princess Diana's family, is just up the road, as is Holdenby House and Coton Manor Gardens. Billing Aquadrome has a whole host of water sports, and a little further afield you can visit the Stoke Bruerne Waterways Museum, Sulgrave Manor, Canons Ashby and Draycote Water Country Park. Stratford-upon-Avon, Oxford and Warwick are within easy driving distance.

Units: 5
Rent: £100 to £300 a week
Other costs: electricity is on a meter and read at the end of the visit
Heating: storage heating, open fires and stoves
A cot and a high chair are available
Open all year

East Portlemouth, Nr Salcombe, Devon   map 1

GARA ROCK HOTEL – ☎ *Salcombe (054 884) 2342.*

H/SC *Take the road to the coast from the A379 at Frogmore.*

The hotel was originally a row of coastguard's cottages and there are glorious views of the cliffs and the sea, and the surrounding National Trust land. You can see a sandy cove down below which can be reached via a footpath.

Great care is taken here to make life as easy as possible for parents, with plenty of cots and high chairs and a baby listening system. There's lots for the children to do – apart from the beach, there are acres of grassy garden in which there is a heated outdoor swimming pool and paddling pool, a hard tennis court and an exceptionally good adventure playground. There are swings and a roundabout for tiny children. Inside is a games room with table tennis and table football and the hotel organises various entertainments like the weekly Magic Show and children's party. A play group is organised for two hours a day on five days of the week for under tens, and this is run by a trained nanny. Trips on a traditional Cornish fishing boat can be booked. A sauna, sun bed and gymnasium have been added to the hotel's facilities, and there is now a room for teenagers, aptly called the Wreck Room.

All the family can enjoy the superb walks in this beautiful part of Devon, even though there is so much to do at the hotel that you need never leave its grounds. When we last called in on a sunny summer day people were having lunch on the lawns and up above the swimming pool a barbecue was in full swing. A lovely setting in which to enjoy a meal.

This hotel manages to care for families extremely well and offers outstanding value for money. It is worth recording that last year saw the 30th anniversary of the Richards family's ownership of the hotel.

Nearby: If you fancy some sightseeing, there is much to choose from within easy reach. The children will no doubt vote for a visit to the National Shire Horse Centre and the Dartmoor Wildlife Centre; enthusiasts will head for the Dart Valley Railway; while the Dartington Cider Press Centre has an array of craft shops and a couple of restaurants. Buckfast Abbey, the Torbay Aircraft Museum, and Compton Castle are all nearby, as is the busy resort of Torquay.

BAR SNACKS (12–2pm) £2–9: Millbay mushrooms, Tandoori prawns, spaghetti carbonara, farmer's lunch, seafood submarine sandwich;
DINNER (7.15–8.30pm) £17: prawn kromeski, roast Aylesbury duck, pudding and cheese
Children: own menu, half portions
£ medium
Best Bargain Break: a range of breaks depending on the season
Children: free up to 5 years, 50% or 80% of the adult rate thereafter up to 13
Facilities: 20 cots and 15 high chairs, and a baby listening system
21 rooms, 10 family Access/Visa
Closed end Oct-Easter • Ale – Palmer's
P – own car park

SELF-CATERING

The hotel has thirteen self-catering apartments, whose guests can use all the hotel's facilities. These can accommodate either four or six people and have well-equipped kitchens. The rents range from £240 to £670 a week.

To qualify for inclusion in the Guide hotels must offer the basic facilities of a cot, a family room and an evening meal. Self-catering establishments must provide cots and high chairs.

East Stoke, Nr Wareham, Dorset   map 2
KEMPS COUNTRY HOUSE HOTEL – ☎ *Bindon Abbey (0929) 462 563.*

On the A352 west of Wareham.

Facing south to the Purbeck Hills, this Victorian rectory, built, according to a stone plaque on the facade, in 1874, is marked at the entrance by some towering pine trees. The very large lawned area at the side of the hotel gives children some space to run in safety, and there is also a climbing frame here.

The interior is handsome, with well-proportioned rooms, which are stylishly decorated; with a particularly pretty restaurant, light and bright and looking out to the gardens. The conservatory is also a pleasant place to have a snack or a meal.

Nearby: The coast is not far away and the best sandy beaches are at Swanage and Studland. Railway buffs could take in a ride on the Swanage Railway and Durlston Country Park also lies in that direction. There are many other attractions within reach: Corfe Castle, the Tank Museum, the Tutankhamun Exhibition and the Sea Life Centre at Weymouth. There are excellent amenities in the vicinity including a leisure centre, squash and tennis courts, fishing, riding and water sports.

BAR SNACKS (12–2pm) £2–4: paté, moussaka, steak & kidney pie; LUNCH (12–2pm) £8: chicken liver paté, grilled local plaice, pudding or cheese;

DINNER (7–9.30pm) £17: smoked haddock mousse, soup, roast fillet of pork, pudding or cheese
Children: own menu, half portions
£ high
Best Bargain Break £89 per person, 2 nights – dinner, b & b
Children: free up to 7 years; £5 from 7 to 12
Facilities: 2 cots and 1 high chair; baby listening to every room
15 rooms, 4 family   Access/AmEx/Diners/Visa
No smoking in dining room   🅿 – own car park

Edburton, West Sussex   map 3

TOTTINGTON MANOR – ☎ Steyning (0903) 815 757.

North of Shoreham, off the A2037 and A281.

This attractive pub and hotel sits in its own grounds of four acres amid lovely Sussex countryside. You can sit in the spacious lawned garden and gaze at the low and gentle hills around you.

The handsome building is 16th century in origin and behind the black and white front there is a section built from brick and timber in an attractive herringbone design. An interesting feature of the hotel is a priest hole below the cellars; the escape tunnel emerges beyond the garden in a copse of trees.

There is plenty of space for families within the pub: for example a pleasant family dining room off the entrance hall and also a very comfortable residents' lounge with a number of easy chairs. You should take a look at the miniature Ford Model T and the grand piano, which are made from icing sugar.

One of the owners, David Miller, was a chef at the Ritz and we are not surprised to hear that the food is gaining an excellent reputation.

Nearby: There is plenty to do and see in the vicinity. If you like a walk you can try the South Downs Way which you can reach from Tottington via a bridle path. Riding, squash, tennis, golf and fishing are all available within a few miles of the hotel. Sightseers should head for the Amberley Chalk Pits Museum, Petworth House, the Devil's Dyke, Parham House, Lewes Castle and the Bluebell Railway. Youngsters will no doubt relish a visit to the Bentley Wildfowl & Motor Museum and the Wildfowl Trust at Arundel.

BAR SNACKS (12–2.15pm & 7–9.15pm) £1–9: taramasalata, salmon mousse, moussaka, spicy home-made sausages, sirloin steak;
DINNER (7–9pm) £15: smoked salmon, chicken Kiev, Italian trifle
Children: half portions
£ high
Children: nominal charge only
Facilities: 1 cot and 2 high chairs
6 rooms, 1 set interconnecting

EDINBURGH

- Ale – Adnams, Bateman's, Fuller's, King & Barnes
- 🅿 – own car park

Also recommended in the Family Welcome Pub & Restaurant Guide.

Edinburgh, Lothian   map 11
THRUMS HOTEL, 14 Minto Street – ☎ (031) 667 5545.

Not far from the city centre, on the south side.

The hotel is very convenient for the centre of Edinburgh and is in an area with many small hotels and guest houses. It has been constructed from two large Georgian buildings, in which many of the original features have been retained. The comfortable and well-decorated lounge has plenty of sofas and easy chairs and the large bay window gives it a bright appearance. The six family rooms have plenty of space and are attractively decorated.

An agreeable aspect of this hotel is its dining room, since part of it is housed in a conservatory, which in its turn looks out to the sizeable lawned garden with its pretty borders of flowers. It is a peaceful retreat away from the city bustle. There is also a stretch of lawned garden at the front.

Nearby: Edinburgh is a fine city with so much to see and do: the famous Castle, the Palace of Holyroodhouse, the National Gallery, Huntly House Museum, the Museum of Childhood, the Royal Botanic Garden, and so on. Within easy reach are many other attractions: the Almondell and Calderwood Country Park and Beecraigs Country Park; and the city is surrounded by castles – at Dirleton, Hailes, Tantallon and Lauriston for example.

LUNCH (12–1.30pm) £4: soup, cold buffet, pudding;
DINNER (5.30–8pm) £7: prawn cocktail, sirloin steak, pudding
Children: own menu, half portions
£ low
Children: cots free; half price up to 12 years
Facilities: 3 cots and a high chair
15 rooms, 6 family   No credit cards
Open all year except Xmas & New Year
🅿 – own car park

Erlestoke, Nr Devizes, Wilts   map 2
LONGWATER – ☎ Devizes (0380) 830 095.

On the B3098 west of Market Lavington. Turn off at Erlestoke Post Office.
The modern brick farmhouse was built in 1980 in a very agreeable style, and is

the focal point of the farm of about 160 acres. This is an organic farm and there are some rare breeds of sheep and longhorn cattle here. The farm's produce will be served to you for dinner.

The rooms are spacious, and all furnished to a high standard of comfort. The owner's collection of china figures and pottery is on display in the lounge, which has delightful views over the surrounding countryside.

The farm has its own area of parkland and two lakes, one of which is stocked with roach, perch, carp etc. Guests are welcome to fish here. The little valley has been made into a conservation area, and several types of wild fowl breed there; the family also breed wild fowl and some are kept in pens on the lawns. You can sit on the large patio and overlook the spacious lawns which run down to the lakes.

All the rooms here have en suite bathrooms, and the family room has a double-bedded room and an adjoining twin-bedded room.

Nearby: It is a lovely spot and there is so much of interest to the holiday maker: the whole of Salisbury plain lies at your feet, with the fine cities of Bath and Salisbury within reach. There are many interesting sights to see: Stonehenge, Longleat Safari Park, Avebury, Bowood House, the fascinating village of Lacock and its abbey, and Barton Farm Country Park.

DINNER (7pm) £11: soup, roast beef, pudding & cheese
Children: half portions

£ low
Children: nominal charge for cot; half price thereafter
3 rooms, 1 family
Open all year, except mid-December to 7 January
No credit cards   No music
P – ample

Evesham, Hereford & Worcs   map 2
ABBEY MANOR FARM – ☎ *Evesham (0386) 443 802.*

SC   *On the B4084, just north west of the town centre.*

This farm was derelict when Pru Jeffery and her family acquired it and you will now find, apart from the delightful main house, four self-catering cottages. The farm has a place in history since it lies on the site of the Battle of Evesham which was fought in 1265.

It is difficult to believe that you are so close to the town of Evesham when you first take in the lovely views across the countryside, and all that peace and quiet that surrounds the farm. And yet you can walk, within a few minutes, to the local supermarket (don't worry, you cannot see it from the cottages).

Lime Tree Cottage is self-contained and we were amazed at the age of some of the beams which have survived in the building. The rooms are all in line down

EVESHAM

the cottage: a large living room, with views on three sides, and a wood-burning stove; then a spacious and well-equipped kitchen; and then a double and a twin-bedded room. The antique furniture and wooden doors are fully in keeping with the cottage and there are neat stretches of garden on all sides, including a large stretch of lawn at one end which doubles as a tennis court (bumpy) in the summer.

The other three cottages are housed in a large brick barn. Two of them sleep four people and the other (Pippins) can accommodate six, in a double and two twin-bedded rooms. The well-equipped kitchens are in each case integrated with the living rooms. We were impressed, above all, with the care which has gone into the design and decoration of the cottages. All the furniture, much of it antique, has been individually chosen: it might be a Georgian dresser or a Victorian chest of drawers, and the old wooden doors complement the ancient beams and pillars. There is a lovely old herb garden in front of these cottages.

There is plenty of garden in which to loll and it includes a large lawned area with bench tables. A barbecue is set up here in the summer. Alongside is about five acres of rough pastureland and orchard where the children can play.

On a practical note there is a laundry room (the machines are coin operated) and you can easily walk to the centre of Evesham.

Nearby: There is an enormous amount to see and do in the area. The local Almonry Museum is worth a look and there are several other historic buildings in the vicinity including Snowshill Manor, Sudeley Castle, Bretforton Manor, Ragley Hall and Coughton Court. Stratford upon Avon is close enough, as is Warwick with its wonderful castle. The children will perhaps vote for a visit to the Cotswold Farm Park, Folly Farm Waterfowl Centre, the Cotswold Wildlife Park or Bourton on the Water, which has a motor museum, a model village and Birdland. There are leisure centres in Pershore and in Evesham.

Units: 4
Rent: £130 to £310 a week
Other costs: none
Central heating: provided
2 cots and 2 high chairs
Open all year

Exbourne, Nr Okehampton, Devon map 1
EASTERBROOK FARM – ☎ *Exbourne (083 785) 674.*

SC *On the B3217 just north of the village.*

If you value peace and seclusion you will be well suited by this farm, which is situated in the middle of the countryside between the village of Exbourne and Monkokehampton, both of which have a pub and a post office.

The farm covers around seventy acres, and guests are welcome to wander about the land and, if they wish, to help with the haymaking, apple picking or the mucking out of the horses, of which there are several. Children will be glad to hear that there are many other animals, too: goats, ducks, chickens, and several cats and dogs. The gardens and paddocks around the house are ideal spots for children to play.

Two of the cottages, close to the main house, have been converted from an early 19th century stone barn. One of them, the Shippen, has an open plan ground floor and both have spacious, comfortably furnished living rooms, with woodburning stoves, and the kitchens are equipped to an excellent standard. Both cottages have two bedrooms and these are bright and attractive, the more so because of the skilful use of skylight windows. The Granary is very suitable for families because, as well as a double bedroom, it has a bedroom with a single bed and two bunk beds.

Across the yard there is the detached Stable Cottage, a delightful building of 18th century vintage. The ground floor is open-plan with the oak beams in place and a spiral staircase leads to the two bedrooms, which also have their full quota of original beams. There is a twin and a double bedroom and a small bathroom.

Central heating is laid on for all the cottages and there is a laundry room. Mrs Pryce can supply pre-cooked meals and she will also cook a dinner for guests in her own house. Pets are accepted and stabling is available if you arrive on horseback.

This is an ideal place for a family holiday and the rents are very reasonable.

FAR SAWREY

Nearby: This is a splendid base if you intend to enjoy the many amenities in Devon. Dartmoor is only a few miles to the south and Exmoor around twenty to the north. Horse riding, walking, fishing and golf can all be done in beautiful surroundings. The beaches to the north or the south can be reached without difficulty. There are many interesting places to visit: Lydford Gorge, the remarkable Castle Drogo, Becky Falls, Morwellham Quay, the Dartmoor Wildlife Park and the Parke Rare Breeds Farm, and the Maritime Museum at Exeter.

Units: 3
Rent: £125 to £250 a week
Other costs: none
Heating: central and night storage heating
One cot available
Open all year

Far Sawrey, Cumbria   map 9

THE SAWREY HOTEL – ☎ *Windermere (05394) 43425.*

On the B5285, one mile from the west side of the Windermere car ferry.

The hotel is situated close to the famous lake and the ferry runs every twenty minutes during the summer and is always busy. The core of the building is of 18th century origin, and various additions have been made over the years; for example the stables were made into a bar, called the Claife Crier, and for parents who fancy a sustaining glass of Theakston's it is useful to know that there are various alcoves, away from the bar, where they and their children can settle down. There is a good range of bar snacks available here at lunchtimes. This hotel offers excellent value to families, especially if you take advantage of their four-day or weekly terms in the off-peak periods.

Nearby: The village of Near Sawrey is famous as the home of Beatrix Potter, and a pilgrimage to her house, Hill Top, at Near Sawrey will no doubt be on the programme. In the heart of the Lakes, you will hardly be short of holiday diversions, even on the simplest level of walking through the lovely countryside, or enjoying the watersports which are available on the lakes. Within easy reach are Fell Foot Park; Grizedale Forest with its wildlife centre and various nature trails; the Steamboat Museum at Windermere; John Ruskin's house, Brantwood which you can also see from the deck of the steam yacht "Gondola", which cruises on Coniston Water; the Lakeside and Haverthwaite Railway; and so on.

BAR SNACKS (11.30am–2.30pm) £1–6: roll mop herring, Cumberland sausage, local smoked trout, sirloin steak;
DINNER (7–8.45pm) £13: 5 courses, changed each day
Children: half portions

£ low
Best Bargain Break £51 per person, 2 nights – dinner, b & b
Children: cots £5; half price to age 13
Facilities: 3 cots and 2 high chairs; and baby listening to each room
17 rooms, 3 family   No credit cards
Open all year except Xmas   No music
• Ale – Theakston's, Jennings   **P** – own car park

Faringdon, Oxon   map 3

BELL HOTEL, The Square – ☎ *Faringdon (0367) 240 534.*

Centre of town on the A420.

This is very much a traditional inn in the centre of town. It was built in the 17th century and the bar retains much of its historic past. At the back of the pub is a quiet courtyard with bench tables and in summer it is strewn with trailing roses and flowers grown in old Thames boats.

Food is served in the bar and in the restaurant all week, and traditional Sunday lunches are also served. You will usually find an enterprising and keenly priced special bar meal in the evenings; perhaps moules marinières or a tray of hors d'oeuvres with crusty bread and a bottle of wine for under a tenner for two people.

There is a residents' lounge off the entrance hall and this is comfortably furnished and has a variety of old prints on the walls. We were most impressed with the standard of accommodation here. One of the family suites is superb: a huge room with a vaulted roof supported by oak beams.

Nearby: You are surrounded by delightful countryside here with the charms of the Cotswolds and the Vale of the White Horse within easy reach, as is Oxford itself. The children will want to visit Coate Water Park, the Cotswold Wildlife Park or Lydiard Country Park; whereas the adults' steps might turn to Blenheim Palace, Buscot Park or the Great Western Railway Museum.

BAR SNACKS (12–2pm & 6–10pm) £1–6: crab & mushroom Mornay, steak & kidney pie, Southern fried chicken, whole grilled plaice, sirloin steak;
DINNER (7.30–9.30pm) £13: sweet pickled herrings, escalope of pork, pudding or cheese
Children: small portions
£ medium
Best Bargain Break £60 per person, 2 nights – dinner, b & b
Children: cot or extra bed £5
Facilities: 1 cot and 2 high chairs, and a baby listening line for each room
11 rooms, 3 family   Open all year
Access/AmEx/Visa   • Ale – Wadworth's

FERSFIELD

P – own car park

Also recommended in the Family Welcome Pub & Restaurant Guide.

Fersfield, Nr Diss, Norfolk   map 8
STRENNETH FARMHOUSE – ☎ Bressingham (0379 88) 8182.

Off the A1066 just west of Diss.

A lovely old Norfolk brick farmhouse, which was probably built in the 17th century. It has been renovated to an excellent standard and most of the bedrooms have en suite facilities. The downstairs rooms have inglenook fireplaces, and one lounge is for non-smokers. All the rooms will take either a cot or an extra bed, and children's suppers are served at 6pm. There is a pool table and a dart board available.

The house is surrounded by open countryside, and there is plenty of garden here too: large grassy areas at the side and the back, with a play area for children with a swing, slide and climbing frame.

Nearby: Diss is right on the Suffolk border, and if you are interested in wildlife, Banham Zoo is nearby as is the Kilverstone Wildlife Park and the Otter Trust at Bungay. Bressingham Gardens has a children's nursery, a steam museum and a narrow gauge railway which takes visitors around the perimeter. Further afield and near the coast you will find the Suffolk Wildlife and Rare Breed Park and the Pleasurewood Hills Theme Park.

✗ DINNER (7.30pm) £12
Children: own menu
£ medium
Children: cots free; half price up to 14 years
Facilities: 2 cots and 2 high chairs; baby listening system
9 rooms, 2 family   Open all year
Access/AmEx/Visa   No music
P – ample

Forest Row, East Sussex   map 4
ROEBUCK HOTEL (Embassy Hotels), Wych Cross – ☎ Forest Row (0342) 823 3811.

On the A22 London-Eastbourne road.
Although it is situated on a busy main road, this pleasant hotel has a lovely position with the Ashdown Forest spread out around it. The 17th century half-

timbered building has been extended here and there, but the hall is notable for its beams and fine staircase. The public rooms are spacious and well-furnished with strategically placed alcoves, including one with a pool table.

Although there is nothing specifically for children, the beautifully kept gardens are very spacious with a lovely array of trees, shrubs and flowers. There is also a courtyard which, lit up at night, is an attractive sight. There is also the whole of Ashdown Forest in which to ramble.

Nearby: There is a visitor centre in the Ashdown Forest and the Ashdown Forest Farm has several rare breeds of animals and nature lovers can also visit Springhill Wildfowl Park. Wakehurst Place is within easy reach, as is the Bluebell Railway. If you go a little further south you can visit the Bentley Wildfowl & Motor Museum, Lewes Castle, Firle Place, and Drusillas.

BAR SNACKS (12–2pm) £2–6: club sandwich, filled jacket potatoes, fisherman's pie, chicken tikka, beef casserole;
LUNCH (12.30–1.45pm) £15: soup, pork Cantonese, pudding or cheese;
DINNER (7–9.15pm) £16: smoked mackerel salad, medallions of beef, pudding or cheese
Children: half portions
£ high
Best Bargain Break £40 per person per night – dinner, b & b
Children: free to age 16
Facilities: 2 cots and 2 high chairs; baby listening on three lines
31 rooms, 3 sets interconnecting   Access/AmEx/Diners/Visa
Open all year   **P** – own car park

Fownhope, Hereford & Worcs   map 2

GREEN MAN INN – ☎ *Fownhope (043 277) 243.*

H/SC   *In the centre of the village on the B4224.*

We were delighted to find this handsome pub some years ago. It is situated in beautiful countryside, very close to the lovely River Wye. It is a classic 15th century inn with most of the essential attributes: a black and white, part-timbered facade, a low-beamed bar, and above all a friendly atmosphere. One of its most celebrated landlords would not have had any trouble with drunken customers – he was Tom Spring, bare-knuckle heavyweight champion of England.

You will always find food on the go here, and the dining-room, housed in an old barn, is a lovely sight – very spacious, with black beams and pillars, and an outlook on one side to a very large grassy garden with lots of trees, and flowers. There are swings and a climbing frame for the children.

The bedrooms are well furnished and very comfortable, and indeed their style and ambience put many a three star hotel to shame. Of the three family rooms two have a double and single bed and the other a double and two singles. The pub has the great advantage, too, of having a separate room off the main bar where children can sit with their parents. It is the Buttery, a comfortable and spacious room with plenty of wooden settles and tables. The adults have a good selection of real ales to sample including Marston's.

Nearby: The pub is close to Hereford with its famous cathedral, and the delightful Wye Valley meanders in crazy loops south to Ross-on-Wye and beyond. Guests can fish the Wye since the landlord has fishing rights to a mile of river. There are many castles to see on the Borders including the famous triangle of the Skenfrith, Grosmont and White castles. The Falconry Centre at Newent will certainly be on the children's visiting list, as will the Wye Valley Centre with its maze, butterfly house and bird centre.

✘ BAR FOOD (12–2pm & 7–10pm) £1–7: plaice & chips, grilled trout, Tom Spring's steak sandwich, steaks, lasagne verdi;
DINNER (7.15–9pm) £10: garlic mushrooms, grilled plaice, pudding or cheese
Children: own menu, half portions
£ medium
Best Bargain Break £64 per person, 2 nights – dinner, b & b
Children: £2.50 under 5 years; £10 from 5 to 12
Facilities: 3 cots and 3 high chairs; and 3 baby listening lines
20 rooms, 3 family   Open all year
Access/AmEx/Visa   No music
• Ale – Hook Norton, Marston's, Sam Smith's
No smoking in guests' lounge   P – ample

SELF-CATERING
Mr and Mrs Williams have two cottages for rent. Deepwood is on the Hereford to Ross-on-Wye road and is situated in an unspoilt stretch of woodland. There are lovely views over the Wye Valley. The cottage has a double and a twin bedroom and a child's room. It has a delightful garden. Fern Cottage is in Fownhope and has a double and a twin bedroom, with a sofa bed also provided. There is a pleasant garden. Linen is provided and the electricity is metered. The rents vary from £100 to £230 a week.

Also recommended in the Family Welcome Pub & Restaurant Guide.

Garthmyl, Powys   map 6
PENLLWYN LODGES – ☎ Berriew (0686) 640 269.

SC *About a mile south of Garthmyl on the A483.*
The lodges are scattered over sixteen acres of wooded hillside, and each of the red cedar buildings has around half an acre of its own grounds, so you are never cheek by jowl with your neighbours. They are all of different designs and a marvellous job has been done in siting the lodges amongst the woodland, where the natural contours and character have been carefully preserved.

The lodges, which sleep either four, six or eight people, have been furnished and equipped without any stinting by the owners, Derek and Sandra Field. They all have fitted woollen carpets, central heating, comfortable furniture and fully equipped kitchens. It is no surprise to learn that the lodges have received the top classification from the Welsh Tourist Board. Every dwelling has its own parking space and a patio or a verandah. You can sit outside and enjoy the lovely views.

There is plenty of space here where the children can play and the adults relax. Fishermen can enjoy the canal which is stocked with carp, chub and tench and game fishing is available nearby. A lake, over 100 yards wide, has been excavated and is also stocked with fish. It is a pleasant place to have a picnic, and the children can make friends with the ducks, geese and swans. There are other animals, too, including dogs and Charlie, the Vietnamese black pot-bellied pig.

This is an attractive and very well-organised holiday complex, where families can enjoy the surroundings.

Nearby: As well as fishing, clay pigeon shooting can be arranged, and there is a riding school no more than three miles away. The sandy beaches of the coast are not too far away and there are many interesting places to visit: the castles at Powis and Montgomery; the Welshpool and Llanfair Railway; Lake Vyrnwy; and the beauties of South Shropshire with the lovely towns of Clun, Ludlow and Church Stretton.

Units: 22
Rent: £175 to £495 a week. Short breaks are available.
Other costs: electricity is metered
Heating: central heating
4 cots and 2 high chairs available
Open all year

Gellilydan, Nr Blaenau Ffestiniog, Gwynedd   map 5

TYDDYN DU – ☎ *Blaenau Ffestiniog (0766) 85281.*

Close to the junction of the A470 (to Blaenau) and the A487 (to Porthmadog).

The farmhouse was built of stone in the traditional Welsh style in the 17th century, and was once the home of Edmund Prys, who helped to translate the Bible into Welsh. The house has great charm and character, with an abundance of oak beams, exposed stonework and an inglenook fireplace, with a 12 foot slate beam, in the lounge.

This working farm is set in extensive grounds in the heart of the Snowdonia National Park. The front garden is a relaxing place to sit; there are brightly coloured flowers in hanging baskets and you look over open countryside. Children are welcome to help feed the animals: pet lambs and goats, rabbits and ducks wander around quite freely. They can also ride the two Welsh mountain ponies. There is room to play informal games of cricket, football and tennis.

The bedrooms have oak-beamed ceilings, tea and coffee making facilities and colour television. The double bedroom has its own bathroom. A cottage alongside the farmhouse is an ideal place for a family to stay since it has a large

GLENELG

bedroom with a double and two single beds. It is good to report that the owner, Mrs Williams, cooks meals for vegetarians, if you have one in the family (as we have). All the food is wholesome and freshly prepared.

Nearby: It is a good area for holidays with a long stretch of coastline nearby. The sandy beach at Harlech is about nine miles away, and the town also has a famous castle, a fine golf course and a swimming pool. Portmeirion Village is close by, as is the Ffestiniog Railway, the Llechwedd slate mines and the dry slope skiing at Trawsfynnydd. The farm itself has a Roman site, which guests are welcome to visit.

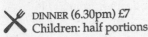 DINNER (6.30pm) £7
Children: half portions
£ low
Children: babies 80% discount; half price from 2 to 7 years; 30% discount from 8 to 13
Facilities: a cot and a high chair; and baby alarms
4 rooms, 1 family   Open all year
No credit cards   Unlicensed
No smoking in dining room and bedrooms
P – ample

Glenelg, Highland   map 12
GLENELG INN – ☎ *Glenelg (059 982) 273.*

Off the A87 and west of Loch Duich.
If you crave some peace and quiet, if you have the urge to forget the travails of everyday life, this is the place to visit. The Glenelg Inn is situated in a beautiful

part of Scotland, close to the short crossing to the Isle of Skye.

The inn was made from an old coaching mews right by the shores of Glenelg Bay. It has been refurbished in relaxed style, and the interior is notable for the low ceilings and huge wooden beams. The occasional stag's head will regard you balefully from a wall. The dining room is an attractive spot with pine furniture and warm red rugs and curtains.

The bedrooms are bright and simply furnished and have a charm of their own. Residents can use a pleasant sitting room, with very comfortable sofas, a huge and ornate grandfather clock and a fine array of family portraits. The bar is a busy and lively place.

The Glenelg has an expanse of lawns which lead down to the sea and picnic tables are set out on a patio. It's a lovely spot to sit on a summer's day.

Nearby: This is a place to enjoy the countryside – walking, horse riding, fishing or just lazing about. The scenery is wonderful, whatever you do. There is also plenty to see including the Lochalsh Woodland Garden and the Eilean Donan Castle. You can drive north to the Torridon Mountains Centre and the Beinn Eighe Nature Reserve. Across on Skye there are two museums and Dunvegan Castle to see.

BAR SNACKS (12.30–2.30pm & 7–9pm) £2–4: houmous & pitta bread, local smoked salmon, tarragon chicken, Hungarian goulash, seafood pilau;
DINNER (7–8.30pm) £18: smoked salmon, pork fillet, chocolate mousse, cheese
Children: half portions
£ medium
Children: half price up to 5 years; three quarters from 5 to 16
Facilities: 1 cot
6 rooms, 2 family   Open Easter to October
Access/Visa   No smoking in dining room
P – own car park

Glengairn, Nr Ballater, Grampian   map 12
GAIRNSHIEL LODGE – ☎ *Ballater (03397) 55582.*

A few miles north of Ballater on the A939 where it meets the B976.

For tranquillity, wide open spaces and a really relaxing atmosphere, this superb granite hunting lodge, which is said to have been used by Queen Victoria, is the place to be. It really has an idyllic position alongside the River Gairn, and has over four acres of grounds where the children can play and the adults can relax.

All sorts of equipment are available for indoor and outdoor games: a pool table, dart board, juke box, board games and a piano; there is a trampoline, baseball

GLENGAIRN

equipment, croquet and mountain bikes, and fishing in the Gairn. Of course it is a great place for walking, skiing, fishing, horse riding and golf; and Aboyne, about twenty miles away, has a sports centre and a swimming pool.

Mr and Mrs Duguid manage to run the Lodge in an informal and easy-going way, and it is an ideal spot for families since five of the bedrooms are family sized.

Nearby: If you like to see the sights you can start with some famous castles: Crathes and Balmoral are the most illustrious, and Craigievar and Corgarff are also within easy reach. Aberdeen is about an hour's drive away and the Transport Museum at Alford is rather closer at hand.

DINNER (7.30pm) £9
Children: half portions
£ low
Best Bargain Break £150 per person per week – dinner, b & b
Children: half price to 10 years; two thirds from 10 to 16
Facilities: 1 cot and 1 high chair
9 rooms, 5 family   Open Xmas to October
No credit cards accepted   No music
P – own car park

If you wish to recommend an establishment to the Guide please write to us – report forms are at the back of the book. We need your help to extend and improve the guide.

Glenshee, Tayside map 11

BLACKWATER INN – ☎ Glenshee (025 082) 234.

About ten miles north of Blairgowrie on the A93.

This large and welcoming inn, which began life as a sawmill, is situated in lovely countryside; there is plenty of peace and quiet here and it's a great place for the outdoor life – walking and riding, pony trekking, fishing, skiing, golf and sailing. Even hang gliding can be arranged if you feel brave enough.

The pub itself is busy and lively and you are as likely to find a crowded bar at teatime as you are at 1 pm. Families are very welcome and are well cared for; there are four family rooms, a couple of cots and a high chair, and baby listening can sometimes be arranged. Food is available both in the bar and in the restaurant throughout the day and includes a children's menu and half portions for smaller appetites.

There is about half an acre of informal garden, which includes a rock garden and a rustic climbing area for children. Nearby there is also a small garden centre and a herb garden.

Nearby: This is an excellent spot to stay if you are touring the Grampian and Highland areas, since the Blackwater Inn is close to Blairgowrie and to Braemar, with its famous castle, to the north. Not that you will be short of golf courses to play or castles to see. There are dozens of courses within an hour's drive, including the superb Rosemount course at Blairgowrie, and a number of notable castles: Glamis, Blair, Balmoral and Braemar, for example. Nature lovers should visit the Loch of the Lowes or the Hermitage Woodland Walk;

and the handsome town of Pitlochry lies in one direction and J.M. Barrie's birthplace in the other at Kirriemuir.

✖ (10am–9pm) £1–10: garlic mushrooms, lasagne, grilled salmon steak, chicken supreme, steaks
Children: own menu, half portions
£ low
Best Bargain Break £32 per person, 2 days – b & b
Children: free up to 4 years; half price from 5 to 9; 20% discount from 10 to 14
Facilities: 2 cots and 2 high chairs; and a baby listening patrol
8 rooms, 4 family   Open all year
Access/Visa   P – own car park

Glyn Ceiriog, Nr Llangollen, Clwyd   map 6
GOLDEN PHEASANT HOTEL – ☎ *Glyn Ceiriog (069 172) 281.*

On the B4500 west of Chirk.
This country hotel is a welcoming sight. Set in the beautiful Ceiriog Valley, the hotel has its own flower-filled garden, two tiled patios and a play area for the children. Inside is a very comfortable lounge which looks away to the hills. The splendid Pheasant Bar has dark wooden settles, stuffed game birds in glass cases, many items of militaria, an old stove with the original tiles on the fireplace surround, and a fine carved wooden mirror. A lovely place to have the odd tincture or two.

At lunchtimes and in the evening you can eat from the bar menu and the dining room offers a full menu. If you are keen on country pursuits, such as fishing and shooting, the hotel provides excellent facilities; and they have their own riding centre as well.

Nearby: This is a lovely part of the Border country and naturally there are interesting castles to view, at Chirk and Powis for example. The mansions of Erddig and Plas Newydd are worth a visit, and the Llangollen Steam Railway will take you on a trip through the delightful Dee Valley. Pistyll Rhaeadr and the Lake Vyrnwy Visitor Centre are both within easy reach.

✖ BAR SNACKS (12–3.30pm & 7–10pm) £2–5: salads, bacon & egg, cottage pie, gammon;
LUNCH (12–2pm) £10: seafood au gratin, lamb chops, pudding;
DINNER (7–8.30pm) £18: Italian salad, Welsh lamb, pudding or cheese
Children: own menu, half portions
£ high
Best Bargain Break £105 per person, 2 nights – dinner, b & b
Children: free up to 18 years
Facilities: 4 cots and 2 high chairs; baby listening to all rooms

18 rooms, 3 family   Access/AmEx/Diners/Visa
Open all year   No music
P – own car park

Glynarthen, Nr Cardigan, Dyfed   map 5
PENBONTBREN FARM HOTEL – ☎ *Aberporth (0239) 810 248.*

Off the A487 north east of Cardigan. There is a sign on the road.

We first came across this hotel a few years ago and were most impressed by the great care which has obviously been taken with the conversion of these old stone farm buildings. The bedrooms, most of which can take an extra bed and a cot, have been built in what were once the stables, the granary and the barn. The whole project has been done in a stylish and charming way.

Opposite the bedrooms you will find the main public rooms which include a bar and a pool room, and a restaurant which has a Welsh harp which is played regularly.

Mr and Mrs Humphreys also have an interesting farm museum, and a nature trail. There is a riding school nearby.

Nearby: The hotel is in a marvellous spot for walking, riding and fishing; and there are some excellent beaches nearby – Penbryn, Tresaith and Mwnt, for example. There is a wild life park at Cardigan, and a splendid stretch of coastline leads down to St David's with its famous cathedral; there is a Marine Life Centre, too. Further afield you can visit the Pembrokeshire castles: Manorbier, Tenby, Carew and Pembroke; and the Manor House Wildlife Park near Tenby. Oakwood Park at Narberth offers a lot of entertainment for the whole family.

✗ DINNER (7–8pm) £11: cawl, Teifi salmon, pudding
Children: own menu, smaller portions
£ medium
Best Bargain Break £72 per person, 2 nights – dinner, b & b
Children: free up to 16 years
Facilities: 2 cots and 2 high chairs; and a baby listening system
10 rooms, 7 family   Access/Visa
Open all year
No-smoking in dining room   **P** – own car park

Please let us have reports – good or bad – on any establishments listed in the Guide as soon as possible after your visit.

Great Malvern, Hereford & Worcs   map 2

ELM BANK, 52 Worcester Road – ☎ Malvern (0684) 566 051.

In the centre of the town.

The house is an elegant building in the late Regency style and its rooms have the advantage of being spacious, with high ceilings. They all have views either of the Severn Valley or the Malvern Hills.

This comfortable house has an agreeable and quiet sitting room and you can enjoy the sight of the surrounding countryside from the terrace or the well maintained lawned garden; it is enclosed so the children can play there in safety, and a see saw is provided for them. Another great benefit for guests is free admission to the Splash in Malvern with its pools and water slides.

Nearby: Elm Bank is just a few minutes' walk from the centre of the town and from the Winter Gardens and the Festival Theatre. The three cathedral cities of Worcester, Gloucester and Hereford are within easy reach, as is the Wye Valley. The Animal and Bird Gardens are just south of Malvern and Spetchley Park and Worcester Woods Country Park are in the other direction. Other attractions include Elgar's birthplace, Hanbury Hall and Witley Court.

✘ DINNER (6.30pm) £10
Children: half portions

£ low

Best Bargain Break 20% discount from November to February

HADLEIGH

Children: free up to 2 years; £10 from 2 to 12
Facilities: 1 cot and 1 high chair; baby listening by arrangement
6 rooms, 3 family Open all year
AmEx only No music
No smoking in dining room & bedrooms P – own car park

Hadleigh, Suffolk map 4

EDGEHILL HOTEL, 2 High Street –☎ Hadleigh (0473) 822 458.

In the centre of the town.

The original house was built in 1590 but was substantially rebuilt in the early 18th century and looks every inch a stately Georgian building. The present owners have done a marvellous job of restoring the house and it is a delightful place in which to stay.

The lounge is spacious and very comfortably furnished, as are the bedrooms and especially a recently completed one with a 19th century four poster bed. In the lounge guests will find several board games and a good selection of books.

At the back of the hotel there is a pleasant garden with a lawn on which the adults can loll and the children can play.

Nearby: Hadleigh itself is an attractive place and there are other delightful towns nearby such as Lavenham, with its great array of remarkable buildings, and Long Melford, where Melford Hall is worth a look. Within easy reach you can visit Gainsborough's House, Flatford where John Constable lived, Clare

Castle Country Park with its nature trails and picnic areas, and the adults will no doubt relish a visit to the Cavendish Manor vineyards.

DINNER (7pm) £14
Children: half portions
£ low
Best Bargain Break £40 per person, 2 nights – dinner, b & b
Children: £5 for a cot or extra bed
Facilities: 1 cot and 1 high chair
12 rooms, 2 family   No credit cards
Open all year except Xmas and New Year
P – own car park at rear   No music

Hartland, Devon   map 1

WEST TITCHBERRY FARM – ☎ *Hartland (0237) 441 287.*

Off the B3248. Take signs for Hartland Point/Lighthouse.

This pleasant house dates back to the mid-18th century, and the farm comprises about 150 acres, on which sheep, pigs and cattle are bred. It is in a very peaceful spot, no more than half a mile from Hartland Point and the lighthouse.

The house sits inside a walled garden, and rambling roses run along the tops of the walls. It is quiet and secluded inside, with lawns in front of the house and a patio area. Guests are free to wander around the farm, and a converted barn houses a games room with a table tennis table and a dart board.

It is a comfortable and spruce house, with a light and airy lounge where guests will find a good collection of books. The dining room, with separate tables for guests, is a welcoming sight with its large inglenook fireplace. You will certainly eat fresh food here, since most of the meat and vegetables are grown on the farm. A self-catering cottage on the farm can accommodate six to eight people.

Nearby: This is a good spot for a holiday. You can for example walk along a coastal path to a beach, which is sandy at low tide, although it is a bit of a climb to and from the beach. The Hartland Quay Museum has much of interest about the vicinity, and several walks around the beautiful coastline start from here. Clovelly is nearby, and just down the coast are many beaches where you can loll about: Widemouth Bay and Crackington Haven for example. It is a great area for surfing, too. The busy tourist resorts lie to the north around Ilfracombe, with the attendant attractions: Watermouth Castle, Exmoor Bird Gardens, Arlington Court. Braunton Burrows is one of Britain's biggest nature reserves.

DINNER (6.30pm) £7
Children: portions of any size

HASTINGS

£ low
Children: reductions up to 11 years
Facilities: 2 cots and 1 high chair; baby sitting by arrangement
3 rooms, 1 family   Open all year except Xmas
No credit cards   Unlicensed
P – ample   No music

Hastings, East Sussex   map 4

BEAUPORT PARK HOTEL (Best Western), Battle Road – ☎ *Hastings (0424) 851 222.*

On the A2100 between Battle and Hastings.

This hotel is a splendid Georgian mansion which was once the home of Sir James Murray, who was second in command to General Wolfe at Quebec. It has a lovely setting in about thirty acres of parkland, which includes a formal Italian garden with superb trees, and a tranquil sunken garden.

There are excellent facilities too: a hard tennis court, an outdoor giant chess board, a putting green, a boule pitch, a croquet lawn, and a heated outdoor swimming pool. Next door there is a riding school and six squash courts; and golfers should be in their element since there is both a 9 hole and an 18 hole golf course.

Nearby: Hastings Castle and Battle Abbey, which is actually built on the land where William the Conqueror defeated Harold. Parents will perhaps favour a visit to the Carr Taylor vineyards; and within a reasonable radius you can visit Rudyard Kipling's home, Bateman's, Herstmonceaux Castle and Drusillas, with its zoo, miniature railway, large adventure playground, restaurant and pub.

BAR SNACKS (10.30am–9.30pm) £1–5: soup, paté, vegetarian pancake, coquille fruits de mer, ploughman's;
LUNCH (12.30–2pm) £12: duck paté, roast leg of lamb, pudding or cheese;
DINNER (7–9.30pm) £14: seafood cocktail, supreme of chicken Marsala, pudding or cheese.
Children: own menu, half portions
£ high
Best Bargain Break £82 per person, 2 nights – dinner, b & b
Children: free up to 16 years
Facilities: 4 cots and 2 high chairs, and a baby listening service on four lines
23 rooms, 1 family   Access/AmEx/Diners/Visa
Open all year   No music
P – own car park

Nr Heathfield, East Sussex　　　　　　　　　　　　　　　　map 4

WEST STREET FARMHOUSE, Maynards Green – ☎ *Horam Road (04353) 2516.*

On the B2203 just south of Heathfield in the village of Maynards Green.

This is a delightful brick farmhouse, built in an L shape, parts of which date back to the 17th century. It is surrounded by nearly four acres of grounds, a large part of which comprises smooth lawns: a lovely spot for the children to play and for the adults to relax.

The attractive and comfortable bedrooms, a twin and a double, share a bathroom and each can accommodate a cot. Guests also have the use of a comfortable sitting room and they have their own dining room. All these rooms have lovely views over the garden and the countryside to the rear of the house.

Nearby: This is a delightful part of England, with glorious countryside all around and with the coastline from Brighton eastwards within easy reach. Nature lovers will head for Drusillas Park, the Seven Sisters Country Park and the Bentley Wildfowl Trust (there is also a motor museum here). Bateman's, where Rudyard Kipling wrote many of his books, is nearby, as is Herstmonceux Castle, Michelham Priory and the Bluebell Railway.

 DINNER (7pm) £8
Children: half portions
£ low
Children: babies free; half price from 3 to 10 years
Facilities: 1 cot and 1 high chair; baby listening by arrangement
2 rooms　Open all year
No credit cards　Unlicensed
P – own car park

Helton, Nr Penrith, Cumbria　　　　　　　　　　　　　　　map 9

BECKFOOT HOUSE – ☎ *Bampton (093 13) 241.*

Off the A6 south of Penrith.

The house is actually about a mile south of the village of Helton, which has a pub and is itself six miles or so from Penrith. It is quite a stately house, built of stone in the mid-18th century, with a large and immaculate lawn at the front with a charming sundial. It is surrounded by a variety of fine trees and at the back of the house the ground slopes up to a small paddock which is also encircled by trees. There is plenty of room for children to play, and they have an adventure playground. There is easy access to the fells with many delightful walks and masses of wild life to spot.

The rooms are beautifully proportioned and include a spacious sitting room which is furnished with a variety of comfortable easy chairs. You have splendid views of the gardens and the countryside beyond, and an open fire for cooler evenings. It is good to report that the television is in a separate (and cosy) room and there are board games and children's toys available.

This is very much a house where families are made welcome and there are cots and high chairs as well as three family rooms. As you would expect of this handsome and spacious place, they are of a generous size and very well furnished and decorated: one has a double and two single beds, and the others each have a double and a single bed. All the bedrooms here have their own en suite facilities.

Nearby: There is much to do and see in this part of Cumbria, especially if you like walking, riding or water sports. Ullswater is a few miles away, as is Haweswater Nature Reserve. Up the road is the pretty village of Askham which lies next to the huge Lowther Park with its deer park and nature trails. It also has an adventure playground and a miniature railway. A sprint down the motorway will take you close to all the other tourist attractions of the Lakes – Grasmere, Ambleside, Coniston, Windermere and so on.

DINNER (7pm) £10
Children: half portions
£ medium
Children: free up to 5 years; half price thereafter up to 12
Facilities: 1 cot and 2 high chairs
6 rooms, 3 family   Open March to November
No credit cards   No music
No smoking in dining room   P – ample

Hereford, Hereford & Worcs   map 2

GREEN DRAGON HOTEL (THF), Broad Street – ☎ *Hereford (0432) 272 506.*

In the main street.

There has been an hotel on this site for nearly a thousand years, and the 19th century stucco facade disguises a much older building. It is indeed a very smart and rather grand hotel with some delightful rooms: a stately oak-panelled dining room, a plush bar and a large and elegant lounge. The hotel was totally refurbished a couple of years ago. Although there are no permanent family rooms, several of the bedrooms are spacious enough to accommodate a cot and an extra bed.

Nearby: Hereford is famous for its cathedral, and is also an attractive town in its own right, and is ringed by delightful countryside. If you follow the Wye Valley south you can have a look at the Wye Valley Visitor Centre with its maze, butterfly house and craft workshops, and there is a bird park next door. There are many castles on the borders – Grosmont, Skenfrith, Raglan and

White Castle – and the ruins of Llanthony Priory are worth a look.

✳ BAR SNACKS (12.30–2pm) £1–4: soup, raised pies, ploughman's;
LUNCH (12.30–2pm) £8, 2 courses: roast rib of beef & Yorkshire pudding, pudding or cheese
DINNER (7–9.30pm) £15: smoked duck & avocado, roast poussin, pudding or cheese
Children: own menu, half portions
£ high
Best Bargain Break £50 per person per night – dinner, b & b
Children: free up to 16 years
Facilities: 5 cots and 3 high chairs; and a baby listening system
87 rooms   Access/AmEx/Diners/Visa
Open all year   No music
• Ale – Bass   No smoking in restaurant   **P** – own car park at rear

---

Hevingham, Norfolk   map 8
MARSHAM ARMS HOTEL, Holt Road – ☎ *Hevingham (0605) 48268.*

On the B1149 north of Norwich.

This appealing inn, smartly decorated under its tiled roof, stands in the countryside about seven miles from Norwich and was originally a hostel for farm labourers, and built in the 19th century. The wooden beams and large open fireplace survive from the original design.

The building has been extended over the years and especially to provide better facilities for families who are welcome to use a spacious and nicely furnished room away from the bar. It is good to report that it is a no smoking area.

There is a terrace with tables and chairs and wooden benches – a pleasant place to sit in the sun and try the pub's excellent range of real ales. Alongside there is a children's play area, which is surrounded by trees.

Eight well-equipped twin bedrooms, all with their own bathrooms, have recently been added to the pub's facilities, and they all have sofa beds and can easily accommodate a family of four.

Nearby: The Broads are quite close and it is not too long a drive to reach the coast where two quiet and sandy beaches can be recommended – at Sea Palling and Happisburgh. This stretch of coast is, mercifully, undeveloped. There are many tourist attractions within reach: Norfolk Wildlife Park, Thrigby Hall wildlife gardens, Blickling Hall, and on the north Norfolk coast, Felbrigg Hall, the Norfolk Shire Horse Centre and the North Norfolk railway.

✳ BAR SNACKS (12–2pm & 6–10pm) £2–10: lasagne, cold buffet, steaks, whole lemon sole, supreme of chicken;
DINNER (6.30–9.30pm) £15: scampi, fillet steak, pudding or cheese

HIMBLETON

Children: own menu, half portions
£ medium
Children: free up to 5 years; £8 from 5 to 14
Facilities: 2 cots and 3 high chairs; 2 lines for baby listening
8 rooms   Open all year
• Ale – Adnams, Bass, Greene King
Access/AmEx/Visa   🅿 – own car park

Also recommended in the Family Welcome Pub & Restaurant Guide.

Himbleton, Nr Droitwich, Hereford & Worcs   map 2

PHEPSON FARM– ☎ *Himbleton (090 569) 205.*

H/SC   *South east of Droitwich. Can be reached from the A422 or the B4090.*

This handsome 17th century farmhouse, with its appealing oak-beamed rooms, is at the centre of a working farm of 170 acres, on which beef and sheep are reared.

Families will receive a warm welcome from Mrs Havard who provides a couple of high chairs and a cot. One of the family suites is in the recently converted granary alongside the farmhouse and contains separate double and twin bedrooms, each of which has a bathroom. Up above is a self-catering apartment with a double bedroom and a sofa bed. Linen, electricity and heating are included in the rent which varies from £125 to £200 a week.

There is a charming and comfortable lounge for guests and a separate dining room where you will eat breakfast. Mrs Havard no longer does evening meals but there are several pubs nearby which welcome families.

Guests are welcome to walk the farm, as long as they observe the obvious rules of the country code, and there is no shortage of lovely walks in the surrounding area, plus fishing, horse riding, golf, etc. You can also relax in the lawned gardens, and there is a swing for the children, who have ample room to play: there are eight acres of woodland for example.

Nearby: There is so much to do and see in this part of England. Hanbury Hall, Spetchley Park, the Worcester Woods Country Park, Elgar's birthplace and the Jinney Ring Craft Centre are all on the doorstep; and a little further east are Stratford-upon-Avon, Ragley Hall, Charlecote Park and the city of Warwick with its famous castle.

£ low
Children: various reductions according to age
Facilities: a cot and 2 high chairs
5 rooms, 1 family, 1 set interconnecting
Open all year except Xmas and New Year
No smoking in bedrooms   No music
P – plenty

Holsworthy, Devon   map 1

LEWORTHY FARM – ☎ *Holsworthy (0409) 253 488.*

Three miles south of Holsworthy on minor roads.

The farmhouse dates back to Saxon times, and is a large and comfortable home. Everything here is done to ensure that a family can have an active and gregarious holiday. Most evenings during the season, for example, there will be an entertainment – a conjuror, a barn dance, a fancy dress competition, or a sing-song. The excellent facilities for families include several family rooms, a good supply of cots and high chairs, and baby listening by arrangement.

The very large lawned garden includes a huge fig tree, which still bears fruit, and a good-sized lake on which guests can take a boat or do some fishing;

HOLSWORTHY

anglers can also fish in the neighbouring river.

The children have their own play areas on the lawn and in the barns – skittles, table tennis, badminton, toys and board games are all available, and there are even two ponies which they are allowed to ride under supervision. All sorts of other activities are organised: snooker and darts; pony trekking on Dartmoor; clay pigeon shoots which are arranged by Mr Cornish; archery and croquet; and there is a nine hole pitch and putt course and a tennis court.

Added to which this is a wonderful spot for nature lovers: red deer, buzzards, pheasant, herons, kingfishers and many other species can be seen.

Nearby: The sandy Cornish beaches are not far away, including those at Bude which are so popular with surfers: Sandy Mouth, Widemouth Bay and Crackington Haven. The Tamar Otter Park will also perhaps be part of the children's holiday programme, and there are castles to see at Launceston and Tintagel, plus Hartland Quay and Clovelly.

DINNER (7pm) £9: soup, steak & kidney pie, fresh fruit & cheese
Children: own menu, half portions
£ low
Children: discounts from 75% to 25%
Facilities: cots and high chairs available; and baby listening can be arranged
14 rooms, 3 family, one set interconnecting
Open all year   No credit cards accepted
No smoking in dining room   Licensed
P – ample

Holywell, Clwyd

map 6

GREENHILL FARM – ☎ Holywell (0352) 713 270.

On the Holywell to Greenfield road, almost opposite the Royal Oak.

This is a most attractive farmhouse, built of stone on a timber frame in the 16th century. The original beams are much in evidence in the comfortable lounge, which also has an open fire. The dining room was built about a century later and is notable for its partly wood-panelled walls.

From the farm you will have superb views of the Dee Estuary and Hilbre Island; and just beyond the Island you will perhaps be able to see the great golf course at Hoylake. You can sit on the spacious lawns and admire it all, and the children can head for the play area with its swings, slide, Wendy house and climbing frame. Guests are welcome to roam the 120 acres of the farm, which supports a herd of pedigree cattle. If the weather is unkind there is a games room with snooker, darts, toys and board games. On a more utilitarian front the Jones family also provide a washing machine and dryer.

Nearby: There is much to see in this part of the world. The Greenfield Valley Heritage Park is on the doorstep, and there are castles to see at Rhuddlan, Ewloe and Flint. Just a bit further on you can visit Loggerheads Country Park

HOPE COVE

(near Mold), and there is a sports and water centre in Holywell, and the Sun Centre in Rhyl.

✕ DINNER (6.30pm) £6: home made soup, steak & kidney pie, pudding
Children: half portions
£ low
Children: cot £2; half price up to 10 years
Facilities: 1 cot and 2 high chairs; baby listening can be arranged
3 rooms, 1 family   Open 1 March to 31 October
No credit cards accepted   Unlicensed
🅿 – ample   No music

Hope Cove, Kingsbridge, Devon   map 1
THE COTTAGE HOTEL – ☎ *Kingsbridge (0548) 561 555.*

Look for Hope Cove off the A381 and take Inner Hope Road.

A comfortable family hotel which has an idyllic position overlooking two safe beaches, which are protected by a grassy headland on one side. From the terrace and the two acres of sloping garden you look out to Thurlestone across Bigbury Bay. There are swings in the garden and a good-sized playroom upstairs with table tennis, space invaders, a piano and a wide window overlooking the sea.

We have had several reports about this hotel and one in particular praised the helpful and hard-working staff, who clearly understand how to look after families.

Nearby: This is one of the loveliest parts of Devon and not the least of the attractions are the many sandy beaches; at Hope Cove itself, Salcombe, Bantham Bay and Thurlestone, for instance. The Devon South Coast Path runs through Hope Cove. The children will certainly enjoy a visit to the National Shire Horse Centre and the Dartmoor Wildlife Park; while Buckfast Abbey, the Dart Valley Railway, the Torbay Aircraft Museum and Compton Castle are all within reach.

✕ BAR SNACKS (12–1.30pm) £1–9: steak & mushroom & potato pie, plaice & chips, ravioli, lobster salad;
DINNER (7.30–8.30pm) £16: prawn cocktail, soup, roast turkey, pudding and cheese
Children: own menu, half portions
£ medium
Best Bargain Break £39 per person per night – dinner, b & b
Children: £2 under one year; £6 from 1 to 3 years; £10 from 4 to 8; £13.50 from 9 to 12 years (includes meals)
Facilities: 6 cots and 6 high chairs; a baby listening system
35 rooms, 5 family   No credit cards accepted

Closed Jan   No music
🅿 – own car park

Hutton, Nr Weston-super-Mare, Avon   map 2
MOORLANDS – ☎ *Bleadon (0934) 812 283.*

In the village, which is south of Weston-super-Mare and can be reached from the A371 or A370.

This is a most attractive Georgian house in a village which sits at the foot of the Mendip Hills. The garden spreads over two secluded acres, with lawns, trees, rockeries, a lovely display of flowers and a kitchen garden, a paddock where pony rides are arranged. It is relaxing and safe for children to play; there is a slide, a climbing frame, and a garden badminton set. Both the dining room and the comfortable lounge look over the gardens and beyond to the wooded hills.

The outlook of Mr and Mrs Holt is stated in their brochure: that they receive visitors into their own home as guests and try to make them feel at home. That certainly includes children, since there are six rooms which can accommodate two adults and a child. Two of them have a double and two single beds.

There is a vegetable garden and the owners use as much of their own, and local, produce as possible.

Nearby: If you like an active holiday you could hardly be in a better spot: golf, fishing and a dry ski slope are available in the locality. The traditional seaside resort of Weston-super-Mare is quite close and it has an excellent leisure centre. Glastonbury and Wells are nearby; as are Cheddar Gorge, the Wookey Hole caves, and Ebbor Gorge and the East Somerset railway. A bit further afield nature lovers can head for Chew Valley Lake and Cricket St Thomas Wildlife Park.

✘ DINNER (6.30pm) £8
Children: half portions
£ low
Children: under 2 years £4; half price thereafter
Facilities: 4 cots and 3 high chairs; baby listening by arrangement
8 rooms, 5 family   Open January to October
Access/AmEx/Visa   No music
No smoking in dining room   🅿 – own car park

Please let us have reports – good or bad – on any establishments listed in the Guide as soon as possible after your visit.

Ilfracombe, Devon   map 1

LANGLEIGH COUNTRY HOTEL, Langleigh Road – ☎ Ilfracombe (0271) 862 629.

On the west side of the town; best to get a map from the hotel.

This hotel has been recommended in the "Family Welcome Guide" for many years, and is in a delightful and quiet spot on the outskirts of the town. It more than lives up to its description as a country hotel; it is situated in several acres of lawned and wooded grounds and is encircled by gentle hills. A stream runs along the boundary of the gardens.

The core of the house dates back to the 16th century, and one of Nelson's admirals, Bowen, built on a rather elegant Regency facade.

The rooms have lovely proportions and are very restful – they have that lived-in and welcoming feel of a large family house. Families are very well looked after here: there are several cots and high chairs, and a baby listening system. This is also connected to two cottages in the grounds, and they each have two bedrooms and a sitting room. We looked at two of the family rooms, which were both very comfortable and well-furnished and have their own bathrooms, as have all the rooms in the hotel. The owners asked us to point out that they have several dogs (Welsh springer spaniels) – just in case any of the children are nervous of them.

Nearby: Ilfracombe is a thriving seaside resort and there are plenty of sandy beaches where a family can enjoy themselves. For a change of scene Exmoor is near, with its many lovely walks, and there are many other places to visit: Exmoor Bird Gardens, Watermouth Castle, Arlington Court, the Maritime Museum at Appledore, Dartington Glass, Dunster Castle, the West Somerset Railway, and so on.

DINNER (7.30–9.30pm) £9: crab & tarragon quiche, chicken Florentine, pudding and cheese
Children: high teas, half portions
£ medium
Best Bargain Break £51 per person 2 nights – dinner, b & b
Children: free to age 1; 25% of the adult cost to 5; 50% to 14
Facilities: 5 cots and 4 high chairs; and a baby listening system
9 rooms, 2 cottages, 4 family   Open all year
Licensed   Access/Visa
P – own car park

SOUTHCLIFFE HOTEL, Torrs Park – ☎ Ilfracombe (0271) 862 958.

Near the centre of the town.

The owners of this large Victorian building, Mr and Mrs Anderson, have attacked the family market with great resolve and everything here is geared up for parents with young children.

Apart from the many cots and high chairs, there is a children's playroom with all sorts of toys, a Wendy house and a small model railway. Board games can also be made available, and cartoons are shown on the video in the playroom. There are loads of books around the hotel, plus a games room for older children with a pool table and darts. Just as useful for parents is a kitchen where food can be prepared for small children; and there is also a washing machine, a spin drier, an iron, etc on the premises.

The lounge, with its comfortable chairs and sofas, overlooks the garden, as does the dining room.

The attractive rear garden has a lawn on two levels, a fine display of flowers, and a couple of copper beech trees. You can sit happily in the sun, and there is room for the children to play. They have a swing and the owners provide various garden games.

You can be assured that the food will be of good quality here, because the owners used to run an excellent wholefood restaurant in Shrewsbury – the Good Life, which is still recommended in the 'Family Welcome Pub & Restaurant Guide'.

Nearby: Ilfracombe is a popular holiday resort with many attractions and if you fancy a change from the beaches there is a good indoor swimming pool. The children will no doubt enjoy a visit to Watermouth Castle, Exmoor Bird Gardens and Combe Martin Wildlife Park; while the adults will perhaps argue the case for Braunton Burrows nature reserve, Arlington Court and Dunster Castle. The beauty of Exmoor is on the doorstep, too.

DINNER (6.30pm): garlic mushrooms, pork in cider, pudding and cheese
Children: own menu, half portions
£ low
Best Bargain Break £165 per person per week – dinner, b & b
Children: first child free up to 5 years (before July 14 and after 1 September); one third of full rate up to 2 years; half from 2 to 11; three quarters from 12 to 14
Facilities: plenty of cots and high chairs; baby listening system
14 rooms, 4 family, 4 sets interconnecting
Open April to September   No credit cards accepted
No smoking in dining room and play room
P – own car park

Inchbae, by Garve, Highland   map 12
INCHBAE LODGE HOTEL – ☎ *Altguish (09975) 269.*

On the A835 north west of Garve.
The journey to Inchbae Lodge is a joy in itself, through some of the loveliest glens in the Highlands and passing Loch Garve and Rogie Falls. Six miles

from the nearest village, Inchbae is a remote former hunting lodge, now a charming and informal hotel with a reputation for good food.

The hotel sits alongside the River Blackwater and there are magnificent views of the heathered hills in every direction, with Ben Wyvis towering over the scene. If you value peace and tranquillity, Inchbae is the place for you, and it is an ideal base for a country loving family who want to tour the Highlands.

The seven acres of grounds are not 'gardened'; they are mowed by tractor and provide a lovely setting for the hotel. The children will love the freedom and all the space. Younger children should be supervised, however, since there is an unfenced pond, but there are safe play areas in an enclosed area of the grounds.

Guests can fish in the river at the bottom of the garden, and the children can make friends with the various animals: pet rabbits, chickens, sheep, dogs, cats and cattle. If the weather is inclement all sorts of games and puzzles are available in the hotel.

Nearby: All sorts of outdoor pursuits can be arranged – fishing, clay pigeon shooting, hill walking, golf and riding – and the area is a prolific one for wildlife. From Garve station you can take a trip by train to the Kyle of Lochalsh and then over the sea (a short ferry trip) to Skye for the day. If you fancy some sightseeing in other directions you can visit the Corrieshalloch Gorge, the Beinn Eighe Nature Reserve, and the Torridon Mountains Centre; near Inverness you can see the Loch Ness Monster Exhibition, Urquhart Castle, Cawdor Castle and the battlefield of Culloden.

BAR SNACKS (12–2pm & 5–8.30pm) £1–9: sweet pickled herring, mussels, sirloin steak, fillet of haddock, haggis;
DINNER (7.30–8.30pm) £17: summer salad, spiced parsnip soup, peppered steak, pudding
Children: half portions
£ medium
Best Bargain Break £99 per person, 3 nights – dinner, b & b
Children: free of charge
Facilities: 2 cots and 2 high chairs; baby listening system
12 rooms, 3 family   Open all year except Xmas
No credit cards   No music
P – own car park

Nr Inverness, Highland   map 12
KILRAVOCK CASTLE, Croy – ☎ Croy (066 78) 258.

Just off the A96 east of Inverness.

This impressive castle has been the home of the Rose family since the 15th century and now offers twenty bedrooms to guests who will find a quiet and relaxed atmosphere and a considerable degree of comfort. The furniture is superb and the family portraits and mementoes are a reminder of the castle's historic past.

The castle is the home of Baroness Rose and is run with Christian principles in mind. Grace is said before meals and after breakfast and dinner you have the option to listen to a short comment on a verse from the Bible. The prices charged, which are inclusive of dinner, are very reasonable for such splendid surroundings.

The castle is situated in a large wooded estate which is notable for many rare trees. With all the woodland and gardens, which incorporate a river and nature trails, it is a lovely place to relax and is of great interest to nature lovers. The facilities are also excellent and include a squash court, a tennis court, a putting green and croquet lawn, swing ball and table tennis. There is also a billiards room.

Nearby: Horse riding and fishing can be arranged locally and there is a fine championship golf course at Nairn, which also has a sandy beach. The Highlands are easily accessible and there are many places of interest within reach: Cawdor Castle and Urquhart Castle, Fort George, the Loch Ness Monster Exhibition, the Landmark Visitor Centre, Culloden battlefield, the Highland Wildlife Centre, the Glenmore Forest Centre and the Rothiemurchus Estate.

LUNCH (1pm): sandwiches, light lunch or full meal;
DINNER (7pm) soup or starter, main course, pudding (included in the price)
Children: half portions

INVERURIE

£ low
Children: babies free; half price up to 5 years; three quarters price from 6 to 16
Facilities: 3 cots and 2 high chairs; baby listening system
20 rooms, 8 family   Open May to September
No credit cards   Unlicensed
No smoking in restaurant and drawing room
P – ample   No music

Inverurie, Grampian   map 12

THAINSTONE HOUSE HOTEL – ☎ *Inverurie (0467) 21643.*

One mile East of Inverurie on main A96.

The building stands on the site of a medieval manor which was destroyed during the Jacobite uprising and was rebuilt in 1820 in the neo-classical style. It is a handsome sight, and is set in the rolling countryside of the Don Valley.

It is a lovely, secluded spot set in fourteen acres of gardens and woodland. There is a play area with a swing and a slide and swingball and boule can be played. One of the many walks takes you to the camp used by Robert the Bruce before the battle of Barra in 1308.

Plans for a radical expansion of the hotel may come to fruition this year with the addition of over 40 bedrooms (many of them family rooms), a swimming pool, a gym and other amenities.

Nearby: The sea is not too far away and Cruden Bay has a sandy beach with a golf course close by. Pennachie Forest has many superb walks which are well marked, and Pitmedden Garden and Forvie Nature Reserve are also within easy reach. There are many castles to see – Fyvie, Drum, Crathes and Castle Fraser – and the children will no doubt relish a visit to Storybook Glen, south of Aberdeen.

BAR MEALS (12–2pm & 6.30–9.30) £1–11: Aberdeen smokie, fillet of sole, steaks, lamb & vegetable casserole;
DINNER (6.45–9.15pm) £19: paprika chicken sautée, soup, Aberdeen Angus steak, pudding or cheese
Children: own menu, half portions
£ high
Best Bargain Break £80 per person 2 nights – dinner, b & b
Children: free up to any age
Facilities: 2 cots and 2 high chairs; 3 baby listening lines
8 rooms, 3 family   Access/AmEx/Diners/Visa

Open all year • Ale – Heriot and guests
P – own car park

Kames, Nr Tighnabruaich, Strathclyde map 11
KAMES HOTEL – ☎ *Tighnabruaich (0700) 811 489.*

South west of Kames off the B8000.

This appealing, black and white building has been a hotel since the 19th century and was once an inn for the drovers who brought cattle across the Kyles of Bute. It is in a delightful spot on the Cowal Peninsula, with Loch Fyne on one side and the Kyles of Bute on the other. The hotel has its own free moorings off Kames Pier and has a safe beach just across the road.

The hotel has recently been refurbished in a most attractive style, with lots of wood panelling in the lounge and the bars; and the elegant and spacious dining room has a high ceiling and a huge carved wooden fireplace. Among the three family rooms, one can accommodate a family of five since it includes a double and a single bed and bunk beds.

In the lawned garden you can sit and admire the splendid views across to the Isle of Bute and watch the world and the yachts go by. There is a children's play area with swings, a slide and a climbing frame.

Nearby: This is a great spot for fishing, since the hotel has access to three hill lochs and two rivers, the Kilfinan and the Glendaruel, and can also arrange sea fishing. You can play golf on a course which is only half a mile from the hotel, and sailing can be organised. If you fancy some sightseeing you can head for the Younger Botanic Garden, the Kilmun Arboretum and Inveraray Castle. The scenery through which you will travel is magnificent.

BAR MEALS (12–9.30pm) £1–7: haddock, rump steak, shepherd's pie, ham & mushroom crunchie;
DINNER (7–9pm) £17: Waldorf salad, pork marsala, pudding or cheese
Children: own menu, half portions
£ medium
Children: cot free; £2 from 2 to 5 years; £5 from 5 to 14
Facilities: 2 cots and 2 high chairs; plug-in baby alarm
10 rooms, 3 family   Open all year
Access/AmEx/Diners/Visa   • Ale – Tetley, McEwan's
P – own car park

Hotels were asked to quote 1992 prices, but not all were able to give an accurate forecast. Make sure that you check tariffs when you book.

Kelso, Borders   map 11

EDNAM HOUSE HOTEL, Bridge Street – ☎ *Kelso (0573) 24168.*

Go to the centre of town and look for the hotel sign.

We are, as always, happy to include such a splendid hotel, which offers real value – at a time when many hotels overcharge disgracefully for mediocre service and facilities.

It's a grand Georgian mansion, built of sandstone – a noted fishing hotel which was once owned by the Duke of Roxburghe. The beautiful interior retains its 'ducal' air with lots of carved wood and ornate plasterwork (in the main lounge there is a relief of Zeus chasing Aurora). The three acres of gardens have a croquet lawn and a long balustrade overlooking a lovely stretch of the Tweed. Handy for the town (once described by Sir Walter Scott as the most beautiful in Scotland) and many places of historic interest – and the staff will arrange other activities for you and your children: riding, golf, etc.

Nearby: There are numerous interesting places to see in the locality including the remarkable Floors Castle and the ruins of Kelso Abbey. There are abbeys at Dryburgh and Jedburgh also and Sir Walter Scott's house, Abbotsford, is not far away. Bowhill, Traquair House, Dawyck Botanic Garden, Kailzie Gardens and Neidpath Castle are all within easy reach.

✘ BAR LUNCHES (12.30–2pm, not Sun) £1–4: smoked mackerel salad, fried haddock, eggs au gratin, roast lamb;
DINNER (7–9pm) £16: warm duck & orange salad, soup, braised brisket of beef, pudding or cheese
Children: high teas, half portions
£ medium
Best Bargain Break £77 per person, 2 nights – dinner, b & b
Children: free up to 2 years, sliding scale up to 14 years
Facilities: 4 cots and 2 high chairs; and a baby listening system
32 rooms   Closed Xmas & New Year

Access/Visa   No music
🅿 – own car park

Nr Keswick, Cumbria   map 9
MANESTY HOLIDAY COTTAGES – ☎ Borrowdale (07687) 77216.

SC   *Off the B5289 south of Keswick.*

The character of these traditional Lakeland buildings, situated at the foot of fells with such resonant names as Catbells and Maiden Moor, has been faithfully preserved by the owners, Cheryl and Alan Leyland, whose family have owned them for 150 years or so.

The original farmhouse and the dairy now contain three cottages, which sleep from two to seven people in spacious, traditionally furnished surroundings. Guests have the benefit of wonderful views of the countryside: across the valley to the fells and towards Skiddaw, Castle Crag and Glaramara.

The adjacent converted barn, known as Cocklety How, is also available to rent. It has two double bedrooms and one single and has the same spectacular views of the fells.

Each of the properties has its own parking space and a garden; with the exception of Manesty Dairy (for two people only) which does, however, have its own verandah.

If you fancy some peace and quiet and enjoy the outdoor life this is an excellent place to spend some time. Manesty is only a stone's throw from Derwentwater and the Lodore Falls and the little village of Grange is less than a mile away.

Nearby: This is a wonderful spot for walkers and Mr Leyland can advise you about the various routes. All sorts of watersports are available on Derwentwater and fishermen are also well catered for. All the attractions of the Lakes are within easy reach: Grasmere, Hardknott Roman Fort, the Steamboat Museum at Windermere, Fell Foot Park with its water sports facilities, picnic areas and adventure playground, Grizedale Forest Visitor Centre and the Ravenglass and Eskdale Railway.

Units: 4
Rent: £110 to £350 a week (short breaks available)
Other costs: electricity
Heating: central heating
4 cots and 2 high chairs
Open all year

Kilchrenan, by Taynuilt, Strathclyde map 11
CUIL-NA-SITHE HOTEL – ☎ Kilchrenan (086 63) 234.

On the B845 at Kilchrenan.

This hotel has a wonderful situation on the northern shore of Loch Awe, and you look across the waters to the hills beyond. Guests can take full advantage of the fishing on the loch, or merely have a quiet day's boating with a picnic on one of the many islands.

The hotel is a tall Victorian building with stepped gables and a comfortable and cosy interior, which includes a bar and a sitting room. Of the six bedrooms, two are family rooms with en suite bathrooms, but plans are afoot to add more. It is also hoped to add a games room in due course.

There is plenty of room in the three acres of grounds for children to play and for parents to relax. The sloping lawns have a wide variety of trees and flowers, including laburnum, cherry and Japanese maple trees, azaleas and rhododendrons.

Nearby: In addition to the delights of Loch Awe, the area has magnificent scenery and is a sheer delight for the nature lover. A little further south is Inveraray with its famous castle, and Oban is to the north west, with a Sea Life Centre close by. Oban is of course a thriving resort and is indeed the "gateway to the islands and Highlands." You can reach Glencoe, scene of the infamous massacre in 1692, quite easily and it is wonderful walking country, and has a great variety of wildlife.

BAR SNACKS (12.30–9pm) £2–8: lasagne, steak pie, trout, salmon; DINNER (7–9.30pm) £11: whitebait, grilled salmon, pudding or cheese
Children: own menu
£ low
Best Bargain Break £75 per person, 3 nights – dinner, b & b
Children: cot £3; half price thereafter up to 10 years
Facilities: 2 cots and 2 high chairs, and a baby listening system
6 rooms, 2 family   Open all year
Access/Visa   🅿 – own car park

Kimbolton, Nr Leominster, Hereford & Worcs map 2
RATEFIELD FARM – ☎ Leominster (0568) 412 507.

Off the A49 north of Leominster. Turn opposite the Stockton Cross Inn.

After travelling down a long farm lane, over several cattle grids and past fields with their grazing sheep, you will come to this neat stone farmhouse which was built at the end of the 18th century. It is the hub of a 100 acre livestock farm, which takes in some National Trust property. The farmland was once the deer park of Berrington Hall, and the pastures and woodlands were landscaped by Capability Brown.

Both the dining room and the lounge, which has a log fire for cooler evenings, have good views of the countryside. The family bedroom can easily cope with a cot or an extra bed.

Much of the food you will eat is produced on the farm – eggs, vegetables, beef and lamb – and even the bread is baked on the spot, and Mrs Mears will cook vegetarian dishes, if warned in advance.

There is a safely enclosed garden where children can play and the owners have mapped out a nature and history trail around the farm. One of the paddocks now comprises a barbecue area, a small above-ground swimming pool, a badminton court, swingball and children's swings. It is also planned to instal a tennis court.

Guests are welcome to see how the farm is run; the rearing of young calves and the work of the sheep dogs will especially appeal to children, and there is a children's pony.

Nearby: Leominster itself is an interesting town, especially to antique hunters, and towns such as Hereford, Worcester, Malvern, and Ludlow are all within easy reach as is the Wye Valley, the delightful Welsh Border areas, and Clun forest. The West Midlands Safari Park at Bewdley is only a short drive away, as are Croft Castle, Berrington Hall, the Severn Valley Railway, the Wyre Forest Visitor Centre, Witley Court and Elgar's birthplace. It is of course a splendid area for walking, horse riding and fishing, and there are plenty of golf courses.

DINNER (7pm) £7
Children: half portions
£ low
Children: £7 up to 5 years (incl. evening meal); £9 from 5 to 12
Facilities: 1 cot and 1 high chair
Open all year except Xmas and early March
3 rooms   AmEx only
Unlicensed· No music
P – ample

Kingscote, Glos   map 2

HUNTER'S HALL – 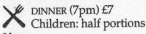 *Stroud (0453) 860 393.*

On the A4153 west of the junction with the A46.

This impressive old coaching inn, built of mellow stone, stands alone opposite the turning to Kingscote Village.

It is very much a pub which welcomes families and has plenty of space to cope with the large number of people who gather to eat and drink here. There is a good-sized bar and a large dining room on the other side of the pub.

Upstairs there is a lot more space including a room specifically designed for families. It is a pleasant spot, nicely decorated and well furnished with pine tables. At very busy times you can overflow into a beamed function room alongside.

The garden is really delightful: it is huge with an immaculate lawn and is beautifully laid out with bushes and small trees. There are lots of tables; and a play area with swings, a mini assault course, and a fort. Barbecues are held here at weekends.

The various bedrooms are in the converted outbuildings alongside the inn and the one family room is ideal for a family of four, since it has two bedrooms, a small dining area and a small kitchen.

Nearby: This is a delightful part of the world with some interesting towns in which to browse – Tetbury and Malmesbury, for example. You can easily reach the Wildfowl Trust at Slimbridge and Berkeley Castle, with its remarkable history, is quite close, as is the famous Westonbirt Arboretum.

BAR SNACKS (12–2pm) £2–8: beef crumble, steak & kidney pie, rump steak, cold buffet, vegetable pie
DINNER (7.30–9.45pm) £15: seafood pancake, fillet of lamb, pudding or cheese
Children: own menu
£ medium
Best Bargain Break £49 per person, 2 days – b & b
Children: cot free; extra bed £5
12 rooms, 1 family   Open all year
Access/AmEx/Diners/Visa   P – own car park
• Ale – Bass, Hook Norton, Uley, Wadworth's

Also recommended in the Family Welcome Pub & Restaurant Guide.

Kinlochlaggan, Nr Newtonmore, Highland   map 12
ARDVERIKIE ESTATE – ☎ *Laggan (05284) 300.*

SC   *South west of Newtownmore on the A86.*

One of the great advantages of staying at one of the properties on the Ardverikie estate is the presence of a sandy private beach at the end of Loch Laggan. Guests can roam the large estate at will, there are miles of roads and tracks which take you into the hills among small lochs. The scenery is superb and you will relish the peace and quiet.

There are five houses scattered around the estate and the largest of them is Gallovie Farmhouse which can sleep up to sixteen people when some are children.

It has its own garden, with a large lawn and a sandpit, and the beach is only about a mile away. Inverpattack Lodge is also big and can sleep up to ten people. It stands in its own grounds in an elevated position above the road. The latter is of course a hazard to children, but they have loads of room to play at the back of the house where there are birch woods, a stream and the hillside. There are fine views south over the fields, and the beach is about a mile and a half away.

Forest Cottage can sleep up to ten people, while Pinewood and the Ardverikie Gate Lodge (not suitable for small children because of its spiral staircase) sleep three to four.

The houses are comfortably furnished with families in mind; the furniture is functional and unfussy. The houses are situated in beautiful surroundings, while the beach is ideal for play and relaxation.

Nearby: Apart from the walks, boats can be hired in summer at the loch and fishing, pony trekking and golf are available locally. In addition to active outdoor pursuits there are plenty of places to visit: the Highland Folk Museum, the Highland Wildlife Park, the Rothiemurchus Estate, Glenmore Forest Park, the Landmark Visitor Centre and the Loch Garten Strathspey Railway are all within easy range. Farther north you can reach Cawdor Castle, Culloden, Urquhart Castle and the Loch Ness Monster Exhibition.

Units: 5
Rent: £200 to £650 a week
Other costs: £5 for linen per bed in the larger houses
Heating: night storage heaters, gas convector heaters and open fires
Cots and high chairs available
Open all year

Kinross, Tayside   map 11

GREEN HOTEL (Best Western), The Muirs – ☎ *Kinross (0577) 63467.*

Close to Junction 6 of the M90 – follow the signs to Kinross.
The old coaching inn, in its strategic position on the road between Perth and

LAMPHEY

Edinburgh, has grown into a sizeable hotel with a marvellous range of facilities for the traveller and the holiday maker. New rooms are being added, to form a courtyard, and should be in place in the early part of this year.

There are a large indoor swimming pool and a paddling pool, a squash court, a curling rink during winter, a games room with pool and table tennis, a small fitness room, two 18 hole golf courses over the road and fishing can be arranged at Loch Leven. There is a putting green and a croquet lawn, or you can sit in the delightful lawned and wooded garden with a glass of something to refresh you.

At weekends bar food is available throughout the day and some of the ingredients are grown in the hotel garden.

Nearby: Apart from the hotel's own courses, this is an excellent base for a golfing holiday with many fine courses within easy reach including Gleneagles, St Andrews, Carnoustie and Rosemount. Riches, indeed. Lochleven Castle on its island, where Mary Queen of Scots was imprisoned in 1567, is worth a look, as are Aberdour Castle and the ruined Castle Campbell. A dash up the motorway will take you to Perth and the famous Scone Palace.

BAR SNACKS (12–2.30pm & 6–10pm, 12–10pm from Fri to Sun) £1–9: omelettes, croque monsieur, haddock & chips, rump steak, scampi;
DINNER (7–9.30pm) £17: sweet herring, soup, roast leg of lamb, pudding or cheese
Children: own menu, half portions
£ high
Best Bargain Break £120 per person, 2 nights – dinner, b & b
Children free up to 15 years
Facilities: 5 cots and 6 high chairs; and a baby listening system
47 rooms, 7 family   Closed Xmas week
Access/Diners/Visa   No music
P – own car park

Lamphey, Dyfed   map 1

THE COURT (Best Western) – ☎ Lamphey (0646) 672 273.

On the A4139 – you can see the hotel from the road.

At the end of a long, sweeping drive stands this splendid Georgian mansion with a classically pillared entrance. It looms over open fields and is next door to the ruins of Lamphey Palace.

There are twelve acres of lovely gardens, mostly lawns and trees, in which to roam, and detached to one side of the hotel a well-designed heated indoor pool with a paddling pool, a sun terrace and a mini-gym.

Among the fourteen family rooms there are eight studio suites which incorpor-

LAMPHEY

ate a twin-bedded room, a sitting room with a double sofa bed and a bathroom – ideal for families.

Nearby: There is much to do in the vicinity including sailing (the hotel can arrange yacht and boat charter), golf at Tenby (reduced green fees for guests), fishing, riding, squash and tennis. There are many sandy beaches: at Tenby, Saundersfoot, Manorbier, Barafundle Bay and Broad Haven for example. There are many castles to visit: Manorbier, Tenby, Carew and Pembroke; Caldey Island can be reached from Tenby; and the Manor House Wildlife Park, Oakwood Leisure Park and Pembrey Country Park are within easy reach.

BAR SNACKS (12–2pm) £1–7: sirloin steak, grilled local trout, salads;
DINNER (7.15–9.30pm) £15: vichyssoise, noisettes of local lamb, pudding or cheese
Children: own menu, half portions
£ high
Best Bargain Break £33 per person per night – dinner, b & b
Children: free up to age 16
Facilities: 5 cots and 2 high chairs; and a baby listening system to every room
31 rooms, 14 family, 6 sets interconnecting
Open all year   Access/AmEx/Diners/Visa   P – own car park

Hotels were asked to quote 1992 prices, but not all were able to give an accurate forecast. Make sure that you check tariffs when you book.

LANHYDROCK

Lanhydrock, Nr Bodmin, Cornwall   map 1
TREFFRY FARM COTTAGES – ☎ *Bodmin (0208) 74405.*

SC *Just off the B3268 south of Bodmin.*

It was no surprise to learn that the conversion of the 18th century farm buildings had attracted an official commendation. The work has been done with sympathy and style.

Treffry was once the home farm of the Lanhydrock estate, and that National Trust property is just a couple of hundred yards away and deserves a visit. Treffry is still a dairy farm of around 200 acres and guests are encouraged to join in the farming activities, but at certain times only.

The cottages have an air of privacy and seclusion, a result perhaps of the thick stone walls and of their not overlooking each other. Great efforts have been made to furnish them in a comfortable and traditional way: good furniture with cheerful fabrics, wood burning stoves, exposed wooden beams and baskets of flowers. The kitchens have excellent equipment. There are unusual touches in several of the cottages: the upstairs studio in Swallows Cottage, the gallery bedroom in Churns Cottage and the Waterwheel in Cogwheels Cottage.

The accommodation is varied. The smallest cottage suits two adults and two children and the largest can take up to eight persons.

On a practical level there is a laundry room and a pre-cooked meal service.

The children have an excellent play area, with climbing frames and swings and the owners, Mr and Mrs Smith, were planning to extend this for the current year. The picnic area has a barbecue and there is both an adventure trail and a woodland trail, so that all the family can have their fun. The farm pony, Fred, will give the younger children rides during the week.

It is a lovely spot for a family holiday and is very well placed for many other activities.

Nearby: The splendid Lanhydrock House is on the doorstep and Pencarrow House is also very close, as are the ruins of Restormel Castle. The children will enjoy Dobwalls Theme Park (recommended in the Family Welcome Leisure Guide) and Newquay Zoo and the Dairyland Farm Park will also appeal to them. Bodmin Moor, a lovely spot for riding, walking and contemplation is near and there is a wonderful choice of safe and sandy beaches on either coast: Newquay and Crantock Bay, Vault Beach and Lantic Bay. The coastal walks are magnificent. Bodmin has swimming, squash and tennis and there is excellent fishing and golf to be done.

Units: 7
Rent: £100 to £495; short breaks available
Other costs: linen on hire; electricity on meters
Heating: central heating
Cots and high chairs: 4 of each available
Open all year

Lanteglos, Nr Camelford, Cornwall   map 1

HOTEL LANTEGLOS – ☎ Camelford (0840) 213 551.

Off the A39.

This hotel is run for families by a family who have taken the utmost care to provide everything necessary for parents and children to have a good holiday.

It's a lovely stone country house in twenty acres of delightful garden, sheltered by mature trees and with a stream running through it. It was built as a rectory for the local church by the famous architect, Augustus Pugin. There are splendid facilities – plenty of indoor and outdoor play areas, including a 'rumpus room' and woodland fort, and a spacious heated swimming pool and paddling pool in the lawned gardens.

A splendid conservatory has been built alongside the bar and its great advantage is that it looks over a play area. So the adults can sit there in peace and still keep an eye on their offspring. There are a hard tennis court, squash court and two badminton courts, and free golf is available at certain times at nearby

LAVENHAM

Launceston. By the middle of the year Bowood Park golf course, next door to the hotel, will have opened. Guests will have direct access, priority tee times and reduced green fees. There are children's entertainments on most evenings.

Nearby: If you should wish to venture forth for other entertainment, there are safe and sandy beaches close at hand: Daymer Bay and Trebarwith Strand for example. The famous Bodmin Moor is a few miles south, and nature lovers will perhaps head for the Tamar Otter Park or the Tropical Bird Gardens at Padstow. Wesley's Cottage, Pencarrow, Lanhydrock and the Farm Park near Bodmin are other nearby attractions.

BAR SNACKS (12–2pm & 6–10pm) £1–6: Cornish fish pie, chicken curry, scampi, sirloin steaks;
DINNER (7.30–9.30pm) £13: egg mayonnaise, chicken Indienne, pudding or cheese
Children: high teas
£ medium
Best Bargain Break £33 per person per night – dinner, b & b
Children: first child under 5 is free, and the second one at certain times; thereafter, children are charged on a sliding scale from £4 to £20 a day
Facilities: 30 cots and 30 high chairs; a baby listening system
16 rooms, 11 family   Access/Visa
Closed Nov-Feb   • Ale – Tinner's
P – own car park

Lavenham, Suffolk   map 4

THE GREAT HOUSE, Market Place – ☎ *Lavenham (0787) 247 431.*

In the centre of town.

The town has so many beautifully preserved mediaeval buildings; over 300 are listed as being of historic significance. The Great House was built in the 14th and 15th centuries, and acquired a new front when it was renovated in the 18th century. Its other claim to fame is that it was the home of the writer Stephen Spender in the fifties.

It is now a delightful hotel and restaurant, which has been decorated and furnished with great style and taste. The four rooms justify their description as suites, since they all have sitting areas. Two of them have separate and spacious sitting rooms, and the newest suite has two double bedrooms and a lounge.

You are offered excellent value for money here, and that goes for the food as well as the accommodation. The menu has an enterprising choice of dishes, and you can have a snack for as little as £3, or an excellent three-course lunch for £9. The three course Sunday lunch costs around £13 (£7 for children). The whole family, from babies to grandmothers, are welcomed here, in the French

LAVENHAM

tradition: which is not surprising since the management is French. We were not surprised to learn that the hotel won a 'value for money' award last year.

At the back of the hotel there is a paved terrace, with plenty of space. It is surrounded by flowers and greenery and can be left open to the weather or completely covered, at the top and the sides, with canvas. A marvellous solution to the problems presented by the English weather.

Below the terrace there is a walled garden which has the merit of being a sun trap. It is in two sections, both lawned; at one end there is a barbecue, and at the other some swings for the children.

Nearby: The town is a splendid place in which to browse, as are the neighbouring ones of Long Melford and Sudbury. The children will enjoy Clare Castle Country Park and the adults will enjoy Cavendish Manor Vineyards. You can also reach Ickworth, Gainsborough's House in Sudbury, Blakenham Woodlands Garden and the Colne Valley Railway with ease.

BAR SNACKS (12–2pm) £3–6: fish soup, marinated salmon, blanquette of pork, lasagne Bolognese;
LUNCH (12–2.30pm) £9: mussels marinière, grilled lamb cutlets, pudding or cheese;
DINNER (7.30–10.30pm) £14: Scotch salmon, roast lamb fillet, pudding or cheese
Children: half portions
£ high
Best Bargain Break £47 per person per night – dinner, b & b
Children: free up to 3 years; £8 from 4 to 12

Facilities: 2 cots and 2 high chairs; baby listening system
4 rooms, 3 family   Access/AmEx/Visa
Open all year, except 3 weeks in January
🅿 – at front

Ledbury, Hereford & Worcs   map 2

WALL HILLS COUNTRY GUEST HOUSE, Hereford Road – ☎ *Ledbury (0531) 2833.*

Off the A438 west of Ledbury

This handsome and spacious red brick Georgian house stands on the side of a hill which overlooks the pleasant town of Ledbury, and beyond you have superb views of the Malvern Hills. The front entrance is bright and welcoming with a porch full of pot plants and hanging baskets of flowers. The large walled garden has plenty of space for guests to relax, and mostly consists of lawns, but with well-established shrubs and flower beds. The several acres of grounds includes a 15th century cruck barn, and there is an Iron Age fort on a neighbour's land.

You will receive a very friendly and enthusiastic welcome from Mr and Mrs Slaughter, who have plenty of space for their guests: the sitting room is large and comfortable and has French windows looking out to the walled garden, and the dining room is similarly spacious and attractive. All the bedrooms are large and can take an extra bed or cot and have views of the surrounding countryside. The family room has loads of room and includes a double bed, a single bed and a sofa bed, and has its own bathroom.

Nearby: Ledbury is excellently placed for holidaymakers to take advantage of the lovely countryside all around, and the many attractive towns such as Hereford, Gloucester, Malvern and Cheltenham. The Wye Valley is close by and there are many other attractions, such as the castles at Eastnor and Goodrich, the Falconry Centre at Newent, the Nature Reserve at Knapp, the Malvern Hills Animal and Bird Gardens, and the Birtsmorton Waterfowl Sanctuary.

🍴 DINNER (7.30–9pm) £13: bacon & mushrooms, seafood gratin, fresh fruit tart
Children: high teas, small portions
£ low
Children: cots £3; £6 from 2 to 5; £9 from 6 to 11
Facilities: 2 cots and 1 high chair; baby listening by arrangement
3 rooms, 1 family   Access/Visa
Open all year except Xmas and New Year

No smoking in dining room   **P** – ample

Leominster, Hereford & Worcs   map 6
ROYAL OAK HOTEL, South Street – ☎ *Leominster (0568) 2610.*

In the middle of town on the A49/A44.

This friendly and welcoming hotel is situated in the town centre in a pleasant Georgian building, which has steadily been refurbished over the years. The lounge bar, with its oak beams and open fires, is a pleasant spot to settle in for a drink and a snack; and the Cellar Bar, with its brick arched alcoves, is an excellent alternative.

Although there are no permanent family rooms, several are large enough to take an extra bed, and there are two sets of interconnecting rooms.

It is a good hotel to know about if you are in the area with your family not least because of the very competitive prices. There is an extensive bar menu with lots of daily specials and an interesting vegetarian menu with such homemade dishes as rice and bean burgers, potato and cheese and leek bake, vegetable lasagne and so on. All the food is freshly cooked.

Nearby: Leominster is an interesting town with an array of antique shops, and all around there is delightful countryside. If you go north, perhaps via Croft Castle, you can enjoy the lovely expanses of South Shropshire, and perhaps see the fine town of Ludlow, Clun with its castle and the Carding Mill Valley at Church Stretton. The Severn Valley Railway is within reach, as is the Midland Motor Museum at Bridgnorth. To the south lies Hereford and the Wye Valley.

BAR MEALS (12–2pm & 6.30–9pm) £2–8: omelettes, salads, steaks, trout;
LUNCH (12.30–2pm) and DINNER (7–9pm) £15: prawns with crudités, fillet steak, pudding
Children: own menu, half portions
£ medium
Best Bargain Break £38 per person 2 nights – b & b only
Children: no charge
Facilities: 4 cots and 4 high chairs; a baby listening system
18 rooms, 2 sets interconnecting   Access/AmEx/Diners/Visa
Open all year
• Ale – Hook Norton, Wood's, Wadworth's
P – own car park

Linwood, Nr Ringwood, Hants   map 3
HIGH CORNER – ☎ *Ringwood (0425) 473 973.*

H/SC   *Off the A338.*

An old drovers' track leads to this pub and it is well worth the effort to visit this delightful old place, a rambling, 17th century building with dormer windows and a big chimney at one end. It is in a lovely woodland setting with a large garden which has a marvellous play area for the children – slides, swings, ropes, climbing frames and a Wendy house.

Families are particularly well looked after with several areas in the pub where they can sit together over a meal or a drink: the Stable bar, which is housed in an attractive old barn; the conservatory which is alongside; and finally the Lego Room, which has three Lego play units to keep the children amused.

There is a wide ranging and enterprising choice of food available every day, and barbecues at the weekends in summer. Sunday lunch is good value at around £8.

The High Corner is a welcoming and well-organised inn, in a lovely spot, where families are made very welcome. All the bedrooms have their own bathrooms and, in addition to a triple bedroom, three other bedrooms can accommodate an extra bed.

If you fancy some exercise, the inn has its own squash court, and stabling is also available if you arrive with a horse.

Nearby: The beauties of the New Forest are on your doorstep and the sea is only a short drive away. Bournemouth, for example, has an excellent family beach and many entertainments. Bolderwood Arboretum has some lovely walks, Furzey Gardens give fine views of the New Forest, and you can easily reach Broadlands, Paultons Park, Beaulieu, the New Forest Butterfly Farm and the Dorset Heavy Horse Centre.

✗ (12–2pm & 7–10pm) £1–9: curry, fried plaice, grilled Avon trout, chicken Malabar, salmis of pheasant
Children: own menu
£ high
Children: from £4 (cot)
Facilities: 2 cots and 3 high chairs; and a baby listening system
8 rooms, 1 family   Open all year
Access/AmEx/Diners/Visa   🅿 – own car park
• Ale – Boddington's, Wadworth, Wethered

Also recommended in the Family Welcome Pub & Restaurant Guide.

SELF-CATERING
There is also a self-catering chalet in the garden. It has a double bedroom, a bunk bedroom for up to three children and a sofa bed, and is fully equipped. The rent varies from around £200 to £375 a week and you can also book it for short breaks (a minimum of three nights).

Little Faringdon, Nr Lechlade, Oxon   map 3
LANGFORD HOUSE – ☎ *Faringdon (0367) 52210.*

SC   *Just off the A361 north of Lechlade.*
The four cottages, all built of stone and of 18th century vintage, lie within the private estate of the Lady de Mauley in the tiny hamlet of Little Faringdon, a peaceful and appealing place which is yet only a mile from the town of Lechlade.
No. 1 Church Cottage is a lovely little cottage, verging on the 'picture post-card' with roses around the front door. You step into a comfortable sitting room with a kitchen at one end and a small pantry and there are two bedrooms up above, a double and a twin. At the back there is a small patio and a good-sized, enclosed lawn. A cot and a high chair are provided.
The Stable Cottage is in the courtyard of Langford House and has its attractive sitting room on the first floor. There are two twin-bedded rooms, one with a bathroom and the other with a shower room. The dining room is downstairs, with a well-equipped kitchen. A washing machine is provided, as is a cot and a high chair.
The other two cottages are not suitable for young children. The Old Cottage

sleeps two people only, and is another delightful building, with a spacious and comfortable sitting room and a lovely lawned garden enclosed by stone walls. The Garden Cottage, part of which was once the summer house, is superbly designed on one floor. There are two bedrooms and two bathrooms, a large and appealing sitting room which looks out to a delightful walled garden, and a sitting cum dining room with a well-equipped kitchen alongside.

We were struck by the tranquillity of Little Faringdon and above all with the great care and attention to detail which has been applied to the cottages. As well as using the cottage gardens, guests can also enjoy the extensive gardens around Langford House.

Nearby: This is an excellent spot from which to explore the Cotswolds, with so many interesting towns and villages within reach including Oxford, Burford and Stow-on-the-Wold. You can visit the Cotswold Wildlife Park, Blenheim Palace, Bourton-on-the-Water with its motor museum, miniature village and Birdland, Sudeley Castle, Sezincote and the Cotswold Water Park. There is trout fishing to be had nearby, water skiing at South Cerney, a leisure centre in Swindon; and golf and horse riding are readily available.

Units: 4
Rent: £150 to £450 a week
Other costs: electricity is on meters; central heating is a separate charge
Heating: night storage
2 cots and 2 high chairs provided
Open all year

Littlehempston, Nr Totnes, Devon map 1
BUCKYETTE FARM – ☎ *Staverton (080 426) 638.*

Just north of Totnes off the A381. The farmhouse brochure has precise directions.

This solid looking farmhouse stands high above the surrounding countryside, and was built in 1860 from stone quarried on the farm, the site of which was mentioned in the Domesday Book.

You will find peace and quiet at this farmhouse and the rooms, as befits a house built in the Victorian age, are spacious and high-ceilinged. The delightful sitting room has French windows on to a little terrace, which is covered by an awning with wisteria trailing across it.

Families are particularly welcome here, and there are several cots and high chairs on the premises. Baby listening can also be done for guests on occasion. The four family rooms have plenty of space; three with bunks as well as a double bed, and another with bunks and twin beds. All the rooms have their own bathrooms or shower rooms.

You will eat real food at Buckyette. Mr and Mrs Miller grow a good selection of fruit and vegetables, bake their own bread, and you will even be offered home-made marmalade for breakfast. We saw the finishing touches being put to the evening's steak and kidney pie when we called in.

Nearby: There is room to stretch your legs on the fifty acres of farmland, and there are unrivalled holiday facilities in this part of the world. Dartmoor with its lovely walks is nearby, and pony trekking, fishing, riding, golf and swimming are all readily available. There are plenty of safe and sandy beaches, and no doubt the children will relish a visit to the National Shire Horse Centre, the Parke Rare Breeds Farm and Paignton Zoo. Buckfast Abbey, and the castles at Totnes and Compton are within easy reach; and for railway enthusiasts, the Dart Valley Railway is just up the road.

DINNER (6.30pm) £8
Children: high teas
£ low
Children: cot free; half price up to 7 years; two thirds from 7 to 14
Facilities: 3 cots and 2 high chairs; baby listening by arrangement
6 rooms, 4 family   Open April to October
No credit cards   No music
P – own car park

Llanarmon D.C., Clwyd   map 6
WEST ARMS HOTEL – ☎ *Llanarmon (069 176) 665.*

West of Chirk on the B4500.

A great deal of redecoration has been done to this handsome hotel. The building is now painted a pristine white, and inside, the heavy beams and large and splendid fireplaces attest to its great age – it was built in the 16th century.

It is very smart and comfortable and there are a couple of lounges where families can park themselves. The bar is notable for a 13th century confessional which is said to have been looted, long ago, from Llangollen Abbey. We looked at a couple of suites which have been recently refurbished in excellent style, and they would be very suitable for family occupation. It should also be emphasised that all the bedrooms are large enough to accommodate an extra bed.

There is a large and delightful lawned garden which spreads alongside the river – a lovely place to be on summer days. Families are welcomed here and will be well looked after by the Alexander family.

Nearby: The hotel sits in glorious countryside, a lovely place for walking, horse riding and fishing. It is on the border and there are several castles to see: Chirk and Powis, for example. The mansion at Erddig and Plas Newydd and the Chwarel Wynne Mine Museum are in the vicinity. The falls of Pistyll Rhaeadr and the Lake Vyrnwy Visitor Centre are well worth a visit.

LLANBRYNMAIR

🍴 BAR SNACKS (12–2pm & 6.30–9pm) £2–6: Ceiriog trout, casserole of game, lasagne, plaice, vegetable bake;
DINNER (7.30–9pm) £18: Waldorf salad, escalope of pork, pudding and cheese
Children: own menu, small portions
£ high
Best Bargain Break £51 per person per night – dinner, b & b
Children: cots £5; extra beds £10
Facilities: 2 cots and 2 high chairs; informal baby listening
14 rooms, 2 suites   Access/Visa
Open all year   No music
🅿 – own car park

Llanbrynmair, Powys   map 5
BARLINGS BARN – ☎ Llanbrynmair (0650) 521 479.

SC *Off the A470 east of Machynlleth. Take the road to Pandy and after one and a half miles there is a sign to Barlings Barn.*

This delightful, 18th century stone farmhouse has a wonderful position in the hills above Llanbrynmair and commands superb views of the valley below. The

LLANBRYNMAIR

owners have renovated the house and restored the adjoining barn, The Wanws, and the latter is one of the self-catering units. Like the farmhouse, roses and honeysuckle cling to the walls and the original features have been retained wherever possible: stone walls and an oak-beamed fireplace, for example. The kitchen has a stripped pine table, old pews and chairs and a Welsh dresser, and is very well-equipped; there is a microwave oven as well as a cooker, a washing machine and a dryer. There is a twin and a double bedroom.

The two 'Barling Barnlets' are recently built suites of two storeys. The bedroom is downstairs and from the living room up above you have magnificent views of the hills and the valley.

This is certainly a place to get away from it all and there are excellent facilities available at Barlings: a heated swimming pool encased in a plastic bubble, a squash court (and Terry Margolis is a qualified coach so you can improve your game with a few lessons), a sauna, a solarium and a pool table. Alternatively you can sit at your ease and enjoy the beauty of the surroundings while the children can run freely in the paddock.

Terry and Felicity Margolis have thought of everything to make your stay an enjoyable one. There are no hidden extras; the rent pays for everything including the central heating, the squash court, swimming pool and sauna. Groceries can be ordered in advance of your arrival; and a good range of meals, cooked on the spot at Barlings, can also be ordered.

It is a delightful place where you will be looked after in a very friendly and relaxed fashion.

Nearby: There is much to see and do in this beautiful part of Wales – riding, walking, fishing and golf for a start; and the beaches at Tywyn, Aberdovey and Borth can easily be reached. Northwards lies the Snowdonia National Park

LLANDUDNO

and the Coed-y-Brenin Forest, with its many waymarked trails. The Centre for Alternative Technology is well worth a visit, as is the Lake Vyrnwy Visitor Centre. Railway buffs can visit the Fairbourne and the Talyllyn Railways.

Units: 3
Rent: £180 to £410 a week (short breaks available)
Other costs: none
Heating: central heating
2 cots and 2 high chairs
Open all year

Llandudno, Gwynedd   map 5

AMBASSADOR HOTEL, Grand Promenade – ☎ Llandudno (0492) 876 886.

On the Promenade near the Pier.

We wanted to recommend some hotels in this famous and traditional North Wales resort and this smartly decorated and well maintained hotel stands out among the many sea front establishments. It is a handsome Victorian building with a corner position and marvellous views of Llandudno Bay, and of the promenade and its gardens. A great asset is the presence of two conservatories along the front of the hotel.

The hotel certainly caters for families, as the presence of sixteen family rooms and a good supply of cots and high chairs will attest. The hotel has no garden of its own, but you hardly need it with the great sweep of the beach almost at your feet. There are donkey rides, Punch and Judy shows and all the other attractions of a traditional seaside resort. Above all (literally) is the Great Orme Country Park, with its fine examples of wild life. You can get to the top by car, cable car, Victorian tramway or even on foot, and magnificent views await you.

Nearby: There are many things to do and see in this part of Wales: the castles at Conwy, Penrhyn and Gwydir; the zoo at Colwyn Bay and Llyn Padarn Country Park; Bodnant Gardens; the Gwydir Forest; and the great expanse of Snowdonia itself.

BAR SNACKS (12–1.30pm) £1–5: chilli con carne, plaice meunière, spaghetti Bolognese, pizza;
DINNER (6.30–7.30pm) £10: plaice goujons, roast duck, pudding or cheese
Children: half portions
£ low
Best Bargain Break £142 per person 7 nights – dinner, b & b
Children: free up to 5 years; £10 from 5 to 8; £14 from 9 to 11; £16 from 12 to 14

LLANDUDNO

Facilities: 4 cots and 4 high chairs, but no baby listening
68 rooms, 16 family   Open all year
No credit cards accepted   No music
No smoking in restaurant and in one lounge
P – own car park

ST TUDNO HOTEL, The Promenade – ☎ *Llandudno (0492) 874 411.*

We are firm fans of this excellent seaside hotel, which is furnished with great style and care, and welcomes all the family, from babies to grandmothers. The St Tudno sets a standard to which few hotels in the traditional seaside resorts aspire. It is not of course an inexpensive hotel, but it offers marvellous value for money.

Alice Liddel, Lewis Carrol's "Alice", stayed at the hotel when she was eight and was no doubt pleased that it was situated opposite the pier and close to the beach. There are donkey rides and Punch and Judy shows on the beach.

The hotel has an indoor heated swimming pool near the coffee lounge. The various public rooms are elegantly furnished and comfortable. The Garden Room restaurant is particularly appealing and has the benefit of being air-conditioned and a non-smoking area. It is a lovely setting in which to sample the excellent food which has a deserved reputation for quality, based as it is on the best available local produce. Older children can join their parents for dinner, but the younger ones are served high tea in the coffee lounge at 5.45pm.

Nearby: Llandudno has its own long and sandy beaches and there are many others to enjoy along the coast. The Great Orme Country Park rises nearly 700 feet from the sea and has a wide variety of wildlife. You can reach the top on foot, by car, cable car or Victorian tramway. There are several castles in this part of Wales: Conwy, Penrhyn and Gwydir – and Bodnant Garden is a wonderful sight. The children will no doubt like to visit the Welsh Mountain Zoo, Gwydir Forest and the Cwm Idwal Nature Trail. There is also a dry ski slope and a toboggan run about half a mile away.

BAR LUNCHES (12.30–2pm) £3–13: scallops & monkfish, local plaice, Welsh fillet steak, poached local salmon;
DINNER (6.45–9.30pm) £23: scallop & prawn mousse, soup, roast leg of Welsh lamb, Bakewell tart, Welsh farmhouse cheese
Children: own menu, half portions
£ high
Best Bargain Break £110 per person, 2 nights – dinner, b & b and Sunday lunch
Children: £8.50 for cots; £13 under 5; 50% discount from 5–12; 25% thereafter
Facilities: plenty of cots and 4 high chairs; baby listening system
21 rooms, 4 family, 2 suites   Access/AmEx/Visa
Open all year   No music

LLANGOLLEN

No smoking in the sitting room and the restaurant
P – own car park

Llangollen, Clwyd   map 6

HAND HOTEL (Mount Charlotte), Bridge Street – ☎ *Llangollen (0978) 860 303.*

In the centre of town.

The hotel was a coaching inn in the 18th century on the London to Holyhead road and stands above the River Dee in the centre of this picturesque town which holds the famous International Eisteddfod every year.

One of the advantages of this hotel for families is that food is available throughout the day from midday onwards, with a small gap between the end of the bar lunches and the beginning of afternoon tea. The bar snack menu offers an excellent choice of food at a reasonable price, and the Sunday lunch at around £8 is good value, too.

The Hand is a friendly and relaxing hotel, which charges reasonable prices.

Nearby: Apart from the fishing this is good walking country and you might begin by walking to the top of the ruined 8th century Castell Dinas Bran. There are fine views from there. There is a canal museum in the town and the Llangollen Steam Railway will take you on a trip along the Dee Valley. The great mansion of Erddig, Plas Newydd, Chirk Castle and the Lake Vyrnwy visitor centre are all well worth a visit. The town is properly called the 'gateway to Wales' and Snowdonia is only thirty miles or so to the west.

BAR SNACKS (12–2pm & 6–8.45pm) £1–4: cold buffet, scampi & chips, Cumberland sausage, club sandwich;
DINNER (6.45–8.45pm) £15: garlic mushrooms, fillet of lemon sole, pudding or cheese
Children: half portions
£ high
Best Bargain Break £45 per person per night – dinner, b & b
Children: free to age 14
Facilities: 2 cots and 2 high chairs; and a baby listening system
58 rooms, 6 family   Access/AmEx/Visa
Open all year   • Ale – McEwan's
P – own car park

To qualify for inclusion in the Guide hotels must offer the basic facilities of a cot, a family room and an evening meal. Self-catering establishments must provide cots and high chairs.

Llangors, Nr Brecon, Powys   map 2
RED LION HOTEL – ☎ *Llangors (0874) 84238.*

In the centre of the village, on the B4560, east of Brecon.

This is an attractive building, long and low and built of stone, and was originally a row of cottages, some dating back to the 17th century. There is a little wooden porch; and hanging baskets of flowers and roses decorate the walls, and you hardly notice the recent extension by the car park. The hotel is situated opposite the church in the middle of the village.

The owners have made many improvements since they took over, and they had an excellent basis from which to work: stone walls, old wooden beams and open fireplaces. It is a pleasant and comfortable place to stay and the facilities include a residents' sitting room and a games room, and a garden with lawns on three levels and borders of flowers.

The owners certainly welcome families and also lay on children's meals: boiled eggs and soldiers for example. The adults can choose from the bar menu or an extensive restaurant menu.

Nearby: This delightful part of Wales has many attractions. The Brecon Beacons National Park is close, and from its mountain centre you can start many lovely walks across Mynydd Illtud, a gentle stretch of moorland. It is excellent fishing country, too, and pony trekking, sailing, water skiing, wind surfing and climbing can also be arranged. Opera buffs will no doubt head for Craig y Nos Park, in whose castle the legendary Adelina Patti once lived; and railway buffs can ride on the Brecon Mountain railway.

✘ BAR SNACKS (12–2pm & 7–9pm) £2–8: shepherd's pie, liver & bacon casserole, cauliflower cheese, moussaka, cod & chips; DINNER (7–9.30 pm) £11: paté, lamb provencale, pudding or cheese
Children: own menu
£ low
Best Bargain Break £50 per person, 2 nights – dinner, b & b
Children: free up to the age of 12
Facilities: 2 cots and a high chair and a baby listening system
10 rooms, 1 family   Open all year
No credit cards accepted   • Ale – Flowers, Marston's
🅿 – own car park

Llanidloes, Powys   map 6
GLYNGYNWYDD, Cwmbelan – ☎ *Llanidloes (05512) 3854.*

SC   *On the A470, south of Llanidloes and just past the village of Cwmbelan. The stone farmhouse lies on the slopes of a quiet valley just south of Llanidloes*

LLANIDLOES

and there are splendid views of the delightful countryside all around. The building mainly dates back to the 17th century and has its full complement of exposed beams, with flagstone floors, inglenook fireplaces and traditional furniture. Two bedrooms are available on a bed and breakfast basis.

Mr and Mrs Davies recently converted an adjacent barn to provide five self-contained cottages and they made every effort to retain the original features of the fine old timber-clad building.

They have made a splendid job of the conversion, since the two-storey cottages are full of character with their old timbers and excellent furnishings. All the bedrooms have fitted carpets, the kitchens are very well-equipped and there are no extras; electricity, fuel, linen, towels and basic cleaning materials are provided. Each cottage also has the great bonus of a traditional cast iron stove in the sitting room.

Four of the cottages are designed to sleep four people, and one can sleep two people. But the small house, Ty Canol Bach, can be combined with Ty Canol Mawr to accommodate a larger family. Every cottage has two extra folding beds, if required. There is a fully equipped laundry room and a games room.

Guests can enjoy the lawned garden; and a small stream runs from the hill above to form a little pool.

It is a delightful place as a base for a family holiday.

Nearby: This is a beautiful part of Wales, with many lovely walks. You could try the walk up the mountain of Plynlimon for a start. All sorts of activities can be organised in the locality: fishing, sailing and canoeing, pony trekking and golf. Llanidloes has a leisure centre with a swimming pool. On the sightseeing front you can visit the Elan Valley to the south and Lake Vyrnwy to the north. The Offa's Dyke Heritage Centre is also close. There are castles at Welshpool and Montgomery and the sandy beaches on the west coast are only a short drive away.

Units: 5
Rent: £115 to £340 a week
Other costs: none

Heating: night storage and solid fuel stoves
A cot and a high chair are available
Open all year

Llys-y-Fran, Nr Haverfordwest, Dyfed   map 5
IVY COURT COTTAGES – ☎ Maenclochog (0437) 532 473.

SC   *North east of Haverfordwest off the B4329 or B4313.*

Ivy Court sits in the middle of beautiful Pembrokeshire countryside and, to add to its considerable appeal, the Llys-y-Fran Country Park is alongside. You hop over a stile and there is the lake and the wooded valley of the park.

There is excellent fishing in the lake, well stocked with trout, and anglers can hire boats. You can use sailing dinghies and other craft with permission from the Welsh Water Board's on-site staff. If you are feeling fit you can do the seven mile hike around the lake's perimeter and enjoy the huge variety of wildlife.

The eight cottages have been built from early 19th century stone farm buildings. Some are single-storied and some are on two floors but all have been converted with great care and with an eye to retaining as much of the original materials as was practicable. For example we saw how a part of the old wooden manger has been kept as a kitchen screen in one of the cottages. It is nicely complemented by the wooden beams and attractive doors.

The kitchens are all very well-equipped, too, with full sized cookers and refrigerators; microwave ovens are supplied in two of them. Central heating is laid on and some cottages have log burning stoves. There is a service area with washing machines, driers and a deep-freeze.

The cottages are of varying sizes and can each accommodate between four and seven people.

We were not surprised to hear that the three acres of gardens had recently won a 'Wales in Bloom' award. They are organised in a most attractive way, with smooth lawns and arrays of flowers, trees and shrubs. There are alcoves here and there where you can enjoy the tranquillity of it all.

All ages are catered for and the children, for example, have their own play area. It is safely enclosed and has swings, a climbing frame, and a slide. All the family can play croquet and badminton on the lawns.

The owners, Tim and Cathy Arthur, offer a range of oven-ready meals and you can order these in advance of your arrival.

In summary we were most impressed with the stylish accommodation and excellent facilities offered at Ivy Court. All the cottages have been graded by the Welsh Tourist Board as '4 Dragon' or '5 Dragon', the top two categories.

Nearby: Apart from the amenities of Llys-y-Fran Country Park, the Preseli Hills are nearby and it is an easy drive to safe and sandy beaches: Newport and Newgale, for example. If you fancy some sightseeing Haverfordwest has a ruined castle and you could take in the Graham Sutherland Gallery, Scolton Manor and St David's Cathedral.

Units: 8
Rent: £110 to £390 a week (short winter breaks available)
Other costs: none
Central heating: provided
Several cots and high chairs
Open all year

Longhorsley, Nr Morpeth, Northumberland — map 10
LINDEN HALL HOTEL – ☎ *Morpeth (0670) 516 611.*

On the A697 north of Morpeth.

At the end of a long driveway you will find this glorious Georgian mansion built in 1812 from local stone for a local bigwig and set in three hundred acres of splendid parkland. The interior is beautifully maintained and elegantly furnished.

There are excellent facilities: a children's playground with swings, a slide, a roundabout and climbing poles, a hard tennis court, putting green, croquet lawn and large playroom in a vaulted cellar with table tennis and snooker (for adults), lots of toys, and mini-furniture for mini-guests. If you are a jogger the hotel will provide you with a map which gives you various routes from one to four miles. There is even an all weather cricket pitch in the grounds and coarse fishing facilities.

Behind the hotel is the Linden Pub, in a converted granary and built of attractive stone like the hotel. There is a large family room under the rafters with a high chair, and the terrace outside has plenty of tables and chairs and a giant draughts board. They serve meals every day including a children's menu and half portions. It's an excellent alternative to the hotel restaurant.

Nearby: The hotel can arrange all sorts of activities for you – clay pigeon shooting in the grounds, salmon and trout fishing, golf on neighbouring courses and horse riding. It is great walking country, and the hotel can send you on three heritage trails. Some fine country houses are within reach – Cragside, Wallington House and Belsay Hall – and further south you can follow Hadrian's Wall.

PUB (12–2pm & 6–9pm) £1–6: leek & potato pancake, rabbit casserole, steak & kidney pudding, shepherds pie;
LUNCH (12–2pm) £18: French onion soup, supreme of chicken, pudding or cheese;
DINNER (7–10pm) £20: terrine of salmon, roast leg of lamb, pudding or cheese
Children: high teas, half portions

LULWORTH COVE

£ high
Best Bargain Break £65 per person per night – dinner, b & b
Children: free up to 12 years
Facilities: 4 cots and 6 high chairs; and a baby listening system
45 rooms, 4 sets interconnecting, 2 cottages
• Ale – Theakston's   Access/AmEx/Diners/Visa
P – own car park   Open all year

The Linden Pub is recommended in the Family Welcome Pub & Restaurant Guide.

Lulworth Cove, Dorset   map 2
MILL HOUSE HOTEL AND BISHOP'S COTTAGE HOTEL – ☎ West Lulworth (092 941) 261.

On the B3071 between Weymouth and Wareham.
The two hotels sit side by side and share their various facilities. Bishop's Cottage was once the home of Bishop Wordsworth of Salisbury, and is an attractive small hotel, a mix of stone, red tiles and turrets. It sits comfortably in the shelter of Bindon Hill, and is a few yards from the famous horseshoe cove. With tables on the terrace in front, the restaurant on the ground floor and the souvenir shop there is always plenty of gentle activity.
The Mill House is situated opposite the pond and is a handsome building. The garden is terraced and winds its way up Bindon Hill. The squash court should by now have been renovated.

LYDLINCH

The residents' lounge and dining room are on the first floor, along with some of the bedrooms. The latter have a cottagey feel with their sloping walls and dormer windows. The residents have a separate entrance through the garden gate. The heated outdoor swimming pool in the long attractive terraced garden is well sheltered by the surrounding hills and overlooks the cove.

The kitchen produces fresh food for the hotel and the cafe: local fresh shellfish is a speciality and vegetarian meals are also available. Meals can be taken in the Bishop's Cottage restaurant (open all day) or the Mill House restaurant, which has an extensive menu, so the whole environment is very flexible for families.

Nearby: This is a splendid holiday area with lots of interesting coastline to see, and particularly good sandy beaches at Swanage, Weymouth and Studland. The Dorset coastal path runs past Swanage and there is a nature reserve at Studland. Inland there is superb countryside to explore, and the children will no doubt be drawn to the Sea Life Centre at Weymouth and Durlston Country Park. Other places to visit include Corfe Castle, the Swanage Railway, the Tutankhamun Exhibition, Thomas Hardy's Cottage, the prehistoric Maiden Castle and Athelhampton.

✗ LUNCH (12–2.30pm) £1–7: lasagne, steak & kidney pie, plaice & chips, three course lunch;
DINNER (6–10pm) £9: crab cocktail, pork chop, pudding
Children: own menu, half portions
£ medium
Best Bargain Break £49 per person 2 nights – dinner, b & b
Children: cots £2; £7 from 2 to 7; £9 from 8 to 11
Facilities: 6 cots and 4 high chairs; and a baby listening system
25 rooms, 5 family, 2 sets interconnecting
Open all year   Access/Visa
P – limited, but public car park nearby

Lydlinch, Nr Sturminster Newton, Dorset   map 2

HOLBROOK FARM – ☎ Hazelbury Bryan (0258) 817 348.

Just off the A357 two miles west of Sturminster Newton.
You will find this very attractive Georgian farmhouse, built of light-coloured stone, in a quiet setting and surrounded by the green fields of the family-run farm.

At one side of the house there is a sizeable and well-maintained lawn bordered by hedges and shrubs, and in another part of the garden there is a small swimming pool. There are other activities laid on for guests; clay pigeon shooting, with tuition, can also be arranged, for example; and one of the outbuildings has been converted into a games room with a pool table, table tennis and darts. There is also a mini-gym.

The accommodation is all contained within converted stables. They have all been furnished to an excellent standard and many of the original features retained, such as the wooden beams and the stall partitions.

You will find excellent family accommodation here in a very pleasant setting.

Nearby: Sherborne Abbey and the neighbouring ruined castle are close, as are the butterfly gardens at Compton House. Montacute House, Ham Hill Country Park, the Fleet Air Arm Museum and Hambleden Hill can all be reached with ease. A little further away in various directions you can reach Cricket St Thomas Wildlife Park and Longleat, Stourhead and Kingston Lacy, and the Rare Breeds Centre near Gillingham.

DINNER (7pm) £10
Children: half portions
£ low
Children: half price
Facilities: 3 cots and 3 high chairs
5 rooms, 1 set interconnecting   Open all year
No credit cards   Licensed
P – plenty   No music

Lynmouth, Devon   map 1

TORS HOTEL – ☎ (0598) 53236.

On the A39.

The hotel stands prominently over the pretty seaside town of Lynmouth and from the terrace and the various public rooms and most of the bedrooms you have splendid views of the sea and the harbour.

The hotel has been refurbished and the bars and the restaurant are very smartly and comfortably decked out. There is a table tennis room at one end of the hotel and a pool table in another games room. Outside, the hotel has several acres of woodland in which to relax, and a heated swimming pool.

Nearby: You can swim at many of the nearby beaches and fishing, tennis and golf are all available locally. You are on the outskirts of Exmoor and the Park Centre is not too far away near Dulverton. Children will perhaps relish a visit to Watermouth Castle or the Exmoor Bird Gardens, while Arlington Court and Dunster Castle can easily be reached.

BAR SNACKS (12.30–1.45pm) £1–4: cheese & pickles, fish platter, leeky pies;
DINNER (7–8.45pm) £17: tuna & rice & bean salad, soup, navarin of lamb, pudding or cheese
Children: own menu, half portions
£ high
Best Bargain Break £35 per person per night – dinner, b & b

Children: free up to 14 years
Facilities: several cots and high chairs; 4 baby listening lines and 2 baby alarms
35 rooms, 5 family Access/AmEx/Diners/Visa
Closed 4 Jan to 1 Mar **P** – own car park

Machynlleth, Powys map 5
WYNNSTAY ARMS HOTEL – ☎ *Machynlleth (0654) 702 941.*

On the A487 in the town centre.

This 18th century hotel was once a staging post on the Royal Mail from Shrewsbury to Aberystwyth. It is a useful place to know in a tourist area, which, like much of mid-Wales, is not over-endowed with good hotels or inns. Among the twenty rooms there are several which can accommodate a family.

There are two comfortable lounges where you can sit with the children while having a drink. Lunch can be taken in the bar or one of the lounges (they'll move a high chair wherever you want it). There is a buffet lunch and the dinner menu has special dishes each day.

Nearby: The coast is quite close with lovely sandy beaches at Fairbourne and Aberdovey, for example. There are some excellent golf courses also, at Aberdovey and Harlech. The Centre for Alternative Technology is well worth a visit and further north you can reach Lake Vyrnwy and the Coed-y-Brenin Forest with its many nature trails. Railway buffs have several choices: the Talyllyn, the Fairbourne and the Bala Lake railways.

BAR MEALS (12–2pm & 7–9pm) £1–6: garlic mushrooms, sirloin steak, cheesy chicken, cannelloni, fillets of plaice;
DINNER (7–8.30pm) £12: chicken liver paté, poached salmon, pudding or cheese
Children: own menu, half portions
£ medium
Best Bargain Break £72 per person, 2 nights – dinner, b & b
Children: free up to 10 years
Facilities: 3 cots and 3 high chairs; and a baby listening system
20 rooms, 2 family Access/AmEx/Diners/Visa
Open all year • Ale – Wynnstay Wallop
P – own car park

To qualify for inclusion in the Guide hotels must offer the basic facilities of a cot, a family room and an evening meal. Self-catering establishments must provide cots and high chairs.

Maentwrog, Blaenau Ffestiniog, Gwynedd map 5
THE OLD RECTORY – ☎ *Maentwrog (076 685) 305.*

Just off the A487 as you enter the village.

Built in 1740 as a dower house for a local family of landed gentry, this is a handsome house of Welsh stone, and has the great bonus of a very large lawned garden which stretches away at the back and is encircled by trees and bushes. Children are welcome to play here. Nearby is the river which eventually joins the sea at Tremadog Bay.

Several of the rooms can accommodate a family and especially a huge suite on the first floor which stretches the width of the house and has delightful views of the countryside. The rooms are decorated with taste and the breakfast room is particularly charming. The annexe on one side of the hotel has been smartly painted and the rooms are comfortable and well decorated and all have their own bathrooms. They are also slightly cheaper than the rooms in the main house.

In addition to conventional food, the owner provides an excellent vegetarian dinner menu at around £7. Children are offered smaller portions of the adults' food – no junk is served here, we are glad to report.

Nearby: There is a play area in the village, and many other attractions in this lovely part of Wales: the slate caverns near Blaenau Ffestiniog; the famous village of Portmeirion; the Ffestiniog narrow gauge railway; and the Coed-y-Brenin Forest. There are many safe and sandy beaches in the area, especially Black Rock Sands and Harlech.

DINNER (7–9.30pm) £9
Children: half portions
£ low
Children: free up to 10 years (a linen charge of £10 per visit)
Facilities: 2 cots; baby listening via 1 phone line
12 rooms, 4 family   Open all year
Access/Visa   **P** – own car park

Mapledurham, Nr Reading, Berks map 3
MAPLEDURHAM ESTATE – ☎ *Reading (0734) 723 350.*

SC *Off the A4074 north west of Reading. Well signposted on the Wallingford side of the village.*

The estate is so quiet and secluded that it is difficult to realise that Reading is just a few miles away. The core of the estate is the magnificent Elizabethan mansion, Mapledurham House, with its splendid grounds and a lovely old watermill. The mansion and the mill and a riverside park are open to the public at weekends.

MAPLEDURHAM

The various cottages and houses are mostly of 17th and 18th century vintage and several of them are within walking distance of Mapledurham House. The two alms cottages, delightful low-built dwellings of brick and tile, are able each to accommodate six people, by dint of extensions at the rear of the original cottages. They both have large grassy gardens.

The size of the gardens is an excellent feature of all the properties and makes them highly suitable for family occupation. For example, when we visited the Mill House an impromptu family game of cricket was under way in the sizeable back garden. The Mill House is a delightful Queen Anne house of three storeys and made from brick and flint, and can accommodate seven people. Its rooms are well-proportioned and there are two sitting rooms.

The other properties can sleep four to five people, but there are two superb thatched cottages – charming, archetypal English country cottages with pleasant gardens – on the edge of the estate.

The owner, Mr Eyston, whose ancestors have owned Mapledurham for several hundred years, told us that the furniture is comfortable but deliberately functional because of the wear and tear it has to withstand. Nevertheless the manager, Jean Emary, confirmed that there is a constant process of refurbishment.

As well as having their large gardens, guests have access to the large area by the mill and the river, a pleasant place for a picnic and where the children can play. A golf course (18 holes) is currently being built and should be open sometime this year.

Nearby: Mapledurham is well-placed for visits to London, half an hour by rail and a comfortable enough journey outside the rush hours, and you have easy access to many other places of interest: Windsor, with its castle, museum and safari park; the Courage Shire Horse Centre and the Childe Beale Wildlife Trust; Cliveden; and the Bekonscot Model Village. You can reach Oxford easily and the Cotswolds beyond.

Units: 10
Rent: £130 to £340 a week
Other costs: linen on hire; heat and light metered only in winter
Heating: central heating
Several cots and high chairs available
Open all year

Mawgan Porth, Cornwall   map 1
BEDRUTHAN STEPS HOTEL – ☎ *St Mawgan (0637) 860 555.*

On the B3276 – the main coast road from Newquay to Padstow.

The hotel takes its name from the array of huge rocks by the beach said to be the stepping stones of the legendary giant Bedruthan.

It is a modern and spacious hotel which is totally geared to the holiday needs of families; there are masses of cots and high chairs, and almost all the rooms are family rooms. The facilities for adults are excellent including two squash courts, indoor and outdoor heated swimming pools, a tennis court, snooker, table tennis, etc.

The facilities for children are outstanding: as well as the swimming pools there are various play areas (including adventure playgrounds, swings, and an area for football), children's films etc. The 'jungle tumble' play area has a ball pool, tube slide, rope ladders and biff bags; it is indoors and is supervised and has a special toddlers' area. To take the younger children off your hands there is a play group every morning except Sundays. The children's entertainment programme is extensive and includes treasure hunts and craft workshops.

The hotel has a farm and a large market garden so it is not surprising that most of the vegetables and quite a lot of fruit are grown by the hotel. The fish is caught locally, and the bread is made on the spot too. As at the Trevelgue Hotel near Newquay (q.v.), there are some excellent wines at remarkably good prices, and a good selection of vegetarian dishes. The hotel provides a range of home-made puréed foods for babies. All told you get astonishing value for money.

Nearby: You need never leave the hotel, but there is no shortage of outside attractions. Mawgan Porth beach, right in front of the hotel, is safe and sandy and there are several excellent beaches at Newquay, a busy resort about six miles away. It has an excellent zoo. The Lappa Valley Railway will appeal to many families, as will the Dairyland Farm Park, the World in Miniature and Trerice, a superb Elizabethan manor house.

LUNCH (1–2pm) £9: soup, cold buffet, pudding or cheese;
DINNER (7.45–9.30pm) £11: summer vegetable mousse, escalope

of salmon, pudding or cheese
Children: own menu, half portions
£ medium
Best Bargain Break £24 per person per day – dinner, b & b
Children: a quarter to three quarters of the adult rate; free of charge in some off-peak periods
Facilities: 40 cots and 40 high chairs; and a baby listening system in every room
75 rooms, 70 family, 13 sets interconnecting
Closed Nov-March   Access/Visa
• Ale – Bass   No music
No smoking in restaurant, lounge and children's play areas
🅿 – own car park

Minchinhampton, Nr Stroud, Glos map 2
BURLEIGH COURT HOTEL – ☎ Brimscombe (0453) 883 804.

Off the A419 east of Stroud. The hotel brochure has a good map.

Burleigh Court is a handsome Cotswold stone manor house, its facade covered in Virginia creeper. It sits in five acres of immaculate gardens on the side of Golden Valley and you have wonderful views of the surrounding countryside.

The emphasis at the hotel is placed firmly on comfort and style: from the attractive furnishings of the lounge areas and the dining room to the charming and spacious bedrooms, which have each been decorated and furnished in their own individual ways. Ten of the bedrooms can easily accommodate a cot or an extra bed for a child, and there are also two suites. We looked at the ground floor suite, an ideal design for a small family: there is a sitting room as you enter, with a double bed behind a screen and a separate bedroom with bunks for younger children. It has the great bonus of looking straight out to the garden and the swimming pool.

The gardens are a delight, the smooth lawns at the back divided here and there by stone walls, and the swimming pool is a genuine Victorian plunge pool – a fine sight. At the front, a huge expanse of lawn, ringed by mature trees, slopes away from the hotel. A little fountain plays in a corner and there is a play area for the children, with swings, a climbing frame, a rope ladder and a tree house. On the other side there is a large and very smooth putting green and a practice net.

This is a delightful hotel where all the family will receive a warm welcome.

Nearby: The hotel is on the fringe of Minchinhampton Common, where you can play golf, go riding or walking or just browse in the sun. Within a reasonable radius you can reach Berkeley Castle and Sudeley Castle, Westonbirt Arboretum, the Cotswold Water Park, the Wildfowl Trust at Slimbridge, the Cotswold Wildlife Park near Burford, and the various attractions at Bourton-

on-the-Water. All the charms of the Cotswolds lie in one direction and of the lovely city of Bath in the other.

BAR SNACKS (12–2pm) £2–7: savoury cheese peach, sausage & mash, seafood pancakes, steak & kidney pie;
LUNCH (12–2pm) £12: scrambled eggs & smoked salmon, carbonade of beef, pudding or cheese;
DINNER (7–8.45pm) £19: spinach & prawn roulade, piquant lamb, pudding or cheese
Children: high teas, flexible portions
£ high
Best Bargain Break £54 per night – dinner, b & b
Children: £10 b & b
Facilities: 2 cots and 1 high chair; baby listening to each room
17 rooms, 2 suites, 3 sets interconnecting
Open all year except Xmas to 7 January   Access/AmEx/Diners/Visa
No smoking in dining room   No music
P – own car park

Moffat, Dumfries & Galloway   map 11
BLACK BULL HOTEL, Station Road – ☎ *Moffat (0683) 20206.*

In the town centre.
This famous pub opened its doors in 1568, and now looks very smart in its coat of white paint, with black edgings and shutters for the windows. It is a rambling building, long and low, and inside you will find a couple of large and comfortable bars. One of them is more of a brasserie bar these days and families are welcome to eat in there together. On warm days you can sit outside in the courtyard.

There are good facilities for families in this old inn. If you want to sit and have a drink and a snack together you can use the Burns Room, where both the walls and the ceilings are panelled in wood; there are a few tables, banquettes around the walls, and a couple of amusement machines. The poet used to frequent the Black Bull and indeed inscribed one of his poems on a window pane, but it is said that the window is in a Moscow museum.

An alternative is another lounge which has been recently redecorated and refurnished. It is warm and cosy with books on display and its character is much enhanced by the lovely decorative Jacobean ceiling. There is also a children's TV room with video games.

The whole pub was redecorated recently, including the bedrooms, which are smart and functional.

Nearby: The pleasant town has good amenities including tennis courts, bowling greens and a children's play park. The splendid countryside around Moffat offers lovely walks and there are ample facilities for fishing, golf and riding.

MONTGOMERY

The Solway Firth coast can be reached without too much difficulty and there are many places within reach if you fancy some sightseeing: the Robert Burns Centre at Dumfries, Maxwelton House, Drumlanrig Castle and the Hoddom Estate, for example.

✗ BAR SNACKS (11am–2.15pm & 6.30–10pm) £1–5: steak pie, haggis, cheese & potato hot pot, lasagne, roast chicken & salad;
DINNER (6.30–9.15pm) £9: egg mayonnaise, sirloin steak, pudding
Children: own menu, half portions
£ low
Children: no charge
Facilities: 2 cots and 2 high chairs; and 3 baby listening lines
5 rooms, 2 family   Open all year
• Ale – McEwan's, Theakston's   Access/Visa
No smoking in the restaurant
🅿 – small car park or on street

Also recommended in the Family Welcome Pub & Restaurant Guide.

Montgomery, Powys   map 6
LITTLE BROMPTON FARM – ☎ *Montgomery (0686) 668 371.*

On the B4385 two miles east of Montgomery.

The early 17th century farmhouse, built of stone and painted white, is situated in gentle and peaceful countryside and you have fine views of the surrounding hills. It has been the home of the Bright family for over half a century, and you will receive a warm welcome from them.

Inside, there is a wealth of oak beams and open fireplaces, and the house is furnished in fine style with many antiques. In the dining room the guests have their own separate tables, and a lovely Welsh dresser, with its gleaming plates, adorns one wall. The bedrooms are comfortable and well-appointed and two of them have their own bathrooms.

Guests are welcome to explore the farm, which has around 100 acres on which cattle and sheep, including Jacob sheep, are raised. Offa's Dyke footpath actually runs through the adjoining fields – a good starting point for some pleasant walks. There is also a pond in an adjoining field, which attracts a lot of wild life.

Nearby: It is an interesting and relaxing area for a holiday or a break. Montgomery itself is a handsome town with a ruined castle, and if you like outdoor pursuits – walking, fishing, golf, rough shooting – you are in the right place. It is an excellent base for sightseeing too, with the lovely countryside of South Shropshire nearby – Church Stretton, Ludlow and the little towns around Clun, "the quietest places under the sun". Railway fans should head for the

Welshpool and Llanfair Light Railway, which is within easy reach, as is Powis Castle.

✗ DINNER (from 6pm) from £6
Children: small portions
£ low
Children: half price under 10
Facilities: a cot and a high chair; baby listening by arrangement
3 rooms, 1 family   Open all year
No credit cards   Unlicensed
🅿 – own car park   No music

Moonfleet, Nr Weymouth, Dorset   map 2
MOONFLEET MANOR – ☎ Weymouth (0305) 786 948.

Off the B3157 north-west of Weymouth.

We have had consistently good reports, from readers and friends, about this hotel in its lovely setting by Chesil Beach. It has excellent facilities for a family holiday or break: a large indoor swimming pool and children's pool, two squash courts, a four rink indoor bowling green, a gymnasium, two hard tennis courts and a short tennis court, a snooker table, adventure playground, and indoor games such as table tennis and table football. Everyone from grandma to grandchild should find something to amuse them.

The handsome 16th century building, which was restored at the end of the 19th century, has a close association with the classic adventure story, 'Moonfleet'.

Nearby: The huge expanse of Chesil Beach is shingle, but nearby Weymouth has a sandy beach and a Sea Life Centre, which will attract the children. In the other direction lies Abbotsbury, with its ruined abbey and famous gardens and swannery. If you go inland, the lovely town of Dorchester is quite close, and Thomas Hardy's cottage can be seen as well as the Tutankhamun Exhibition. If you are in the mood for sightseeing you can visit the country house of Athelhampton, the tank museum at Bovington Camp, and Clouds Hill, the memorial to T.E. Lawrence.

✗ BAR SNACKS (12–2pm & 7–10pm) £1–4: crudités, salads, daily specials, ploughman's;
DINNER (7–9pm) £10: blue cheese prawn cocktail, ragout of lamb, pudding or cheese
Children: own menu, half portions
£ high
Best Bargain Break £78 per person, 2 nights – dinner, b & b
Children: from 15% to 80% of the adult rate, depending on age
Facilities: 10 cots and 6 high chairs; a baby listening system

MULLION

37 rooms, 10 family, 3 sets interconnecting
Open all year   Access/AmEx/Diners/Visa
• Ale – Hall & Woodhouse   No smoking in one lounge
🅿 – own car park

Mullion, Cornwall   map 1

POLURRIAN HOTEL, Polurrian Cove – ☎ Mullion (0326) 240 421.

Follow your nose through Mullion, past the cricket ground – you may have to ask, although there is a hotel sign.

The roof blew off this hotel at the beginning of 1990 but it is good to report that all is well again with this excellent hotel. From the expansive gardens of the Edwardian building you will have some breathtaking views down to the sea; and if it is action rather than contemplation that you require, there is plenty to divert you: a putting green, hard tennis court, and outdoor badminton court, one squash court and a superbly equipped grassy play area with a slide, trampoline, sandpit and swings, and all enclosed for the parents' peace of mind. Down below is a sandy cove where you can do some surfing.

There is a games area indoors with snooker, bar billiards and table tennis. The leisure club has an indoor swimming pool with a paddling pool and a mini-gym, plus a sauna and a solarium. There is also an outdoor heated swimming pool.

There is a warm and relaxing atmosphere at this hotel, which has everything necessary for a happy family holiday, including children's outings to local attractions.

Nearby: Most of the surrounding land is owned by the National Trust, and there are delightful walks to take. Mullion golf course is just a couple of miles away and there are many attractions within reach: Goonhilly Earth Station, the Flambards Theme Park, Poldark Mine, the Seal Sanctuary at Gweek and St Michael's Mount.

🍴 BUFFET LUNCH (12–2pm) £1–6: chicken & chips, cold buffet, scampi, fisherman's pie, moussaka;
DINNER (7–9pm) £18: quenelle of sole, soup, roast leg of pork, pudding or cheese
Children: own menu, half portions
£ high
Best Bargain Break £150 per person 3 nights – dinner, b & b
Children: free up to 15 years
Facilities: plenty of cots and high chairs, and baby listening system
40 rooms, 4 family   Access/AmEx/Diners/Visa
Open March to November   No music
🅿 – own car park   • Ale – Ruddles

Mundesley, Norfolk   map 8

THORNLEA, 51 High Street – ☎ Mundesley (0263) 720 598.

In the centre of the village.

This is a semi-detached Edwardian house, which has been well modernised and is only minutes from the sea. It has the advantage of a large, grassy garden, which faces south and has several facilities to amuse families: a badminton set, a netball stand, boules which can be used on the lawn, and even a football or two is available.

The owners of this house offer good food and excellent facilities for families. They emphasise that the food is all cooked on the spot from fresh ingredients – no microwave ovens here.

Nearby: Mundesley is an unspoilt place, and that is one of the charms of this part of Norfolk, but there is plenty to do and see. The beach offers safe bathing, and good fishing can also be had locally. It's also a great area for walkers and nature lovers; and for golfers, too, with a course in the village and Cromer and Sheringham fairly close. There is a variety of things to do and see in the neighbourhood: Felbrigg Hall and its fine gardens; the Shire Horse Centre near Cromer; the North Norfolk Railway; Blickling Hall; and the Norfolk Wildlife Park north of East Dereham.

✗ DINNER (6–7pm) £7
Children: half portions
£ low
Children: free up to 2 years; half price thereafter to 12
Facilities: 2 cots and 2 high chairs; and a baby alarm
3 rooms, 1 family   Open all year (except Xmas)
No credit cards   Unlicensed
No smoking in bedrooms   No music
 – own car park

Mungrisdale, Nr Penrith, Cumbria   map 9

NEAR HOWE FARM HOTEL – ☎ Threlkeld (0768) 779 678.

H/SC   *Off the A66 between Penrith and Keswick*

It would be difficult to imagine a more delightful situation than that of Near Howe, a lovely double-fronted farmhouse built of the traditional dark-hued stone of this part of the country. After you have driven up a long and bumpy road you can look back at the moorland which dips and rolls beneath. This is the Mungrisdale Valley over which John Peel and his companions used to hunt.

You will certainly find peace and tranquillity here, not least in the garden

NAIRN

which fronts the house. It has an immaculate lawn, is safely enclosed and ringed with trees, and all around is the glorious countryside. It is a wonderful base for a holiday in an area which has so much to offer: fishing, golf, water sports, walking, or just plain relaxing.

There is a residents' lounge and a games room with a pool table and a dart board, and a few toys. In addition there is a bar in another lounge.

Nearby: If you fancy seeing the sights you are only a short drive away from the popular parts of the Lakes: Grasmere, Windermere, Coniston Water and so on. Much nearer to hand is Ullswater and Derwent Water, and Lowther Park with its nature trails, adventure playground and miniature railway.

✘ DINNER (7pm) £8
Children: half portions
£ low
Children: half price under 12 years
Facilities: 1 cot and 1 high chair
7 rooms, 1 family   Open March to November
No smoking in dining room   No credit cards
🅿 – loads

SELF-CATERING

There are three cottages to let, which have been converted from an old barn and you will have lovely views over the fells. Each has two bedrooms, a double and a twin-bedded room, and a very well-equipped kitchen. Guests have the use of the garden and of the other hotel facilities and there is a laundry room. The rents vary from £140 to £200 per week and include electricity, heating and linen.

Nairn, Highland   map 12

GOLF VIEW HOTEL (Rank), Seabank Road – ☎ Nairn (0667) 52301.

Off the A96 on the west side of Nairn. There is a small sign to Seabank Road.

This large stone hotel was built in 1897 and is a good centre for a family holiday by dint of its excellent facilities, which include an outdoor heated pool, a play area with a climbing frame and a trampoline, a putting green, two hard tennis courts and a games room with table tennis, pool and lots of toys. In addition the Nairn championship golf course is nearby. There are beautiful views across the Moray Firth to the Black Isle and the Northern Highlands. The extensive gardens, with their fine lawns, lead down to the esplanade and the beach.

The emphasis in the restaurant is on traditional and local dishes, and the lunches offer particularly good value. This is a very well-run hotel, which offers excellent food and service. The place exudes a relaxed charm which makes

NAIRN

a stay here a great pleasure.

Nearby: Fishing, swimming, water skiing and sailing can all be organised, and there is delightful countryside all around to explore. Many tourist attractions are within easy reach including Cawdor Castle, the battlefield of Culloden, Fort George, Urquhart Castle, the Landmark Visitor Centre, the Loch Ness Monster Exhibition, Brodie Castle and the Highland Wildlife Centre just south of Aviemore.

✘ BAR LUNCHES (12–2pm) £1–5: terrine, smoked cod, leg of lamb, chicken & sweetcorn pancake;
LUNCH (12–2pm) £21: salmon & prawn terrine, roast loin of pork, pudding or cheese;
DINNER (7–9.15pm) £21: smoked turkey soup, fillet of halibut, pudding or cheese
Children: half portions, high teas
£ high
Best Bargain Break £49 per person per night – dinner, b & b
Children: free to 4 years; £15 thereafter
Facilities: 3 cots and 5 high chairs; baby listening line to every room
48 rooms, 4 family   Access/AmEx/Diners/Visa
🅿 – own car park   No music

Also recommended in the Family Welcome Pub & Restaurant Guide.

INVERNAIRNE HOTEL, Thurlow Road – ☎ *Nairn (0667) 52039.*

Off the A96. Turn into Albert Street towards the sea.

Mr and Mrs Wilkie have refurbished this hotel over the last few years. The house was built in the Italian style about a century ago and is notable for the number of fine wooden fireplaces, especially the one in the dining room, and its wood panelling. The sun lounge is a particularly pleasant place to sit, and there is also a pool room in the hotel.

There are two cots on the premises, along with the three family rooms, plus a couple of high chairs, and all the bedrooms have their own bathrooms. The garden is about an acre in size with a lawned area and a little wood, and a putting green. It has the bonus of overlooking the sandy beach, to which there is a private path.

Nearby: This area of Scotland has long stretches of beach, and Burghead Bay, just along the coast, is a sailing centre where you can hire boats. Sea fishing trips can also be taken from the harbour, or you can fish in nearby lochs and rivers. If you play golf you need look no farther than the Nairn links, a superb championship course, which is a few minutes walk from the hotel. There is an excellent swimming pool near the hotel. If sight seeing is on your agenda, there are many fine castles within reach: Cawdor, Urquhart, Brodie and Fort George, for example. The Culloden Battlefield is not far away and you can also

visit the Loch Ness Monster exhibition at Drumnadrochit.

✖ BAR MEALS (12–2pm & 8–10pm) £3–9: chicken curry, spaghetti Bolognese, haddock, sirloin steak, salmon;
DINNER (7–8pm) £10: prawn cocktail, chicken Suedoise, pudding
Children: own menu, half portions
£ medium
Best Bargain Break £99 per person, 3 nights – dinner, b & b
Children: free up to 10 years
Facilities: 2 cots and 2 high chairs; baby listening system
9 rooms, 3 family   Access/Visa
Open all year except Xmas and New Year
• Ale – McEwan's (sometimes)   No smoking in dining room
🅿 – own car park

Nr Nairn, Highland   map 12
COVENANTERS INN, Auldearn – ☎ *Nairn (0667) 52456.*

Two miles east of Nairn, just off the A96, on the edge of the hamlet of Auldearn.

The inn has quite a history since the rebel Covenanters fought the battle of

Auldearn with the Duke of Montrose in 1645 in what is now the car park. The building began life as a mill and a brewhouse in the 17th century and it is good to report that the original character of the place is still apparent.

The lounge bar, for example, has sandstone walls, a low, oak beamed ceiling, oak tables and settles, and a wood burning stove. It is a warm and welcoming spot. Families are made welcome here, too. Older children and adults can use the snooker table and the dart board, and younger ones are not forgotten, since there is a play area and a good selection of toys.

The restaurant, part of which is a conservatory, has a couple of high chairs and has an excellent reputation for its seafood. Fresh langoustines are usually available.

On sunny days you can sit on the paved terrace where there are several bench tables. There is a small children's play area with a wooden fort, climbing frame, a slide and swings.

Nearby: There are some fine sandy beaches in the area including Burghhead, Nairn and Findhorn, which is a good surfing centre. There are some fascinating places to visit within an easy drive: Cawdor Castle, the Highland Wildlife Park, the battlefield of Culloden, Urquhart Castle, the Loch Ness Monster Exhibition and Brodie Castle. Golfers have a good choice of courses, including the championship links at Nairn, and fishing, horse riding, and water sports are all readily available.

BAR SNACKS (12–2.30pm & 5–9.30pm) £1–10: smoked venison, pickled herring, langoustines, roast pheasant, fillet steak
RESTAURANT (12–2.30pm & 5–9.30pm) £12: gravadlax, venison steak, pudding
£ medium
Best Bargain Break £25 per person per night – dinner, b & b
Children: free up to 12 years
Facilities: 1 cot and 2 high chairs; baby listening to all rooms
8 rooms, 2 family   Open all year
Access/Visa   P – own car park

Also recommended in the Family Welcome Pub & Restaurant Guide.

Nancenoy, Nr Helston, Cornwall   map 1

TRENGILLY WARTHA – ☎ *Constantine (0326) 40332.*

Off the B3291 between Constantine and Gweek.
The inn is situated down the narrow country lanes east of Helston and not far from the Helford River where it cuts deep into the Cornish landscape. There are signs here and there which point the way to the place, and eventually you will find a long, cream-painted building with a garden room at the front. The

latter room is where families are welcome to settle if they have young children in tow and the adjoining entrance hall contains a pool table. Behind is a pleasant and spacious bar and real ale enthusiasts will be glad to hear that there is always a wide choice of beers available and the choice is rotated on a regular basis.

At the back of the bar there is a comfortable and pleasantly furnished lounge with an open fire; and the restaurant is a very pretty and relaxing place. We had a really excellent dinner and a nicely cooked breakfast and greatly enjoyed our stay at this well-run inn.

There are six bedrooms in the pub and some of them can accommodate two parents and a child. On summer days you can take advantage of the covered patio, and the very pretty garden with its array of flowers and bushes. It's a quiet and peaceful spot, and you have a view across the lush valley of a distant village church.

Nearby: There are many sandy beaches nearby and the pick of them for families are perhaps Kennack Sands, Towan and Pendower beaches and the Lizard Peninsula is one of the most attractive parts of Cornwall. There is no end of attractions for holiday makers within easy reach: the Seal Sanctuary at Gweek, Flambards Theme Park near Helston, the Poldark Mine, Godolphin House, St. Michael's Mount, Paradise Park and the Shire Horse Farm near Camborne.

BAR SNACKS (12–2pm & 6.30–9.30pm) £1–8: smoked salmon, trout, dressed crab salad, Trengilly sausage, sirloin steak;
DINNER (7.30–9.30pm) £16: marinated goat's cheese, poached salmon, pudding
Children: own menu, half portions
£ low
Children: cots £2; £8 thereafter
Facilities: 1 cot and 1 high chair; all rooms have baby listening through the phones
6 rooms   Access/AmEx/Visa
Open all year   • Ale – a varying choice
P – own car park

Also recommended in the Family Welcome Pub & Restaurant Guide.

Nettlecombe, Nr Bridport, Dorset   map 2
MARQUIS OF LORNE – ☎ *Powerstock (030 885) 236.*

Off the A3066 and north east of Bridport. Follow the signs for Powerstock first.
This 16th century stone pub is tucked away beneath the old hill fort of Eggardon, and is deep in the Dorset countryside. There are two lovely gardens, where the lawns are surrounded by borders of flowers and you can sit at your

ease under the apple trees. The children have their own play area with swings, a climbing net and frame, and slides.

Parents will be pleased to hear that there is real ale to be quaffed in the bars: two pleasant and comfortable rooms with wood panelled walls.

There is a separate entrance for residents and this leads to the guests' sitting room and the dining room, which has fine views across the countryside. The bedrooms are comfortable and bright and the two family rooms are set up with bunk beds and both have their own bathrooms. Mr and Mrs Bone do the cooking and sensibly encourage children to have smaller portions of the adult's food – not the inevitable chips and things.

Nearby: This splendid holiday area has the excellent beach at Seatown nearby and several others along this fine stretch of coastline from Lyme Regis to Weymouth. The interesting and ancient town of Dorchester is a short drive away, with the Tutankhamun Exhibition nearby. Nature lovers will head for the famous swannery at Abbotsbury or the Sea Life Centre at Weymouth, the Donkey Sanctuary near Sidmouth, or the Farway Country Park.

BAR SNACKS (12–2pm & 6.30–9.30pm) £2–11: devilled whitebait, steaks, chicken Mexican, plaice, vegetarian moussaka;
DINNER (7–9.30pm) £17: Marquis smokie, tenderloin of pork, pudding or cheese
Children: own menu, half portions
£ medium
Best Bargain Break £125 per person, 5 nights – dinner, b & b
Children: under 2's free; half price from 2 to 8 years
Facilities: 1 cot and 1 high chair, and baby listening
6 rooms, 2 family   Access only
Open all year   • Ale – Palmer's
P – own car park

Newbiggin, Stainton, Nr Penrith, Cumbria   map 9
TYMPARON HALL – ☎ *Greystoke (076 84) 83236.*

From Exit 40 of the M6 take the A66 to the west of Penrith. The house is on the edge of the village.

This very attractive, early 18th century farmhouse was built from sandstone and sits in its own sizeable garden. This is laid out in a very pleasing way with a lawn, a pond and some lovely trees including a weeping willow. There is also a patio at one side with a barbecue.

Beyond are the open fields of the farm itself, about 200 acres of them, and guests are welcome to wander about at their will. There is a Shetland pony which the children may ride.

The family room can sleep four people, and there is a pleasant residents' lounge with an open fire, and a separate dining room.

Nearby: This is a lovely house in a splendid spot for a holiday, especially if you are keen on walking, fishing, pony trekking and golf. A sprint northwards up the motorway and a right turn will take you to Hadrian's Wall. Lowther Park with its nature trails, adventure playground and miniature railway is in the vicinity, as is Ullswater; while the more popular parts of the Lakes (Grasmere, Windermere and so on) can be reached quite easily.

✗ DINNER (6.30pm) £7
Children: half portions
£ low
Children: half price under 12 years
Facilities: 1 cot and baby listening by arrangement
3 rooms, 1 family   Open April to October
No credit cards   Unlicensed
No smoking in bedrooms   **P** – ample

Newby Bridge, Nr Ulverston, Cumbria   map 9
SWAN HOTEL (Inter) – ☎ *Newby Bridge (05395) 31681.*

The hotel has a wonderful position by the River Leven at the end of Lake Windermere and its 300 yards of lake frontage has moorings for boats. You can also arrange fishing here.

A secluded garden runs at the rear of the hotel and there is a croquet lawn and a golf practice net. An adjoining field is often the take-off point for hot air balloons.

The indoor facilities include table tennis, darts, a small snooker table and a good selection of board games.

There are three bars, one of which, the Mailcoach Wine Bar, serves hot and cold dishes every day. The Tithe Barn Restaurant is open for lunch on Sunday only (good value at just under £9) and serves dinners each evening with an interesting English menu.

Nearby: You are in the heart of the Lake District and an active holiday can start with all the water sports which are easily available, plus walking, fishing, golf and riding. The Lakeside and Haverthwaite Railway is on the doorstep, as is Fell Foot Park, with its own water sports facilities, picnic areas and adventure playground. Holker Hall, Sizergh Castle, Levens Hall, the Grizedale Forest Centre, Brantwood, Belle Isle and the Steamboat Museum at Windermere are all within easy reach.

✗ WINE BAR (11.45am–2.45pm & 6.30–9.45pm) £1–8: Morecambe Bay shrimps, Mailcoach pie, sirloin steak, fillets of plaice;

DINNER (7–9pm) £16: herring salad, pot roasted leg of lamb, pudding or cheese
Children: own menu, half portions
£ high
Best Bargain Break £46 per person per night – dinner, b & b
Children: cots £3; £15 extra bed (inc. breakfast)
Facilities: 4 cots and 3 high chairs; baby listening system
36 rooms, 6 family   Access/AmEx/Diners/Visa
Open all year, except 10 days in early Jan
• Ale – Boddington's and guests   🅿 – own car park

Newquay, Cornwall   map 1
TREVELGUE HOTEL – ☎ *Newquay (0637) 872 864.*

On the B3276 Newquay-Padstow road.

As at the sister hotel at Mawgan Porth, the Bedruthan Steps (q.v.), the owners have designed this hotel for family holidays and everything is geared to that end. It is a modern, purpose-built hotel with spacious rooms and superb facilities. Even if it is pouring with rain the indoor facilities will keep anyone amused: they include a snooker room, a swimming pool with separate children's pool, table tennis, pool, games machines and lots of space where children can play. There is a playroom and a new indoor jungle trail for young children. For the older children there is a special disco. Nearby is the Fun Factory, which is an indoor play area for under-12's.

Should the sun happen to shine, there is another excellent swimming pool in its own grassy garden; a hard tennis court, paddle tennis court and squash court. There's an adventure playground, a sandpit, and a pirate ship, all within easy viewing and shouting distance of the terrace, upon which you can enjoy your drinks with an easy mind. There are nine acres of grounds in which the children can roam and three acres of garden.

Below the hotel are some lovely sandy beaches. Under-6's can be abandoned to the play group each morning from Monday to Friday and over-6's are taken on various outings and offered Punch and Judy shows, parties, galas, games and magic shows, etc. Parents will be interested in the wine list, which is very reasonably priced, and has some real bargains.

Entertainments are put on every evening, so it is just the place for an active, gregarious holiday for families with young children. The food, by the way, is bound to be fresh – the hotel has its own market garden, makes its own bread and pasta, etc.

Nearby: The busy resort of Newquay is just down the road and has safe and sandy beaches, and it is one of the main surfing centres of Britain. The children will no doubt want to visit the zoo, the Dairyland Farm Park or the World in

Nr NEWQUAY

Miniature; and the Lappa Valley Railway and the lovely Elizabethan house at Trerice are within easy reach.

BAR LUNCH (12–2.15pm) £1–4: burgers, baked potatoes, pizzas, salad;
DINNER (7.30–9pm) £8: pasta in blue cheese sauce, chicken bonne femme, pudding or cheese
Children: own menu
£ medium
Best Bargain Break £30 per person per night – dinner, b & b
Children: varies from free to 25% discount
Facilities: masses of cots and high chairs, and baby listening
70 rooms, 54 family   Access/Visa
Closed Nov-Mar   P – own car park

Nr Newquay, Cornwall   map 1
WATERGATE BAY HOTEL – ☎ *St Mawgan (0637) 860 543.*

H/SC   *On the B3276 north of Newquay.*
We were alerted a couple of years ago by several readers to the presence of this substantial family hotel which is not too far away from the busy resort of Newquay. Not that you need venture there, since there are plenty of facilities at the hotel itself, including a sandy beach, part of which actually belongs to the hotel. The coastal footpath runs close by.

Nr NEWQUAY

Indoors there is a spacious playroom for young children with plenty of toys and games, a slide and a pirate ship; and alongside there is a pool table for older children. The snooker room is confined to adults or children supervised by adults. In addition there is a tennis court and a separate sports hall adjoins the hotel and it has a skittle alley, a fitness room, and a court on which to play badminton, short tennis, etc. There is a putting green on one of the terraces which overlooks the bay, and loads of room for families to relax, including a lounge or quiet room for adults only.

The Coffee Shop (open from 10am to 6pm) offers a good range of snacks and dishes of the day. It overlooks the outdoor swimming pool and paddling pool and alongside it is a small indoor pool.

Nearby: Newquay itself is a busy and lively resort, and, apart from Watergate Bay, there are many safe and sandy beaches in the near vicinity. There are many places to visit, and the children will certainly be interested in the zoo, which has a large play area and a leisure centre attached to it with swimming pools, squash and tennis courts and a golf driving range. There is a leisure park at St Agnes, a farm park (Dairyland) near Newquay and a World in Miniature at Goonhavern, five miles from Newquay. Add the Lappa Valley Railway and the Elizabethan manor house at Trerice, and there is something for everyone.

COFFEE SHOP (10am–6pm) £1–3: soup, salads, ploughman's, hot dish of the day;
LUNCH (12.30–1.45pm) £8: soup, cold buffet or dish of the day, pudding or cheese;
DINNER (7–8.30pm) £14: pilchard salad, roast loin of lamb, pudding or cheese
Children: own menu, half portions
£ low
Best Bargain Break £35 per person per night – dinner, b & b
Children: free at certain times; 25% of adult rate up to 3 years; 50% from 4 to 6; 66% from 7 to 11; 75% from 11 to 14
Facilities: as many cots and high chairs as required; baby listening system to every room
70 rooms, 35 family, 17 sets interconnecting
Open March to November   Access/Visa
No smoking in restaurant   No music
P – ample

SELF-CATERING

Close to the hotel there are three villa flats. One of them is very large and can sleep up to ten people and the others can accommodate four to five. They are well-equipped and the garden has a sandpit, a trampoline and other play equipment. There is a launderette. In addition there are two houses available and they are a couple of miles from the hotel. The large one can sleep nine or ten people and the smaller one four people.

The facilities of the hotel are available to guests, and cots and high chairs, central heating and bed linen are provided. The electricity is metered and you must provide your own towels. The rents vary from £120 to £820 a week.

North Berwick, Lothian   map 11
BELHAVEN HOTEL, Westgate – ☎ *North Berwick (0620) 3009.*

Follow the one-way system along the High Street and straight on to Westgate. This substantial, double-fronted Victorian house has many advantages for families, and especially so if they are golf enthusiasts, since several of the rooms have lovely views across the golf course to the Firth of Forth. The residents' lounge has the same panoramic views across the links.

This is very much a family hotel with three family rooms, a cot and a couple of high chairs; and the friendly owners are willing to do a spot of baby sitting in the evenings. There are plenty of board games in the hotel, plus a small snooker table. Gardens lie to the front and rear of the hotel and the beach is only a short walk across the golf course. Apart from the local beach there are several others in the area, and Gullane, overlooked by the famous Muirfield links, is particularly recommended.

Keen golfers should note that the Belhaven offers a mid-week golfing package: four nights, half board plus five days golf at three different courses. Great value from £115.

Nearby: Apart from the beaches and the golf there is an enormous amount to do and see in this part of Scotland. Edinburgh, with its great variety of sights to see, is not so far away, and closer at hand there are Tantallon Castle, Dirleton Castle and Hailes Castle, the John Muir Country Park, Preston Mill, the Motor Museum near Aberlady, the Museum of Flight and the Duke of Hamilton's house, Lennoxlove.

DINNER (6.30pm) £8
Children: own menu, half portions
£ low
Children: cot free; £7 from 2 to 7 years; £9 from 8 to 11; £14 thereafter
Facilities: 1 cot and 2 high chairs; baby listening can be arranged
8 rooms, 3 family   Open all year
No credit cards accepted   No smoking in dining room
🅿 – on street

If you wish to recommend an establishment to the Guide please write to us – report forms are at the back of the book. We need your help to extend and improve the guide.

Norton, Shropshire map 6

HUNDRED HOUSE HOTEL – ☎ *Norton (095 271) 353.*

On the A442 between Bridgnorth and Wellington.

This hotel and pub has been renovated and adapted with great style by the Phillips family. You enter a bright and airy reception area, with a tiled floor, exposed brick walls, doors with stained glass panels, and bunches of dried flowers and herbs hanging from the ceiling.

The style is continued in the various rooms which make up the bar and restaurant areas. There is a lovely high-ceilinged room with a Colebrookdale cast-iron range and families can sit here together. There are windows on to the sizeable garden, shaded by trees. The two donkeys, Gerrard and Susan, are still on hand to crop the lawns.

The large bar has cast-iron cooking pots and other utensils hanging from the beamed ceilings – a suitable reminder of the old industries of this region, where nearby Ironbridge is regarded as one of the cradles of the Industrial Revolution. The museums there are well worth a visit.

The bar is on two levels, and families can relax at the tables in the eating area which is notable for a huge fireplace. There is a great emphasis on food here, and the menu certainly looks enticing. Some of the produce will come from the hotel's own vegetable garden: mange-tout and asparagus perhaps, as well as the herbs.

It is good to report that food is available throughout the day here from Monday to Saturday, and during the usual Sunday pub opening hours.

The bedrooms are furnished and decorated with great style, and they include a high proportion of family rooms.

Nearby: There is no shortage of entertainment in this part of the world. The beautiful countryside of South Shropshire can easily be reached and a trip through Ludlow to Stokesay Castle and Clun and back through the Carding Mill Valley is recommended. The famous Ironbridge Gorge Museum is close at hand, as is the Midland Motor Museum and the Aerospace Museum at Cosford. The Severn Valley Railway runs from Bridgnorth.

BAR SNACKS (11.30am–2.30pm & 6–10pm) £2–13: savoury pancakes, ratatouille, rack of lamb, steaks, lasagne;
DINNER (7–9.30pm) £18: sole & fennel mousse, rabbit pie, pudding or cheese
Children: own menu, half portions
£ high
Best Bargain Break £95 per person, 2 nights – dinner, b & b
Children: free up to 16 years
Facilities: 4 cots and 4 high chairs, and a baby listening system
9 rooms, 5 family   Open all year
- Ale – Phillips, Flowers, Marston's and guests

Access/AmEx/Visa   No music   🅿 – own car park

Also recommended in the Family Welcome Pub & Restaurant Guide.

Nowton, Nr Bury St Edmunds, Suffolk map 8
HIGH GREEN HOUSE – ☎ *Sicklesmere (0284) 386 291.*

Off the A134 south of Bury St Edmunds.

The quack and waddle of friendly geese might greet you at the garden gate, from where you will see this splendid house. The original part was built in the 16th century and has a steep roof and very tall central chimneys; and the later additions are Victorian.

The house retains its nice wooden doors and the sitting room is particularly attractive with wooden pillars in the walls, a beamed ceiling, a huge open fireplace, and plenty of comfortable chairs.

Several of the bedrooms can take a cot or an extra bed, including one with a four-poster bed – a lovely room in the old part of the house.

The house is surrounded by a large lawned garden. There is an old covered well in the front garden, and apple trees to one side. The lawns are walled or fenced, but there is a pond at the side, so the children must be careful. But there is masses of space to play, and the house is surrounded by open countryside, where there are pleasant walks.

Nearby: This is good fishing country, and if you are in the mood for sightseeing, Ickworth Mansion is nearby; as is Norton Tropical Bird Gardens, and West Stow Anglo-Saxon Village. The delightful old towns of Lavenham and Long Melford, Cavendish Manor Vineyards and Clare Castle Country Park are a short drive away.

✗ DINNER (7.30pm) £9
Children: high teas
£ low
Best Bargain Break £70 per person 3 nights – dinner, b & b
Children: babies free; 20% discount from 2 to 12 years
Facilities: 2 cots and 1 high chair, and baby listening
5 rooms, 1 family   No credit cards accepted
Open all year   No music   🅿 – ample

Hotels were asked to quote 1992 prices, but not all were able to give an accurate forecast. Make sure that you check tariffs when you book.

Onich, by Fort William, Highland map 12

ALLT-NAN-ROS HOTEL – ☎ *Onich (08553) 210.*

Just east of Onich village on the A82.

Beautifully situated by Loch Linnhe this hotel was once a Victorian manor house, and it has lovely views of the mountains and towards the Isle of Mull. All sorts of land-based and aquatic pastimes can be arranged, and this hotel is very much a haven for walkers.

There is a large, rambling garden at the front and the side of the hotel and you have superb views of the loch. It has terraced lawns and trees, with streams and ponds, and there are swings in one of the wooded areas.

Nearby: Any form of water sport can be arranged and some tuition to accompany them. The area is a fisherman's paradise: for salmon or trout, sea fishing or coarse. Walking, climbing, golf and pony trekking can all be arranged and there is a leisure centre in Fort William. If you fancy some sightseeing Glencoe and Ben Nevis are close, and the West Highland Museum is in Fort William. The children will certainly enjoy a visit to the Sea Life Centre near Oban.

✗ DINNER (7–8.30pm) £20: Stilton quiche, soup, fillets of hare with red cabbage, pudding or cheese
Children: own menu, half portions
£ medium
Best Bargain Break £154 per person, 3 nights – dinner, b & b
Children: free to age 3; £8 from age 4–12; £16 from age 13–16
Facilities: 3 cots and 2 high chairs; baby listening through the phones
21 rooms, 1 family   Access/AmEx/Diners/Visa
Open all year except November   No smoking in dining room
🅿 – own car park

ONICH HOTEL (Consort) – ☎ *Onich (08553) 214.*

On the A82 in the village.

This white-painted hotel, with its various modern additions, stands in an exceptional position on the shores of Loch Linnhe and there is a multitude of activities to pursue on land and water.

The hotel has a pool table, and there are swings and a climbing frame on the lawn in full view of the restaurant and sun room. The hotel garden is very attractive; the lawns with their trees and flower beds go down to the shore of the loch. Picnic lunches are available and coin operated washing machines and driers are provided for guests.

It is a friendly and welcoming place, and they even have real ale.

Nearby: Fishing on sea, loch and river and all sorts of water sports can be arranged, as can pony trekking, golf and cruises from Oban. The leisure centre in Fort William has swimming, squash and tennis. The children will relish a visit to the Sea Life Centre near Oban, and Glencoe and Ben Nevis are near at hand. There are many routes for hill walkers and an excellent leaflet maps them out.

BAR MEALS (12–9pm) £1–9: herring & salad, sirloin steak, haddock & chips, cold buffet, lasagne;
DINNER (7–9pm) £14: ham & pepper salad, soup, roast gigot of lamb, pudding or cheese
Children: half portions
£ high
Best Bargain Break £80 per person 2 nights – dinner, b & b
Children: cot £2.50; 75% reduction from 2 to 5; 50% reduction from 6 to 12; 25% reduction from 13 to 16 years
Facilities: 3 cots and 2 high chairs; and baby listening to every room
27 rooms, 6 family   Access/AmEx/Diners/Visa
• Ale – Arrols   Open all year
P – own car park

Ottery St Mary, Devon   map 2
FLUXTON FARM HOTEL – ☎ *Ottery St Mary (0404) 812 818.*

On the Tipton St John Road, which runs south of Ottery St Mary.
This is a handsome 16th century Devon longhouse, in lovely farmland surroundings. It is situated in the Otter valley, and most of the rooms have splendid views to friendly wooded hills across the valley. Although it is no longer a farm, the owners keep some ducks, chickens, and cats.
The delightful gardens spread across a couple of acres, with a stream running

through, and are partly enclosed by an old stone wall. Adults can take their ease on the wide lawns, shaded perhaps by one of the many trees, while the children can have rides on a little railway which runs through the grounds. There is also a trout pond and fishing can be arranged on the Otter.

There are two charming and comfortable lounges, and it is good to report that one of them is non-smoking. The dining room has a large open fire and a beamed ceiling, and there is a small bar.

Nearby: It is an attractive area for holiday makers, with pretty countryside, and the coast is very close with an excellent choice of clean and sandy beaches. Children will no doubt be interested in nearby Bicton Park, the Donkey Sanctuary and Farway Countryside Park. The amazing building, "A la Ronde", near Exmouth is also well worth a visit, as is the Maritime Museum in Exeter, and Killerton House. On the other side of the Exe Estuary you can visit the Dawlish Warren Nature Reserve.

DINNER (6.45pm) £7
Children: own menu, half portions
£ low
Children: babies free; one third of full rate up to 5 years; half price thereafter
Facilities: 1 cot and 1 high chair; baby listening by arrangement
12 rooms, 2 family   Open all year
No smoking in one lounge or dining room
No credit cards   No music
P – own car park

Parkmill, West Glamorgan   map 1

PARC-LE-BREOS RIDING AND HOLIDAY CENTRE – ☎ Penmaen (0792) 371 636.

Off the A4118 west of Swansea.

A spacious Victorian farmhouse which is situated on the delightful Gower Peninsula. It is surrounded by woodland which gives the place a quiet and secluded atmosphere, but the many attractions of this popular holiday area are within easy reach.

Although Parc-Le-Breos is a pony trekking centre you can opt to use it just as a holiday base, or the children can go off on their ponies for the day while the parents do other things. It seems an ideal situation for both parents and children. There are good facilities in and around the house with a large garden where the children can play and where barbecues are held in summer, a television lounge, a disco and a games room with table tennis and a pool table. In the spacious dining room you will sample home grown food, since most of the fruit and vegetables are grown on site.

Nearby: There is a long stretch of excellent beaches: Port Enon, Oxwich Bay,

Three Cliffs (with the ruins of Pennard Castle up above), Pwlldu Bay and Caswell Bay. Two nature reserves add to the interest: the South Gower Coast Reserve stretches from Port Eynon to Worms Head at Rhossili and further east is the Oxwich National Nature Reserve. A little further afield you can visit Penscynor Wildlife Park, Aberdulais Falls, Afan Argoed Country Park, Margam Country Park and the Glamorgan Nature Centre. Nature lovers are well catered for, and so are those interested in fishing, golf, and water sports.

✕ DINNER (6pm) £6
Children: half portions
£ low
Children: half price to 8 years
Facilities: 2 cots and 2 high chairs, and baby listening by arrangement
9 rooms, 6 family   Open all year
No credit cards accepted   No music
Unlicensed   **P** – ample

Peebles, Borders   map 11
CRINGLETIE HOUSE HOTEL – ☎ *Eddleston (072 13) 233.*

Two and a half miles north of Peebles on the A703.

This delightful hotel has been recommended in the Family Welcome Guide from its first edition onwards and has always been a favourite of ours. The house was built in 1861 for the Wolfe Murray family and one of those ances-

tors, Colonel Alexander Murray, had accepted the surrender of Quebec on the death of General Wolfe in 1759.

Cringletie is a most appealing and distinguished sandstone mansion and shows all the exuberance of the Victorian age with its high windows, pointed towers and tall chimneys. It is set in nearly thirty acres of beautiful gardens against a background of gentle hills. You can certainly relax in such a setting, and the children can make use of the play area.

The public rooms are elegantly furnished and well-proportioned, and there is an interesting choice of food; it is not surprising that the hotel has been recommended in the "Good Food Guide" for twenty years. A couple of acres of kitchen garden ensures that the ingredients for your meals are fresh.

Nearby: You are only about twenty miles from Edinburgh with its many attractions. Almost on the doorstep you can visit Neidpath Castle, Kailzie Gardens, Traquair House, Dawyck Botanic Garden and the John Buchan Centre. You are surrounded by lovely countryside if you like walking; and horse riding, fishing and golf are all readily available.

LUNCH (1–1.45pm) £11: smoked haddock mousse, lambs' liver, pudding or cheese;
DINNER (7.30–8.30pm) £23: prawn pot, casseroled venison, pudding or cheese
Children: half portions
£ high
Best Bargain Break £53 per person per night – dinner, b & b
Children: cot £2.50; extra bed £12.50
Facilities: 3 cots and 2 high chairs; and baby listening
12 rooms, 2 family   Open early March to 1 Jan
Access/Visa   No music
No smoking in dining room and one lounge
P – own car park

Also recommended in the Family Welcome Pub & Restaurant Guide.

PEEBLES HOTEL HYDRO – ☎ *Peebles (0721) 20602.*

On the main road.

A gigantic Victorian spa hotel, in thirty acres of grounds, whose portals you need never leave because everything you want is on site. The huge chandeliers, glass domed roofs, and miles of corridor hark back to a more expansive age.

The many and varied facilities include an excellent fenced-in children's playground, a 'commando course' for older children, two squash courts, badminton, three hard tennis courts, a volleyball court, a pitch and putt course, a putting green and an indoor heated pool in the leisure centre, which has been named 'Bubbles'. Sensibly there is a playpen in the Ladies changing room.

There is a vast games room with three table tennis tables, two snooker tables

PENALLY

(for over 18's only), table football and space invaders, and in addition a playroom which is supervised and has toys, a slide, a rocking horse and a video. During the summer season the hotel has a number of full-time children's supervisors; and there are masses of events organised right through the day for children and for adults; plus dances and discotheques almost every night.

Nearby: There are dozens of golf courses and excellent places to walk, ride and fish. Within easy reach you will find Kailzie Gardens, Traquair House, Neidpath Castle, the John Buchan Centre, Dawyck Botanic Garden, Bowhill and Sir Walter Scott's house at Abbotsford.

✕ BUBBLES (12.30–3.30pm & 7–9.30pm) £1–5: paté, salads, beef Stroganoff, dish of the day, grilled salmon;
LUNCH (12.45–2pm) £11: smoked mackerel, cold buffet, pudding or cheese;
DINNER (7.30–9pm) £16: smoked salmon mousse, beef Stroganoff, pudding or cheese
Children: high teas, half portions
£ high
Best Bargain Break £52 per person per night – dinner, b & b
Children: from £5 to £17 (includes breakfast & high tea)
Facilities: plenty of cots and high chairs; and baby listening via the telephones
137 rooms, 25 family   Access/AmEx/Diners/Visa
Open all year   • Ale – Greenmantle
P – own car park

Penally, Nr Tenby, Dyfed   map 1
PENALLY ABBEY HOTEL – ☎ *Tenby (0834) 3033.*

Just off the A4139 west of Tenby.

This delectable 18th century stone manor house, built on the site of an ancient abbey, sits high above the coast road and from its windows and gardens you can see Tenby golf course and Carmarthen Bay beyond. Indeed, the sandy beach is a ten minute walk across the links (reduced green fees available).

The stone walls and gabled windows house some beautifully proportioned and spacious rooms, including a very attractive lounge and dining room, and the pointed arches of the windows are echoed by the same unusual design for the doors. If you fancy a swim, there is a small indoor heated pool; and five acres of rambling lawned garden, with a ruined 13th century chapel, will appeal to the more sedentary guests. The children will also find a Shetland pony in an adjoining field.

This is a lovely and relaxing small hotel in a delightful part of Wales.

Nearby: Tenby is a busy seaside resort with sandy beaches, of which there is a wide choice including Manorbier Bay, Barafundle Bay (owned by the National Trust) and Broad Haven. There are several castles to see: Pembroke, Tenby, Manorbier and Carew, for example; and the children will relish a visit to Manor House Wildlife Park. Caldey Island, with its abbey and Cistercian monastery, can also be visited.

DINNER (7.30pm onwards) £20: spinach & salmon roulade, baked ham, pudding or cheese
Children: half portions
£ medium
Best Bargain Break £40 per person per night – dinner, b & b
Children: £8 to age 5; half price from age 6–14
Facilities: 2 cots and 2 high chairs; baby listening by arrangement
10 rooms, 3 family   Access/Visa
Open all year
P – small car park and on road

Penrith, Cumbria   map 9

NORTH LAKES GATEWAY HOTEL (Shire Inns) – ☎ Penrith (0768) 68111.

Just off exit 40 of the M6.

This hotel was built only a few years ago, and presents a fairly functional face to the multitude of traffic which passes its location close to junction 40 of the M6. But the interior belies these first impressions, and the high vaulted ceilings, with wooden beams, stone fireplaces and excellent furnishings give a smart and spacious tone to the hotel.

The leisure club, unlike many others which lay claim to the description, offers proper facilities and has plenty of space. The pool is sizeable and superbly done under a vaulted pine roof and includes a children's pool; there are two excellent glass-backed squash courts; and an exercise room well-equipped with bikes and other good quality equipment. There is also a snooker room.

The hotel has six family rooms. Apart from two parents, they can accommodate up to three children with bunk beds and a convertible sofa. Since children under 14 stay free these rooms, charged at the standard rate, represent pretty good value if you are on the move with several youngsters.

Unusually for a hotel of this size, proper draught ale is served – a perfect way to round off a busy day in the Lake District or after a couple of hours in the leisure club.

Nearby: Penrith itself is an interesting town, as is Appleby just down the A66. Beautiful Ullswater is on the doorstep while the southern Lakes with all their attractions are not far away: Grasmere, Belle Isle, Lake Windermere. The children will enjoy a visit to Hill Top, the home of Beatrix Potter. Nearer to hand for the hotel is Lowther Park with its nature trails and adventure playground.

BAR MEALS (12–2pm) £4–8: pork with peppers & cream, steak & mushroom pie, meat platter;
LUNCH (12.30–2pm, not Saturdays) £10: clams Louisiana, roast rack of lamb, pudding or cheese;
DINNER (7–9.30pm) £16: hot garlic buttered seafood, daube of lamb Avignon, pudding or cheese
Children: own menu, half portions
£ high
Best Bargain Break £114 per person 2 nights – dinner, b & b
Children: free up to 14 years
Facilities: 5 cots and 5 high chairs; baby listening system for every room
85 rooms, 6 family, 6 sets interconnecting
Access/AmEx/Diners/Visa   Open all year
• Ale – Thwaites   **P** – own car park

Pentire, Nr Newquay, Cornwall   map 1

PORTH ENODOC HOTEL, 4 Esplanade Road – ☎ *Newquay (0637) 872 372.*

West of Newquay on Fistral Beach.

This is an excellent hotel in a marvellous setting alongside the wide sweep of

PENTIRE

Fistral Beach and on the edge of a golf course. A raised patio area is built around the front of the hotel and beyond that the lawned garden.

The comprehensive facilities of busy, touristy Newquay are within walking distance, or you can stay put and enjoy the relative peace and relaxation of the hotel and the surrounding area. Virtually all the rooms have views of the sea and the golf course, and are brightly and comfortably furnished.

Nearby: There is a wide selection of good beaches – Hayle Bay, Harlyn Bay, Bedruthan Steps, Watergate Bay, Newquay's own excellent beaches where major surfing championships are regularly held, Crantock and so on. There is much else to do and see in the vicinity: a zoo at Newquay, a leisure park at St. Agnes, Dairyland Farm Park, the World in Miniature and the Lappa Valley Railway.

DINNER (6.45pm) £7
Children: half portions
£ low
Best Bargain Break £41 per person, 2 nights – dinner, b & b
Children: cot £5; half price from 2 to 8; three-quarters price from 8 to 14
Facilities: 2 cots and 2 high chairs; and baby listening system
16 rooms, 6 family   Open Easter to November
No smoking in dining room   No credit cards
P – own car park   No music

Please let us have reports – good or bad – on any establishments listed in the Guide as soon as possible after your visit.

Pluckley, Nr Ashford, Kent   map 4
ELVEY FARM – ☎ *Pluckley (023 384) 442.*

Off the A20 and west of Ashford.

At the end of a quiet country lane you will find this splendid example of a Kentish yeoman's farmhouse. It was built in the 16th century in the familiar oak beamed and ragstone pattern, and the various buildings have been utilised to provide excellent accommodation. The oast house, for example, has two twin-bedded rooms in the roundel; the stable block has double, twin and family rooms; and the barn has two double bedrooms.

The conversion has been carried out with great care without sacrificing any of the original features of the house, and you would not imagine that such a secluded spot is only a few miles from the M20. Elvey is still a working farm of 75 acres, and guests are welcome to explore the farm. It is H.E. Bates country and you should certainly see some darling buds in May.

The lounge is very comfortable and French windows lead out to a sun terrace with the lawned gardens beyond, with various play areas for the children.

Nearby: This is an excellent base from which to enjoy the many attractions of this part of the country. Wild life enthusiasts will head for Port Lympne Zoo Park or Howletts, and railway buffs can enjoy both the Kent and East Sussex and the Romney, Hythe and Dymchurch railways. Sissinghurst Castle Gardens, Scotney Castle Gardens, Bedgebury Pinetum, Leeds Castle and the historic town of Canterbury are all within easy reach.

 DINNER (7.30pm approx) by arrangement (£14 approx)
Children: half portions
£ medium
Children: cot £5; £15 from 3 to 16 years
Facilities: 3 cots and 2 high chairs; baby listening by arrangement
10 rooms, 6 family   Open all year
Access/Visa   No music
P – ample

Nr Polperro, Cornwall   map 1
LANLAWREN FARM – ☎ *Polperro (0503) 72121.*

SC   *Three miles west of Polperro.*

Lanlawren means the valley of the foxes and the various cottages and apartments have been converted from the granary, barns and stables that once formed part of Lanlawren Manor, an estate which dates from the 13th century.

The apartments and cottages at Lanlawren can accommodate from two to six people. The buildings retain their original stone walls and are well-equipped and comfortably furnished. They all have storage heaters for winter use and, in every case except one (Culver House) have open fires. Many of the properties have exposed stone walls and ancient wooden beams. On a practical level, washing machines are provided. There is room to roam in several acres of lawned and wooded gardens which lead down to a little stream.

Lanlawren has a great bonus for guests with the presence of a leisure club with a swimming pool, sauna, spa bath, solarium, exercise equipment and a games room. The children have their own play area, including sandpits; barbecues are also provided; and there is a small library and a collection of indoor games.

There are also two cottages in Polperro itself, Willy Wilcox and Quay Cottages. They are close to the harbour wall and look across it to the beach and the water. They have the traditional interiors of exposed beams and open fires and each has three double bedrooms. Guests are welcome to use all the facilities at Lanlawren.

You can have a splendid family holiday here, in winter or summer, and you should note that short off-peak breaks are available.

Nearby: The National Trust have the coastal area in their care and there are many delightful walks. There is no shortage of safe, sandy bays either and Lansallos, Lantic and Lantivet Bays are very close and you might even see some grey seals. There are many attractions nearby: Lanhydrock House, Dobwalls Theme Park, Pencarrow House, Newquay Zoo, Trerice House and the Dairyland Farm Park. All sorts of pursuits can be arranged including water sports, fishing, golf, riding, tennis, etc.

Units: 15
Rent: £120 to £700 a week
Other costs: electricity is metered (but not the heating)
Heating: central heating and log fires
Plenty of cots and high chairs
Open all year

Pontfaen, Newport, Nr Fishguard, Dyfed map 5

GELLI FAWR COUNTRY HOUSE – ☎ Newport (0239) 820 343.

H/SC *Off the B4313 south of Fishguard.*

This old and well-established Welsh hill farm has been converted into a hotel with ten bedrooms, and there are self-catering apartments built in the original coach house and mill house. The old mill wheel is still in place.

It is in a lovely spot in the Gwaun Valley at the base of the Preseli Hills and is situated in the Pembrokeshire National Park. It has its own large stretch of pasture and gardens, twelve acres in which the adults can relax and the children can play. There are plenty of grassy areas, an abundance of trees, picnic and play areas, and goats, dogs and cats – a paradise for young children. There is also a heated swimming pool, with a paddling pool alongside.

There are two family rooms here and plenty of cots and high chairs, as well as a plug-in baby listening system. There are various board games in the house and a good selection of children's books. The owners run a food school at the hotel, and the cooking, both traditional and vegetarian, is of a high standard. Good news for families is that children's meals are served through the day until 6 o'clock, and consist mainly of fresh local produce.

Nearby: This is a splendid place for fishing in the many rivers and lakes and in the sea, and for riding, surfing, rough shooting, walking, bird watching and other country pursuits. There are some excellent beaches along the Pembrokeshire coast and a wealth of other things to do and see. Wild life enthusiasts have several parks in the vicinity: at Cardigan, at St. David's (the Marine Life Centre), and further afield at Tenby. There are castles to see at Tenby, Manorbier, Carew and Pembroke, and railway enthusiasts can make a trip to the Gwili Steam Railway near Carmarthen. Oakwood Park at Narberth offers lots of entertainment for the whole family.

BAR MEALS (12–2pm & 5–6pm) £3–5: seafood pie, omelettes, lasagne, cottage pie;
DINNER (7.30pm) £16: lovage soup, roast loin of pork, apple & date crumble
Children: own menu, half portions
£ low
Best Bargain Break £70 per person, 2 nights – dinner, b & b
Children: free up to 12 years

Facilities: 3 cots and 3 high chairs; and a baby listening system
10 rooms, 2 family   Open all year
Access/Visa   **P** – plenty

SELF-CATERING

The Coach House, an attractive stone building, overlooks the swimming pool and has two apartments, each with three bedrooms. There are another seven apartments in the Mill House, another lovely stone building. Some have two and others three bedrooms and several of the apartments have bed settees as well. Cots and high chairs are provided, as is central heating, but an additional charge is made for electricity. The utility room has a washing machine, drier and ironing board. The rents are very reasonable: from £90 to £440 a week.

Redmile, Leics   map 7

PEACOCK FARM GUEST HOUSE – ☎ *Bottesford (0949) 42475.*

Off the A52 west of Grantham.

This farmhouse was built early in the 18th century, and is no longer part of a working farm. Instead it offers most of the facilities necessary for an enjoyable family break or holiday. As you enter the property you will see a big lawn, with several apple trees, and a swing and a see-saw. There is a small covered swimming pool, a summer house, a play room with table tennis and a pool table, and several bikes for guests to use.

A bar area sits alongside one of the two dining rooms, and there is a small patio where you can enjoy a drink on summer days. The guests' sitting room, with windows on two sides, is bright and comfortably furnished with sofas and easy chairs.

A great advantage of Peacock Farm is the presence of four family-sized rooms, and the rooms on the top floor, with sloping ceilings under the rafters, are especially attractive. In the grounds is an excellent family unit, with two beds, two bunk beds and its own bathroom.

The cooking is based on fresh local produce, and the fruit, vegetables and herbs will mostly come from the garden. Real ale fans will be pleased to hear that the bar serves Ruddles bitter.

Nearby: The famous Belvoir Castle is just up the road, and indeed can be seen from several of the rooms in the farmhouse. The interesting town of Grantham is just a short drive away, with Belton House and Woolsthorpe Manor, where Sir Isaac Newton was born, not very far away. Grimsthorpe Castle is a short drive away and west towards Nottingham you will find Colwick Country Park, with its water sports, fishing and a nature reserve; Green's Mill; and the Holme Pierrepoint water sports centre.

DINNER (7–9pm) £11: stuffed pepper, rump steak, pudding or cheese

Children: own menu, half portions
£ low
Children: cot £5; two thirds of the adult rate from 3 to 10 years
Facilities: 2 cots and 2 high chairs; baby listening and a patrol
7 rooms, 5 family   Open all year
Access/AmEx/Visa   • Ale – Ruddles
P – own car park

Rhu, Strathclyde   map 11

ROSSLEA HALL HOTEL (Best Western), Ferry Road – ☎ *Rhu (0436) 820 684.*

On the A814.

Built in the familiar mid-19th century baronial style and extended in the early 1970s, this hotel stands in quiet wooded surroundings on the shores of Gareloch, and a little away from the village. Its connections with the whisky trade are kept up, since each bedroom is named after a distillery.

The gardens are extensive, and indeed elegant with the lawns sheltered by high hedges and mature trees, with fine displays of flowers and shrubs.

On Sundays, parents who want to have a meal in peace can leave their children (from 2 to 12 years) in the care of a trained nanny from 11.30am to 3.30pm. The charge of £1.50 covers their food, toys, and video cartoons.

Nearby: This is a splendid base from which to explore this part of Scotland. Apart from the various water sports which are available it is a great spot for walking, golf, riding and other activities. It is well placed for sight seeing too. The Kilmun Arboretum is close, as is the Younger Botanic Garden. You can quickly reach Inveraray Castle, and a number of country parks – at Ballock Castle and Culcreuch Castle for example. The Brian Marshall Lodge visitor centre and Loch Katrine are a bit further away, and finally Glasgow, with its many attractions, can easily be reached.

✕ BAR SNACKS (12.30–2.30pm & 5.30–7.30pm) £1–8: lasagne verde, salads, burgers, Highlander pie, plaice;
DINNER (7–9.30pm) £15: egg mayonnaise & smoked salmon, roast lamb, pudding
Children: own menu, half portions
£ high
Best Bargain Break £80 per person, 2 nights – dinner, b & b
Children: free up to 12 years
Facilities: a cot and a high chair; and a baby listening line

39 rooms, 3 family   Access/AmEx/Diners/Visa
P – own large car park

Richmond, North Yorks   map 10

KINGS HEAD HOTEL, Market Place – ☎ *Richmond (0748) 850 220.*

In the town centre.

This fine Georgian building looks out over the famous cobbled market place, one of the largest in Britain; alleyways, or wynds, lead off it to some splendid old houses. Up above towers the great keep of the 12th century castle.

It is an attractive town and the Kings Head suits it well. The hotel has been recently refurbished but none of its character has been lost; there is some excellent antique furniture and a fine collection of grandfather clocks. The comfortable dining room, on the first floor, looks out over the square.

The bedrooms have each been decorated in different styles, and part of the charm of the hotel is its relaxed atmosphere. All members of the family are made welcome here.

Nearby: The famous castle is well worth a visit, as is the restored Georgian theatre and the Museum of the Green Howards. The area is wonderful walking territory and the hotel runs special weekend walking breaks in Swaledale. There is a great selection of places to visit within an easy drive: Bolton Castle, Jervaulx Abbey, Fountains Abbey, Stump Cross Caverns, Bolton Abbey, Malham Cove and Ripley Castle.

BAR MEALS (12–2pm) £1–4: ploughman's, filled jacket potatoes, cold meat platter, dish of the day;
DINNER (7–9.15pm) £15: smoked mackerel mousse, chicken supreme, pudding
Children: half portions
£ high
Best Bargain Break £78 per person, 2 nights – dinner, b & b
Children: free up to 16 years
Facilities: 4 cots and 4 high chairs; baby listening system
28 rooms, 1 family   Open all year
Access/AmEx/Diners/Visa   • Ale – Theakston's
No smoking in restaurant, coffee lounge and some bedrooms
P – own car park at rear

Hotels were asked to quote 1992 prices, but not all were able to give an accurate forecast. Make sure that you check tariffs when you book.

Rock, Nr Wadebridge, Cornwall   map 1
GLENEGLOS HOTEL, Trewint Lane – ☏ *Trebetherick (0208) 862 369.*

Close to the centre of the village.

The village faces south across the bay to Padstow, whence a ferry has run since the 14th century. It's an inappropriately named place because a feature of this coast is the long stretches of sandy beach: Polzeath beach for surfers and swimmers, and Daymer Bay where children can cavort in safety.

The hotel, a three-storey, white-washed building, was probably once a farmhouse and now offers a comfortable base for holidaymakers. There is a pleasant lounge with comfortable chairs and sofas (and books and board games are provided), a small bar and a separate dining room. From some of the bedrooms you have views of the estuary.

At the side and the back of the house there are lawned areas with picnic tables and chairs, and a lily pond. You can play swingball and bowls on the lawns, and open fields stretch out around you. A sizeable vegetable plot ensures that your food is good and fresh.

Nearby: This is a pleasant, small hotel in an excellent holiday area, with lots of diversions for holidaymakers. Apart from the many sandy beaches there is good fishing to be had, golf at St Enodoc's, pony trekking and water skiing. Bodmin Moor is within easy reach, as is Pencarrow, a mansion notable for its superb collection of paintings and china. There are tropical bird gardens in Padstow, and further afield a zoo in Newquay and a farm park near Bodmin and Lanhydrock House to visit.

DINNER (6.30pm) £11
Children: own menu
£ low
Children: free up to 5 years; half price from 5 to 12; 25% discount thereafter
Facilities: 2 cots and 2 high chairs; baby listening system
6 rooms, 3 family   Open February to December
Access/Visa   🅿 – own car park

Rockcliffe, Dumfries & Galloway   map 11
BARON'S CRAIG HOTEL – ☏ *Rockcliffe (055) 663 225.*

Follow the sign to Rockcliffe from the A710.

This delightful granite built hotel, with its unobtrusive modern additions, stands in lovely grounds overlooking the Solway and Rough Firth. From the elegant dining room and the airy, high-ceilinged lounges you have splendid views of the water and the wooded hills.

The hotel is set in a dozen acres of woodland, with immaculate lawns and colourful displays of flowers, especially when the massed ranks of rhododendrons are in full bloom. You can sit here at peace or perhaps take some gentle exercise on the putting green.

Nearby: This is a most attractive and unspoiled part of Scotland and there are miles of sandy beach around Southerness. In the vicinity of the hotel there is plenty to do in the way of sailing, fishing, golf (at Southerness, for example), wind surfing, horse riding and walking. If sightseeing is on the agenda there is plenty of scope: Threave Garden, Caerlaverock Castle and the nearby nature reserve, Broughton House and the Gem Rock Museum at Creetown.

✘ BAR LUNCHES (12.30–2.30pm) £1–7: fresh salmon mayonnaise & salad, hot dish of the day, ploughman's, smoked mackerel & salad;
LUNCH (1–2.30pm) £12: soup, smoked salmon, pudding or cheese;
DINNER (7–9pm) £19: potted shrimps, roast venison, pudding, cheese
Children: own menu, half portions
£ high
Best Bargain Break £47 per person per night – dinner, b & b
Children: free up to 12 years
Facilities: 4 cots and 4 high chairs; 3 baby listening lines
26 rooms, 2 family   Access/Visa
Closed end-Oct to Easter   No music
P – own car park

Rogeston, Nr Haverfordwest, Dyfed   map 5
ROGESTON COTTAGES – ☎ *Broad Haven (0437) 781 373*

SC   *Two miles off the A487 to St. David's.*
The owners of Rogeston Cottages, Mr and Mrs Rees, give full and accurate directions in their brochure and you will need them because they are hidden

ROGESTON

away in the delightful coastal countryside of Pembrokeshire.

If you want peace and quiet in beautiful surroundings, this is an excellent choice; and, as a base, Rogeston offers much to do and see in the surrounding area.

The cottages were made from 18th century farm buildings and are grouped round the old cattle yard in two blocks. With one exception they are all single storey and the original stone walls are complemented by wooden beams and panelling, pine furniture and fittings. The cottages have been converted in a generous style. For example, the dried flowers and herbs which appear in abundance and the skilful decorations make such a difference. A great effort is made to ensure that guests feel at home.

The cottages all have a combined sitting and dining room and a bedroom. A couch converts easily into an extra double bed. The kitchens are extremely well-equipped and central heating is provided. The Old Granary, built towards the end of the 19th century, has accommodation for larger families or groups. Each of the two floors has three double bedrooms.

A fully equipped laundry room is provided, and if you tire of cooking a good choice of cooked meals is available: chicken and broccoli crumble, lamb rigatoni, cauliflower and pasta bake for example. All the dishes are low in fat.

Each house has its own private patio but the communal gardens are delightful with smooth lawns and wonderful views of the encircling countryside. There is plenty to do: there is an excellent grass badminton court, swing ball and even a boule pitch. Behind the Old Granary there is another lawn with a children's sand pit. Above all, the children will enjoy the spacious grounds and they can made friends with the animals: the ducks and hens and the Jersey cows.

Nearby: All the pleasures of the countryside lie at your feet – walking (Mr and Mrs Rees can help you to plan your routes), horse riding, fishing in sea or stream and facilities for water sports, golf, swimming, tennis and squash are all available. The nearest beach is Druidston Haven, which is a lovely sandy bay. There are castles galore to see, Pembroke, Manorbier and Carew, for example, and St David's Cathedral is close. There is a small Marine Life Centre at St David's and a butterfly farm.

Units: 7
Rent: £147 to £465 per week
Other costs: none
Central heating: provided
As many cots and high chairs as required
Open all year

If you wish to recommend an establishment to the Guide please write to us – report forms are at the back of the book. We need your help to extend and improve the guide.

Rosedale Abbey, North Yorks   map 10
BELL END FARM – ☎ Lastingham (07515) 431.

SC   *North west of Pickering. The owners provide detailed directions.*

Bell End Farm opened its doors to visitors in 1988 and is a triumph for Richard Castle's enterprise and imagination. A series of dilapidated barns and other farm buildings have been transformed into eight splendid holiday homes which have won three awards. The cottages form an L-shape and are built of stone under mellow red pantile roofs. Excellent use has been made of stone interior walls and exposed wooden beams, and the cottages have been furnished and equipped to a very high standard. It is pleasing to report, for example, that electricity and heating, linen and towels are all provided within the cost.

The cottages vary in size and can sleep from two to six people, and they are all (with the one exception of Park's Delight) suitable for family occupation. High chairs and cots are provided and the stairs have safety gates at top and bottom. The homes have marvellous views of the beautiful countryside, and several of them are designed with the living areas on the top storey to take full advantage of this.

The facilities at Bell End are exceptional. There are two acres of grounds in which the adults can relax and the children can play. The play area includes a climbing frame, sand pit and swing. Indoors, you will find a heated swimming pool and the thoughtful owner provides a playpen here. On a practical note, a washing machine and a drier are available in the utilities area.

Bell End Farm has been constructed with great flair, and with a grasp of detail which is essential if a family holiday is to be a success: for example you can order a meal in advance for your first evening, and frozen meals are also available.

It was no surprise to learn that Bell End Farm was put in the 'Highly Commended' category by the English Tourist Board. It is a splendid place in a beautiful part of England where everyone, especially families, is made welcome.

Nearby: You are in the heart of the North York Moors with wonderful walks all around you, and there are excellent facilities for horse riding, fishing on the Esk, Derwent, Dove and Rye, and golf. Racing fans have a choice of six well-known venues. It is a very good base if you wish to see the sights: Flamingo Land, Eden Camp, Nunnington Hall, Castle Howard, Shandy Hall, Rievaulx Abbey and Mount Grace Priory are all within easy reach, as are the coastal resorts between Whitby and Scarborough.

Units: 8
Rent: £260 to £755 a week (winter breaks available)
Other costs: none
Heating: night storage
Plenty of cots and high chaairs
Open all year

Rowton, Nr Ironbridge, Shropshire   map 6

CHURCH FARM – ☎ *High Ercall (0952) 770 381.*

Off the A442 north of Telford.

The farmhouse was built of brick in the 17th century and sits in a pretty village a few miles away from the M54. There is a pleasant and homely atmosphere: the lounge is very comfortable with a number of sofas and easy chairs, and the dining room has sliding doors on to a patio. The bedrooms are spacious and well-furnished, including a very large family room and a four poster bedroom, which both have their own bathrooms. Mr and Mrs Evans also have two 6/8 berth caravans for rent.

The well-kept garden has a front lawn big enough to stand an informal family game of football or cricket. For the more sedentary, the garden furniture is put out during the warmer weather and you can sit at peace on the patio or amid the many flowers.

This is a working farm with dairy cows, sheep and pigs, and guests (especially children) are encouraged to join in the farm's activities. They will have willing guides in the owners' two children, who welcome some young company.

Nearby: There is much of interest to see in the neighbourhood, starting with Ironbridge with its various museums which commemorate its industrial heritage. Further south there is the Midland Motor Museum at Bridgnorth and the Severn Valley Railway. A lovely day out in beautiful countryside could take in the route to Ludlow via Clee Hill, then to Clun, Bishop's Castle and Church Stretton.

✗ High teas only (a good choice of pubs and restaurants nearby)
£ low
Children: half price
Facilities: 1 cot and 1 high chair; baby listening by arrangement
4 rooms, 1 family   Open all year
No credit cards   Unlicensed
No smoking in dining room and bedrooms
🅿 – ample

St Andrews, Fife   map 11
RUFFLETS COUNTRY HOUSE HOTEL – ☎ *St Andrews (0334) 72594.*

On the B939 to the west of St Andrews.

This attractive and welcoming hotel has a gorgeous garden which stretches over ten acres and has immaculate lawns, lovely climbing plants and fine displays of flowers. The house was designed by Dundee architect Donald Mills in 1924 and he also masterminded the terraced garden to the south of the building. There are two streams in the ground and many topiaried hedges. You can also hone your skills on the 9-hole putting green. A huge vegetable and herb garden supplies the needs of the hotel kitchen.

The hotel is just on the outskirts of the famous town, and provides a restful atmosphere for holiday makers.

Nearby: Apart from its renowned golf course the city houses the oldest university in Scotland, and offers a variety of other attractions in its streets which are a melange of buildings from medieval to modern times. Earlshall Castle lies in one direction and the superbly restored Kellie Castle in the other; in between is Cambo country park with its wildlife and farm animals.

 BAR SNACKS (12.30–2pm) £1–8: grilled plaice, roast rib of beef & Yorkshire pudding, fresh salmon & salad, vegetable & pecan nut lasagne;
LUNCH (12.30–2pm) £11: terrine of smoked salmon, calves liver, pudding or cheese;
DINNER (7–9pm) £21: seafood & oyster salad, roasted quail, pudding or cheese
Children: high teas, half portions
£ high
Best Bargain Break £64 per person, per night – dinner, b & b
Children: free up to 10 years
Facilities: 3 cots and 3 high chairs; and 3 lines for baby listening

ST AUSTELL

20 rooms, 3 family   Access/AmEx/Diners/Visa
Open all year   No music
P – own car park

St Austell, Cornwall   map 1
BOSINVER HOLIDAY COTTAGES – ☎ *St Austell (0726) 72128.*

SC *Off the A390 towards Polgooth.*

Mr and Mrs Milln have been offering self-catering holiday accommodation for around twenty years, and three cottages and fourteen holiday bungalows are grouped in the grounds around their old thatched farmhouse.

One of the advantages of Bosinver is the thirty-seven acres of woods and meadows in which the properties lie. It is quite a haven for wild life and the guests can enjoy the peace and quiet too. There are also some extra facilities which any family will enjoy: an all weather tennis court, a lake in which guests can fish for trout, and an outdoor heated swimming pool and a sauna. The games room is functional but has table tennis, darts, and a pool table. The children have play areas with swings and a see-saw.

The three cottages have all been converted from old farm buildings and are suitable for occupation at any time of the year. They can sleep up to five or six people. The bungalows are not let during the winter months and are comfortable and practical holiday homes, and they are reasonably priced.

Laundry facilities are provided and every unit has its own ironing board. The owners also have a selection of books, jigsaws and board games. Barbecues can be hired.

Nearby: There are many sandy beaches close by, including Vault, Pentewan, Porthpean and Carlyon Bay, and superb coastal walks. All sorts of activities are readily available: horse riding, water sports, golf, tennis and fishing. St Austell has a recreation centre. If you want to see the sights, Polgooth is a lovely old village and Charlestown was a noted port and has a visitor centre. Trelissick Garden, Automobilia, Lanhydrock House, Dobwalls Theme Park, Truro Cathedral, Dairyland Farm Park, Newquay Zoo, Trerice House and the Lappa Valley Railway can all be easily reached.

Units: 17
Rents: £50 to £400 a week
Other costs: linen and cots (£3.50 per person); electricity is on a meter
Heating: electric and solid fuel
Plenty of cots and high chairs
Cottages open all year; bungalows March to November

CARLYON BAY HOTEL – ☎ Par (072 681) 2304.

Off the A390 east of St Austell.
The hotel was built in 1930 and has a marvellous location in 250 acres of grounds, which include an excellent golf course of 6400 yards. The extensive landscaped gardens are a delight, due in no small part to the excellent climate of the Cornish riviera, and you have marvellous views of the bay. You can follow the coastal path and Crinnis Woods, part of the hotel grounds, is a lovely spot to explore.

The facilities here are superb. As well as the golf course, there are two hard tennis courts and an outdoor heated swimming pool. Children are catered for with an adventure paddock which has a tree house, a slide and a trampoline. If the weather is unkind you can enjoy the splendid indoor leisure centre which has an excellent swimming pool, a children's pool, sauna, solarium and spa bath. There are two snooker tables, table tennis and a children's play room.

Everything is in place at this excellent hotel for a relaxing and agreeable family holiday including a high standard of service and comfort. It is good to report that there is an extensive and healthy menu for children and a good choice of vegetarian dishes.

Nearby: The coastline is dotted with lovely sandy bays, including one below the golf course. If you fancy seeing the sights, Charlestown, an 18th century port, is on the doorstep and has a visitor centre; and Mevagissey has a folk museum. There are many other attractions within an easy drive: the ruined Restormel Castle, Lanhydrock, the farm park at Bodmin, Dobwalls Theme Park, Trelissick Garden, the Dairyland Farm Park, Trerice and the Newquay Zoo.

LUNCH (12.30–2pm) £10: whitebait, entrecote steak, pudding or cheese;
DINNER (7.30–9pm) £17: crudités, soup, roast English lamb, pudding and cheese
Children: own menu
£ high
Best Bargain Break £117, 2 nights – dinner, b & b
Children: from £3 a day to 75% of the adult rate
Facilities: 6 cots and 10 high chairs; baby listening system
73 rooms, 2 family, 14 sets interconnecting
Open all year   Access/AmEx/Diners/Visa
P – own car park

St Breward, Nr Bodmin, Cornwall   map 1

COOMBE MILL – ☎ Bodmin (0208) 850 344.

SC *Off the B3266 south of Camelford. The brochure has clear directions.*
The village sits on the edge of Bodmin Moor and the thirty acres of the Coombe

ST BREWARD

Mill estate shelter in the Camel valley below. The river runs right through Coombe Mill, and provides superb salmon and trout fishing, and the valley is a home for a wide variety of birds, animals and plant life.

The properties comprise six stone cottages and twelve log cabins. Four of the cottages have been converted from old farm buildings: a mill, a granary, a stable and a barn. One of them is suitable only for two people while the others will accommodate four. The best features of the old buildings – exposed beams and stone internal walls – have been retained and augmented by excellent furnishings and equipment. They all have wood-burning stoves and the Old Mill has a minstrel's gallery over the spacious living room.

Two cottages, built of granite and with slate roofs, have recently been built and fit in with grand style. Each has one double and two twin bedrooms and is superbly equipped.

These cottages are all set within the landscaped gardens; and the cabins are scattered along the bank of the river and have views of the lakes. The majority of them can sleep four people, with the second bedroom having twin or bunk beds.

One of the great advantages for families of staying at Coombe Hill is the presence of the animals. There is a herd of red deer, Jacob sheep, pigmy goats, Vietnamese pot-bellied pigs, Highland cows and donkeys plus the ducks, geese and swans, and the many wild birds.

It is a great spot for children who also have the benefit of an excellent adventure playground. There is a huge covered barbecue and, on a practical level, a well-equipped laundry room.

Nearby: Apart from all the opportunities for fishermen, the delights of Bodmin Moor lie on the doorstep. There is a long run of safe and sandy beaches on the nearby coast, including Newquay and Bedruthan Steps. All sorts of sports are available: surfing, sailing, swimming, tennis, golf and horse riding. The other attractions are diverse. Famous houses such as Pencarrow, Trerice and Lanhydrock are close; the children will be keen to see the Tamar Otter Park and Newquay Zoo; and Dobwalls Theme Park and the Dairyland Farm Park are not too far away.

Units: 18
Rent: £80 to £550 a week (short breaks available)
Other costs: electricity by meter; high chairs and cots with linen £10 a set
Heating: central heating
Cots and high chairs: 12 of each
Open all year

To qualify for inclusion in the Guide hotels must offer the basic facilities of a cot, a family room and an evening meal. Self-catering establishments must provide cots and high chairs.

ST BREWARD

PENROSE BURDEN COTTAGES – ☎ *Bodmin (0208) 850 277 and 850 617.*

SC *Off the B3266 south of Camelford. The brochure has very clear instructions.*

The cottages are located in delightful countryside, with views over a wooded valley to Bodmin Moor, which is no more than a mile away. They are all converted from old farmbuildings but are scattered, which enabled the owners, Mr and Mrs Hall, to give each cottage its own garden, from where guests can enjoy the views.

The stone cottages have been converted with great care and have exposed oak beams, quarry tiled floors with occasional rugs (fitted carpets in the bedrooms), and wood burning stoves. The furnishings are modern and simple and all the essential equipment is provided without stint. Original paintings by a local artist adorn the walls.

The gardens have picnic tables and chairs and barbecues are provided so that you can have an al fresco meal on those long summer evenings.

You should note that all the cottages are designed for disabled guests (Mr Hall is disabled).

The cottages vary in size but most of them can accommodate four or five people; Jingles is the smallest with room for a couple or a couple with a child, while a recent conversion, Wenford, can sleep up to six.

Penrose Burden is a busy working farm but the work does not impinge on the guests, who are welcome to stroll around the 250 acres. Another asset of the place is free trout and salmon fishing on the Camel, where the Halls have a mile-long stretch, and other water is available via the local Anglers' Association.

There is also an arrangement whereby guests can use the heated swimming pool and tennis courts of the nearby Country Hotel. A range of prepared meals is available and these can be ordered for your arrival or for any evening of your stay at Penrose Burden.

Nearby: For walkers, there is easy access to Bodmin Moor and horse riding, golf and all kinds of water sports can be arranged without difficulty. There are many excellent beaches on the nearby coast (for example Newquay, Bedruthan Steps, Constantine Bay and Harlyn Bay) and interesting coastal walks. The many other attractions include Tamar Otter Park, Pencarrow House, Newquay Zoo, Trerice House, Dairyland Farm Park, Lanhydrock House and Dobwalls Theme Park.

Units: 8
Rent: £130 to £400 a week
Other costs: electricity on a meter
Heating: night storage and wood burning stoves
Several cots and high chairs
Open all year

ST DAVID'S

St David's, Dyfed map 5
WARPOOL COURT HOTEL – ☎ St Davids (0437) 720 300.

Close to the centre of the town.

This hotel has been recommended in the Family Welcome Guide since the very first edition. It is an appealing place, built of grey stone, has extensions here and there and was built in the 19th century as the St David's Cathedral choir school.

It is certainly not lacking in charm and it has a magnificent position on the unspoiled Pembrokeshire coast. There are wonderful views of St Bride's Bay, especially from the large lawned garden, a delightful place to loll on a warm day. It is notable for the statuary dotted around.

There are excellent facilities here including a covered and heated swimming pool, a gymnasium, a pool table and table tennis, an all-weather tennis court, and an outdoor play area for children. Free golf can be arranged at the nearby St David's Golf Club.

The menu is strong on fresh local produce, especially fish, and a vegetarian menu is available.

Nearby: There are lovely beaches here – Whitesand Bay, Newgale Sands and Marloes Sands for example – and the Pembrokeshire Coast path can be followed. The famous Cathedral is within walking distance and the Marine life Centre is just down the road. There is a wildlife park near Cardigan and another near Tenby; and lots of castles to see including Carew, Tenby and Manorbier.

BAR SNACKS (12–2pm) £3–7: smoked salmon, minute steak, garlic mushrooms, Glamorgan cheese sausages;
LUNCH (12–2pm) £11: smoked salmon, noisettes of Welsh lamb, pudding or cheese;
DINNER (7–9.15pm) £23: crab cocotte, escalope of venison, pudding, cheese
Children: high teas, half portions
Facilities: 3 cots and 3 high chairs; and a baby listening system
£ high
Best Bargain Break £102 per person, 2 nights – dinner, b & b
Children: free up to 14 years
25 rooms, 11 family   Access/AmEx/Diners/Visa
Open all year   • Ale – Bass
P – own car park

Please let us have reports – good or bad – on any establishments listed in the Guide as soon as possible after your visit.

St Erme, Cornwall   map 1

TREVISPIAN-VEAN FARM GUEST HOUSE – ☎ Truro (0872) 79514.

On the A3076 north of Truro.

You approach the farmhouse down a short drive, with banks of hydrangeas on one side and trees on the other. It is a 17th century house, which has been modernised and extended to cope with twenty to thirty guests. It is run in efficient and friendly fashion by the Dymond family and offers excellent facilities. The large dining room can seat nearly forty people and has windows on three sides which look on to the farm yard and colourful flower beds. The three lounges include one with a television and video.

An old pig-sty, with stone walls and wooden beams and rafters, has recently been converted into a play room and there is table tennis, a pool table, and table football. The garden is safely enclosed and there are swings, a slide and a trampoline; and a patio area with tables and chairs lies just off one of the lounges.

Trevispian-Vean is a working farm and the children are encouraged to see how the farm is run. They can have donkey rides, too.

Nearby: This is an excellent base for a family holiday in an area which offers a great variety of facilities. There are many excellent beaches to the south – Gyllyngvase Beach at Falmouth, Towan Beach, Pendower, Porthlunay and Vault Beach for example; and in the other direction there is Holywell Bay and Chapel Porth. All around there is a wide choice of things to do and see: the Leisure Park at St Agnes, the World in Miniature, Dairyland Farm Park, Newquay Zoo, the Lappa Valley Railway, etc. A fishing lake has been created below the farmhouse and guests can fish there for carp.

DINNER (6.30pm) £6
Children: half portions
£ low
Children: £6.50 up to 3; £10.75 from 3 to 10; £13 from 10 to 12 (includes evening meal)
12 rooms, 6 family   Open Easter to November
No credit cards   **P** – ample

St Hilary, Nr Penzance, Cornwall   map 1

ENNYS – ☎ Penzance (0736) 740 262.

Off the A30 or A394 east of Penzance.

You approach the house up a long and winding road, bounded by open fields. You will then see the regular stone features of a charming Cornish manor house, with a walled garden: to the left a small lawn with borders of flowers, and to the right a two-tiered lawn with masses of flowers. There is also a patio

ST IVES

area with tables and sun beds, and a grass tennis court.

An adjoining barn has recently been renovated to provide two family suites, each with two bedrooms and a bathroom. A baby listener extends to the sitting and dining rooms and the very useful facility of a laundry room is also provided.

It is a small working farm, and guests are welcome to walk the fields which stretch down to the River Hayle. Older children will no doubt head for the play room, which is housed in an old barn, and where they can play table tennis, darts and pool.

This is a delightful base for a family holiday, in a lovely rural setting, but with the beaches and the towns within easy reach. The food is mostly cooked from home-grown ingredients, with fresh fish and shellfish often available, and even the bread is baked daily on the premises. The children have their high teas at 5.30, so that the adults can relax over their candle-lit dinner.

Nearby: There are numbers of excellent beaches within easy reach - Prussia Cove, Whitesand Bay, Praa Sands, etc – and St. Michael's Mount and Land's End are a short drive away. You can easily reach Paradise Park, Poldark Mine, the Flambards Theme Park, Godolphin House and the Seal Sanctuary near Helston – and no doubt the children will point the way for you. Fishing, pony trekking and golf can all be arranged and there is a wind surfing school nearby at Marazion. The Minack open air theatre stages plays at Lamorna.

 DINNER (7pm) £12
Children: own menu
£ low
Children: two thirds of adult rate up to 10 years
Facilities: 2 cots and 2 high chairs; and baby listening
5 rooms, 2 family suites   Open all year
No credit cards   No smoking in bedrooms
P – own car park

St Ives, Cornwall   map 1

PORTHMINSTER HOTEL (Best Western) – ☎ *Penzance (0736) 795 221.*

On the main road into the town.

A famous resort on the 'Cornish Riviera', a town of steep twisting streets, which has always been popular with artists. Some famous ones have lived here including Whistler, Sickert and Barbara Hepworth whose house is now a museum.

This is an excellent traditional seaside hotel set high above the town and with a commanding view of St Ives bay. The gardens lead down to the sea and a lovely safe beach, to which there is a pathway for guests. There is a heated outdoor swimming pool with children's paddling area and a playground with climbing frame, slide and see-saw. During the summer season table tennis, pool, and darts can be played indoors.

If the weather is unkind you can head for the indoor leisure centre which has a pool, gymnasium, sauna and solarium; and table tennis and darts can also be played.

Nearby: The town has several museums including the Barbara Hepworth and Bernard Leach's pottery is well worth a look. Land's End and St Michael's Mount are quite close, with Paradise Park even closer. South toward the Lizard you can visit the Poldark Mine, Flambards Theme Park, the Seal Sanctuary and Goonhilly Earth Station.

BAR LUNCH (12.15–2pm) £2–6: chef's special, ploughman's, cold buffet, roast of the day;
DINNER (7.15–8.30pm) £15: smoked mackerel, soup, roast duckling, pudding or cheese
Children: own menu, half portions
£ high
Best Bargain Break £72 per person, 2 nights – dinner, b & b
Children: free up to 2 years; one third of adult rate from 2–7 years; half the adult rate from 8–12 years
Facilities: 4 cots and 4 high chairs; 3 baby listening lines
49 rooms, 9 family, 7 sets interconnecting
Open all year   Access/AmEx/Diners/Visa
P – own car park opposite

St Mawgan, Cornwall   map 1

LANVEAN FARM COTTAGES – ☎ *St Mawgan (0637) 860 555.*

SC *Directions are given at the Bedruthan Steps Hotel in Mawgan Porth: the cottages are owned by them.*

St Mawgan is a delightful little village with an agreeable 16th century pub with a splendid garden. The three cottages have all been converted from stone farm buildings and offer comfortable accommodation for families in a quiet setting. They overlook the village and have particularly good views of the ancient church and the surrounding countryside.

Sampson Cottage was a farm house and can sleep four people in a double and a twin bedroom. Bryher Cottage can accommodate five people in a double, a twin and a single bedroom and the cot can be put in the double room. It has a spiral staircase. Barn Cottage was converted from a traditional grain barn and has three bedrooms to accommodate six people.

The cottages are all comfortably furnished, attractively decorated and have well-equipped kitchens. Each cottage has its own lawn with a picnic table and a small barbecue and on a practical level they have washing machines.

There is a great bonus for guests in that all the facilities of the Bedruthan Steps Hotel and the Trevelgue Hotel (at Newquay) are at their disposal. Both hotels have been in the Family Welcome Guide since the very first edition and have unrivalled facilities for families. There are comprehensive leisure facilities and full entertainment programmes (see under Mawgan Porth and Newquay in the Guide).

Nearby: Safe and sandy beaches abound in this part of Cornwall and include the one at Mawgan Porth. Newquay has several excellent beaches and has become a notable surfing centre. For gentler pursuits you can walk along the North Coast Path. Newquay has an excellent zoo and the children will also enjoy the Leisure Park at St. Agnes and the Dairyland Farm Park. Trerice is a wonderful Elizabethan mansion, while Dobwalls Theme Park and Lanhydrock are a little further afield.

Units: 3
Rent: £200 to £570 a week
Other costs: none
Heating: central heating
Cots and high chairs provided for Bryher and Barn cottages
Open all year

Saunton, Nr Barnstaple, Devon   map 1

SAUNTON SANDS HOTEL – ☎ Croyde (0271) 890 212.

H/SC *On the B3231.*

This large hotel, prominently situated above the rolling expanse of Saunton Sands, has an excellent range of facilities for families and succeeds in looking after them well. Some friends of ours, a family of five, regularly take a winter break here and enjoy it greatly.

The facilities include an indoor heated swimming pool with a paddling pool, a hard tennis court, squash court and a mini-cinema; horse-riding, sailing, wind-surfing, fishing, etc can all be arranged by the hotel staff; just down the road is Saunton Golf Club, a splendid links course which offers a stern test for any golfer. A long stretch of lawn overlooks the vast expanse of Saunton Sands, with a play area at one end of the lawns.

One of the great bonuses of this hotel is the presence of a nanny, who is in attendance from 10am to 6pm every day. So the harassed parents can occasionally have a rest, too. It should be emphasised that most of the hotel bedrooms can take an extra bed.

Nearby: Saunton Sands spreads below the hotel and there are many other fine beaches including Woolacombe and Croyde Bay. Nature lovers should see Braunton Burrows, one of the largest nature reserves in Britain, and the children will enjoy a visit to Exmoor Bird Gardens. They will have fun, too, at

Watermouth Castle, and Arlington Court is well worth a visit.

✂ LUNCH (12.30–2pm) £11: whitebait, roast Devon turkey, hot fruit pie;
DINNER (7.30–9pm) £16: soup, poached halibut, escalope of pork, pudding or cheese
Children: own menu, half portions
£ high
Best Bargain Break £124 per person 2 nights – dinner, b & b
Children: free up to 2 years; 60% discount from 2–5; 40% discount from 6–11 years
Facilities: 20 cots and 7 high chairs; baby listening line for every room
94 rooms, 7 family, 12 suites   Access/AmEx/Diners/Visa
Open all year   🅿 – own car park

SELF-CATERING

Seventeen apartments are let on a self-catering basis, and the occupants can use all the hotel facilities. The apartments are extremely well-equipped and many of them look out over the dunes and the estuary. They vary in size and can be rented at prices ranging from £90 to £170 per night.

Sedbusk, Nr Hawes, North Yorks   map 9

THE STONE HOUSE HOTEL – ☎ Wensleydale (0969) 667 571.

Off the A684 near Hawes.
This delightful country hotel is situated amid glorious scenery on the edge of the Yorkshire Dales. It has been highly recommended for many years in the Family Welcome Guide, not only for the outstanding value it represents but also for the warm and friendly welcome which Mr and Mrs Taplin offer.

The house, a listed building, was converted less than a decade ago, and enormous care was taken to preserve its character. An old broom cupboard houses the serving hatch to the tiny bar, and the old library has been retained. There are plenty of books there, and a snooker table and an interesting collection of vintage slot machines.

The food is cooked from fresh produce, and even the sausages are made on the spot. Children can have high teas, and although lunches are not served, the owners will supply packed lunches, if requested.

The hotel also has a niche in literary history. That wonderful writer, P.G. Wodehouse, found a name for his famous butler after meeting the original owner of Stone House, Hugh Grallan, whose own butler was called Jeeves.

Nearby: You may fancy a packed lunch because this is wonderful walking country, or you can vary this with some horse riding and fishing. It's a marvellous part of the world for touring around to see the sights: the Dales Folk

SELKIRK

Museum, Bolton Castle, Jervaulx Abbey and Richmond Castle are all within easy reach; and further away to the south you can visit Malham Cove, Stump Cross Caverns, and Bolton Abbey.

✗ DINNER (7–8pm) £14: watercress soup, roast leg of pork, pudding, cheese
Children: half portions, high teas
£ medium
Best Bargain Break – 5% discount for 3 or more nights
Children: £6 (including breakfast)
Facilities: 2 cots and 2 high chairs; and a baby listening system
15 rooms, 1 family   Access/Visa
Closed Jan & midweek Nov–Mar   No smoking in dining room
🅿 – own car park

Selkirk, Borders   map 11
PHILIPBURN HOUSE HOTEL – ☎ Selkirk (0750) 20747.

Where the A707 and the A708 meet, just out of the town.

The house dates back to 1751, and not long before that date the Covenanters and the Royalists did battle at Philipbaugh which lies in the fields only a short distance away. It became a hotel in 1972 and specialises in family holidays.

In the rambling but well-kept grounds you will find a heated swimming pool, a pets corner, a trampoline, badminton court, adventure playground and a Wendy house. Inside there is also a games room, with table tennis and snooker.

Adults who prefer a less active outdoor existence will find plenty of peace and quiet on the spacious back lawn, which has a number of bench tables and garden chairs.

There is a very flexible system of eating arrangements here. A quick bite menu served from 6pm is a favourite with older children while the comprehensive children's menu is served from 5.30pm at prices ranging from under £1 up to £5.

The management and staff make a big effort to keep their guests happy and the hotel will arrange a nanny for the odd morning or afternoon given reasonable notice.

Nearby: If you are the active type you can go walking, fishing or pony trekking and there is a fine selection of golf courses. There are many attractions within reach – Abbotsford (Sir Walter Scott's home), Bowhill, Traquair House, Floors Castle, the abbeys at Dryburgh and Melrose, and Kailzie Gardens.

✗ BAR SNACKS (12–2pm & 7–9.30pm) £1–9: fresh sardines, lasagne, beef & Belhaven pie, ham & haddie, Swiss rosti;
LUNCH (12–2pm) £14: tarte d'Alsace, roast loin of pork, sherry trifle;

DINNER (7–9.30pm) £23: baked crab, boeuf Bourguignonne, pudding or cheese
Children: own menu
£ high
Best Bargain Break £118 per person, 2 nights – dinner, b & b
Children: from free to £18, depending on age and season
Facilities: 6 cots and 4 high chairs, and baby listening system
16 rooms, 12 family   Access/AmEx/Diners/Visa
Open all year   No smoking in restaurant
P – own car park

Semley, Nr Shaftesbury, Dorset   map 2
BENETT ARMS – ☎ *East Knoyle (0747) 830 221.*

Off the A350 north of Shaftesbury.
The pub was built from the local Chilmark stone in the 18th century by a local landowner, who wanted a village inn where his estate workers could enjoy themselves. It has stood the test of time and is a handsome sight, situated, as is right and proper, on the village green close to the church, and with a small garden to the rear.

If you have children in tow it is nice to know that you are welcome in various parts of the pub; for example there is an eating area which is up several steps from the bar. There is an excellent bar menu at reasonable prices, and a restaurant for more elaborate meals.

Most of the food is cooked on the spot from fresh produce which might include fresh fish from Poole and salmon shipped overnight from Scotland.

Nearby: Beautiful countryside stretches all around you with ample scope for walking and riding, fishing and golf. The lovely city of Salisbury is not too far away, with Wilton House on its fringes. There are many interesting places within reach including Stourhead, Longleat, Montacute House, Brymton d'Evercy, Ham Hill Country Park and Cricket St Thomas Wildlife Park.

BAR SNACKS (12–2pm & 7–10pm) £2–8: scampi royale, trout, steaks, Wiltshire ham with egg & chips, lasagne;
DINNER (7–10pm) £14: herrings in Madeira, rack of lamb, pudding or cheese
Children: half portions
£ low
Children: from free to £5, depending on age
Facilities: 1 cot and 1 high chair; baby listening system
5 rooms   Open all year, except Xmas
Access/AmEx/Diners/Visa   • Ale – Gibbs Mew
P – own car park

Also recommended in the Family Welcome Pub & Restaurant Guide.

Shanklin, Isle of Wight   map 3

BRUNSWICK HOTEL, Queens Road – ☎ Isle of Wight (0983) 863 245.

Near the centre of the town. The hotel brochure has a clear map.

The Queens Road is packed with hotels, but the Brunswick appealed to us most of all. It looks extremely smart, from the freshly painted exterior to the well decorated public rooms.

The core of the hotel is a pleasant Victorian building and the extensions marry in well. The lounge is huge and very comfortably and smartly furnished, and a new restaurant was built last year. These rooms overlook the spacious gardens with well tended lawns and a mass of roses and other bright flowers, and a splendid North American cedar shades some of the lawns.

A great bonus is the sizeable outdoor swimming pool and there is also a well-designed indoor pool, with a sauna and a spa bath alongside.

Just outside the garden is the coastal path which encircles the island, and the hotel sits high above a large sandy beach; a lift gives easy access to and from it.

We were most impressed by this appealing and well-run hotel, which provides an ideal base for a family holiday on the island. It offers good value for money and excellent facilities for all the family, including high teas for the children.

Nearby: It is just a short walk to the centre of the town and to the Old Village and there is a multitude of things to do and see on the Island. High on the children's list there will certainly be a trip to Blackgang Chine, the Flamingo Park, Butterfly World, Robin Hill Park and the Needles Pleasure Park; Carisbrooke Castle, Arreton Manor, Osborne House and the Steam Railway are also very popular.

(7pm onwards) £6 (for residents)
Children: half portions
£ medium
Children: cots free; one third of adult rate up to 7 years; half price thereafter up to 15
Facilities: 4 cots and 4 high chairs; and baby alarms
34 rooms, 10 family, 3 sets interconnecting
Open March to November   Access/Visa
🅿 – own car park

Please let us have reports – good or bad – on any establishments listed in the Guide as soon as possible after your visit.

Slaley, Nr Hexham, Northumberland   map 11

RYE HILL FARM – ☎ *Slaley (0434) 673 259.*

H/SC   *Off the B6306 south of Hexham.*

This is a delightful 17th century stone farmhouse which has been converted with taste and provides excellent facilities for visitors. The building forms an open courtyard with the farmhouse at one end and the guests' bedrooms situated in the central wing. Apart from the lounge cum writing room, the owner provides a utility room and laundry facilities.

There are thirty acres of grounds including a good stretch of garden and a patio, and barbecues are occasionally held. There is loads of room for children to play and they will find a swing, a slide and a climbing frame in the grounds. Indoors, there is a pool table and board games and books are available.

Nearby: Northumberland has sometimes been called the "forgotten county", and if you want glorious, unspoiled countryside, and an area crammed with history – in short a place to enjoy without hustle and bustle – this is the place to be. Hadrian's Wall runs just to the north of Hexham and you can follow the line of forts from the Roman Army Museum near Haltwhistle east to the Roman site at Corbridge. A bit further afield is Kielder Forest and Kielder Water, and the interesting city of Durham.

DINNER (7.30pm) £9
Children: half portions
£ low
Children: free up to 2 years; half price up to 12
Facilities: 1 cot and 1 high chair
6 rooms, 2 family   Open all year
No credit cards   No smoking in bedrooms
🅿 – ample   No music

SELF-CATERING

The Old Byre can accommodate up to nine people. The dining area and lounge are open plan, with a log burning stove. The kitchen is fully equipped and has a dishwasher, microwave oven, fridge freezer and all other necessities. There is a twin bedded room (plus a folding bed), two double rooms, and a bunk bedroom for children. All linen and central heating is included and the rent varies from £200 to £450 a week.

To qualify for inclusion in the Guide hotels must offer the basic facilities of a cot, a family room and an evening meal. Self-catering establishments must provide cots and high chairs.

SOLVA

Solva, Nr Haverfordwest, Dyfed map 5
LLANDDINOG OLD FARMHOUSE – ☎ *Croesgoch (0348) 831 224.*

H/SC *Follow the signs to the farmhouse from the A487. They start at the top of the hill at Solva village. O.S. map reference SM831 271.*

Tucked away in the peaceful countryside the farmhouse can give you a family holiday away from it all. The attractive stone farmhouse was built in the 17th century and its rooms, with old wooden beams and an inglenook fireplace, confirm this. Both the family rooms contain cots and baby listening can be arranged with the owner. A good selection of board games and books is provided.

From the charming dining room you look out through french windows over the extensive gardens, about five acres of lawns and paddocks. There is plenty of room for the adults to relax and for the children to play. In the grounds there is a large pond and some wild garden, swings, and many small animals including two ponies, sheep, calves, poultry and pigs.

Nearby: If you want an active holiday there is plenty to do in the vicinity – fishing, pony trekking, walking, golf, swimming, sailing and surfing, and there are many beaches along the coast. If museums and castles interest you there are many of these: at Scolton Manor, Haverfordwest, Manorbier, Pembroke and Tenby. There are wildlife parks at Cardigan and near Tenby, and a butterfly farm and a Marine Life Centre near St David's. The Oakwood Leisure Park near Narbeth offers a lot of family entertainment too.

✖ DINNER (6.30pm) £7: home made soup, roast turkey, sherry trifle
Children: own menu, half portions

£ low

Children: cot £1; half price thereafter
Facilities: 2 cots and 2 high chairs; baby listening can be arranged
2 rooms, both family   Unlicensed
Open all year except Xmas and New Year   No music
No smoking in dining room or bedrooms   🅿 – ample

SELF-CATERING

Three attractive cottages are available and form an open courtyard. The smallest can sleep four people and the others six; one of them has a small enclosed garden and the other an enclosed forecourt, which makes them very suitable for families with very young children. Cots and high chairs are provided and the inclusive rental varies between £100 and £430 a week. Short breaks are also available, and meals can be taken in the farmhouse by arrangement.

Please let us have reports – good or bad – on any establishments listed in the Guide as soon as possible after your visit.

South Kilvington, Nr Thirsk, North Yorks map 10

HERRIOT COUNTRY HOLIDAY HOMES and THORNBOROUGH HOUSE FARM – ☎ *Thirsk (0845) 522 103.*

SC *The farm is off the A19 north of Thirsk, and the cottages are in various locations in and around Thirsk.*

The six cottages, which are owned by Mr and Mrs Williamson, are charming and well-maintained terraced cottages which are reminiscent of another quieter age. Some have the original exposed wooden beams and all of them are comfortably furnished and have well-equipped kitchens which include microwave ovens as well as electric cookers, dishwashers, washing machines and ironing boards.

The cottages can sleep three, five, six or eight people. Knottsberry Cottage is the smallest property, but it suits a small family since its bedroom has a double bed and a single bed.

Knottsberry is just a few minutes' walk from the centre of Thirsk ('Darrowby' in James Herriot's stories), as is Whitemare Cottage which has two double bedrooms and another bedroom with bunk beds.

The other cottages are within a mile to six miles of Thirsk. Cots and high chairs are available for all the cottages and it is good to report that bed linen, towels, gas and electricity are all included in the rent. There are no hidden extras.

In addition to their cottages, Mr and Mrs Williamson have three rooms in their attractive 18th century farmhouse. There is a family room, a double room and a twin. Evening meals are available, as are cots and high chairs. The tariff is very reasonable at under £30 for bed and breakfast for two people and babies are accommodated free.

Nearby: The Yorkshire Dales have their own distinctive beauty and there are plenty of things to do and see. Walking, swimming, fishing, horse riding, golf and many other pursuits are readily available. Thirsk is a marvellous base if you wish to see the sights, of which there are many within reach. Rievaulx Abbey, Shandy Hall, Castle Howard, Eden Camp, Flamingo Land, Fountains Abbey, Ripley Castle, Jervaulx Abbey and Bolton Castle. The dales and the North York Moors are there to be enjoyed along with the fine towns of Harrogate and York, and Thirsk itself.

Units: 6
Rent: £100 to £250 a week
Other costs: none
Heating: central heating
Cots and high chairs available
Open all year

Stiperstones, Shropshire map 6
TANKERVILLE LODGE – ☎ *Shrewsbury (0743) 791 401.*

H/SC *Off the A488 south of Shrewsbury. The brochure has clear directions. This is a lovely and unspoilt part of Shropshire, made famous by Mary Webb's novels, "The Golden Arrow" and "Gone to Earth". It also provided the setting for Malcolm Saville's adventure stories for children. The original part of the house was a hunting lodge, and has been extended recently. It is a white-painted building, long and narrow, and the four letting rooms are in the modern part. Everything here is simply and efficiently done; and the cot can be accommodated in one of the bedrooms which overlooks the garden.*

Nearby: There is delightful countryside to enjoy in this part of the world, with all of South Shropshire at your feet. The Long Mynd, much of which is owned by the National Trust, the Stiperstones Nature Reserve (with the famous Devil's Chair) and Carding Mill Valley are nearby, and golfers should know that Church Stretton golf course, designed by the incomparable James Braid, is a charming course on the hills. The children will be keen to see the Acton Scott Working Farm Museum near Church Stretton.

Further south are the Clun villages – "the quietest places under the sun" – Ludlow with its famous castle, and the Clee Hills. A round trip would then take you to Bridgnorth via the Severn Valley Railway Station and the Midland Motor Museum and on to Ironbridge with its fascinating museums.

And don't forget Buildwas Abbey, the Roman City at Wroxeter and Wenlock Priory. That should be enough for one day.

✘ DINNER (7pm) £7: courgette & mint soup, Shropshire fidget pie, pineapple pavlova, cheese
£ low
Children: nominal charge for linen
Facilities: 1 cot
4 rooms   Open all year
No credit cards   No music
P – own car park

SELF-CATERING

Ovenpipe Cottage, just across the garden, can be rented. It is a converted barn, built into the side of a hill and the open plan living area is on the top floor. The bedroom downstairs has a double and two single beds and a shower and WC. It's a lovely spot for a small family and the rent, which does not include electricity, ranges from £65 to £125 a week. The village inn and shop is less than a mile away and provides food and provisions until 10 o'clock at night.

Stockbridge, Hants   map 3
GREYHOUND HOTEL, High Street – ☎ *Stockbridge (0264) 810 833.*

In the main street.

The Greyhound looks every inch the traditional English coaching inn, standing in its smart coat of paint in the main street of this attractive and historic market town. The interior is just as smart and has two spacious bars; the lounge is very welcoming with its wooden ceiling beams, solid oak tables, wheel back chairs and bench seats, prints of North West Frontier troops, fishing rods amd so on. It is very comfortable and relaxing. On summer days you can sit on the lawn at the back of the pub and beyond is the River Test. If you are good enough to catch a trout, the chef will be good enough to cook it for you.

All the bedrooms here, including the family room, have bathrooms (with showers) and families can sit together in a separate room in the pub. It also doubles as a breakfast room, and has several tables and chairs and a splendid open fireplace. There is an enterprising and wide ranging menu, with quite an emphasis on fish dishes.

Nearby: This is a good base for a family break since so many attractions are within easy reach. Children will certainly enjoy a visit to the Hawk Conservancy near Andover, to the Marwell Zoo and to the Farley Mount Country Park; while the city of Winchester, Hillier Arboretum, Broadlands and Paultons Park are all nearby.

✕ (12–2pm & 7–9.30pm) £2–11: fresh local trout, game pie, steak & oyster pie, fresh lobster, Dover sole
Children: small portions
£ low
Children: cot £5; extra bed £10
Facilities: 2 cots and 1 high chair
6 rooms, 2 family   Open all year
• Ale – Courage   Access/AmEx/Visa
🅿 – own car park

Also recommended in the Family Welcome Pub & Restaurant Guide.

Stoke Fleming, Nr Dartmouth, Devon   map 1
STOKE LODGE HOTEL – ☎ *Stoke Fleming (0803) 770 523.*

Just off the A379 south of Dartmouth.

A cream-painted Georgian building, with some later additions, comprises the hotel, with some bay windows on the ground floor and a portico entrance. One of its many agreeable features is the large sun terrace where you can relax and enjoy the views: on one side of the pretty village of Stoke Fleming and on the other of the sea.

The hotel has excellent facilities for families. Three acres of attractive garden includes a pond where ducks gather; there is a top quality all-weather tennis court; a heated swimming pool and giant chess and draughts boards. Indoors you will find another swimming pool, a jacuzzi, a fitness room and table tennis.

The hotel has everything you need for a relaxing stay in comfortable surroundings.

Nearby: There is a great selection of sandy beaches and bays in the vicinity, and the whole area offers all kinds of water sports, as well as horse riding, fishing and golf. Within an easy drive there are many attractions. The children will no doubt vote for visits to the National Shire Horse Centre, Dartmoor Wildlife Park and the Parke Rare Breeds Farm. You can also visit the Torbay Aircraft Museum, Buckfast Abbey and the Buckfast Steam Railway, Compton Castle, Morwellham Quay and the nature reserve at Dawlish Warren. All the beauties of Dartmoor also lie nearby.

✕ LUNCH (12–2pm) £8: soup, grilled lamb cutlets, pudding or cheese;

DINNER (7–9pm) £14: egg & prawn salad, supreme of chicken, sherry trifle
Children: half portions
£ medium
Best Bargain Break £70 per person, 2 nights – dinner, b & b
Children: free up to 2 years; 25% from 2 to 5; 50% from 5 to 14; 75% thereafter
Facilities: 4 cots and 4 high chairs; baby listening system
24 rooms, 4 family   Open all year
No credit cards   No music
🅿 – own car park

Stoke Gabriel, Nr Totnes, Devon map 1

GABRIEL COURT HOTEL – ☎ *Stoke Gabriel (080 428) 206.*

Go to the village and you'll find a signpost to the hotel.

We are always happy to visit this very pretty 16th century manor house. It's an elegant, white-painted building with an ornamental balustrade and a square tower, in a quiet village between Paignton and Totnes. It is set in three acres of lovely tranquil sloping land which boasts one of the oldest pink magnolias in England, ancient yews, an old-fashioned knot garden, vegetable garden, and an orchard just made for visiting youngsters to play in. There's also a heated outdoor swimming pool, a croquet lawn and an outdoor play area.

The kitchen uses local produce as much as possible – fruit and vegetables from the garden, salmon and trout from the Dart, and poultry and venison from nearby farms and woods.

There are separate meal times for young children, who are not allowed in the dining room in the evenings.

Nearby: This part of Devon has so many attractions for visitors and especially families on holiday. There is an array of excellent beaches surrounding the busy resort of Torquay and many places to visit, including Compton Castle, Buckfast Abbey and its neighbour, the Dart Valley Railway. Further afield the children can visit the Dartmoor Wildlife Park and the National Shire Horse Centre. The ruins of Berry Pomeroy Castle, haunted of course, are not far from the hotel. Golf is available and trips on the River Dart can also be arranged.

DINNER (from 7.30pm) £21: egg baked with cream & cheese, soup, fresh Dart salmon, pudding and cheese
Children: high teas
£ high
Best Bargain Break £204 per person, 4 nights – dinner, b & b
Children: cot £6.50; £9.50 from 3 to 10 years; £15 thereafter
Facilities: plenty of cots and high chairs; baby listening to every room
20 rooms, 5 sets interconnecting   Access/AmEx/Diners/Visa

Open all year, except February   No music
🅿 – own car park

Stoulton, Hereford & Worcs   map 6

CALDEWELL, Pershore Road – ☎ *Worcester (0905) 840 894.*

On the A44 south-east of Worcester.

The house is very well positioned for travellers and tourists since it is about three miles from junction 7 of the M5 south of Worcester. It is a charming house, part Georgian and part Victorian, with its history on display inside, and a little museum. There is loads of space surrounding the house, with extensive gardens and several acres of woodland. Guests can do a spot of coarse fishing on the small lake, or simply browse in the dinghy.

Families should note that there is now available a double room (with a bathroom) with a connecting door to a twin room, and the other family room is spacious; it has a double and two single beds.

A tennis court, croquet lawn, and children's swings and a climbing frame are also provided. There is even a miniature steam railway in the grounds, and the owners arrange special railway weekends. Several animals – a cow, goats, sheep, and hens – will interest the children, and table tennis can also be played in the house.

Nearby: For holiday makers there is a multitude of choices nearby: Bredon Hill on one side and the Malvern Hills on the other; further afield the Cotswolds and the Wye Valley; and quite close at hand Worcester Woods Country Park, Hanbury Hall, the Avoncraft Museum, and the Malvern Hills Animal and Bird Gardens. Music lovers might be interested in Elgar's birthplace (on the west side of Worcester).

✘ DINNER (by arrangement) £7
Children: half portions
£ low
Children: cot free; half price up to 12 years
Facilities: 1 cot and 1 high chair; baby listening by arrangement
4 rooms, 2 family   Open March to December
No credit cards   Unlicensed
🅿 – ample   No music

If you wish to recommend an establishment to the Guide please write to us – report forms are at the back of the book. We need your help to extend and improve the guide.

Stow-on-the Wold, Glos   map 3

FOSSE MANOR HOTEL (Consort) – ☎ *Cotswold (0451) 830 354.*

On the A429.

This privately owned hotel is housed in a Victorian manor house, most of whose walls are covered in Virginia creeper. It has the great bonus for families of a large lawned garden, which runs to about seven acres and provides loads of space for children to play and for adults to relax. A play area is laid out with a sand pit, swings and a slide, and there is a croquet lawn.

It is a pleasant hotel with several cots and high chairs available. It is of course in the heart of the lovely Cotswolds where there is so much to enjoy.

Nearby: The Cotswold Farm Park, Birdland and the model village at Bourton on the Water, the Folly Farm waterfowl sanctuary and the Cotswold Wildlife Park are all within easy reach as are Sudeley Castle, Sezincote, and Chedworth Roman Villa. The hotel staff can arrange riding, fishing and clay pigeon shooting, and there are several golf courses in the vicinity.

LUNCH (12.30–2pm) £14: prawn & pineapple salad, grilled salmon steak, pudding or cheese;
DINNER (7.30–9.30pm) £17: shish kebabs, lemon sole, pudding or cheese
Children: own menu, half portions
£ high
Best Bargain Break £54 per person per night – dinner, b & b
Children: cot free; £10 up to 10 years; £15 over 10
Facilities: 3 cots and 4 high chairs; and a baby listening system
20 rooms, 2 family, 2 sets interconnecting
Open all year excluding Xmas week   Access/AmEx/Diners/Visa
P – own car park   No smoking in restaurant

Studland, Dorset   map 2

KNOLL HOUSE HOTEL – ☎ *Studland (092 944) 251.*

On the B3351 east of Corfe Castle and north of Swanage.

The owners of this large and well-equipped hotel try valiantly to hold the balance between the various types of guest: on the one hand the facilities and situation of the hotel appeal greatly to families, and on the other the hotel has many regular guests who are not encumbered with children. Some relations of ours had their honeymoon here some years ago!

If you have young children you have to make some compromises – for example you must expect to eat your family breakfast in the children's dining room, a fairly functional area. On the other hand the children can have their lunch at

12.30 and are then supervised in the well-equipped play room (Wendy house, play-pens, toys, etc.) while the parents have their meal in peace. Similarly, children under 8 are not permitted in the dining room at night, but have high tea from 5 o'clock.

The facilities within the hotel and the 100 acres of grounds are extensive and include: a heated swimming pool and paddling pool; a huge play area with a pirate ship and a wonderful and ingenious "Hag" adventure playground; and a par-3 golf course and two hard tennis courts. Indoors there are games such as table tennis, pool, table football, etc. Finally the well-designed leisure centre has a small indoor pool, a fitness room, a sauna and solarium, and a health juice bar. This is primarily a place for adults, but children are allowed in from 11am to midday, and for an hour in the afternoon if the weather is foul.

It is an expensive hotel but its facilities more than justify the expense; and it is in a superb holiday area.

Nearby: The beaches in this area are splendid and indeed the Studland beach, with over three miles of sand, is one of the best and cleanest in Britain. Behind it lies the Studland Heath Nature Reserve, and its neighbour, Swanage Beach, is also clean and sandy. The Swanage Railway is on the doorstep, as is Durlston Country Park and Corfe Castle. Brownsea Island is delightful and has many sandy beaches, too. Sightseers can easily reach the Tank Museum at Bovington, Hardy's cottage and the Tutankhamun Exhibition at Dorchester; and the children will enjoy a visit to the Sea Life Centre at Weymouth.

LUNCH (1pm onwards) £14: hors d'oeuvres, soup, roast loin of pork, pudding or cheese;
DINNER (7.30pm onwards) £16: salade Nicoise, roast loin of lamb, pudding, cheese
Children: own menu
£ high
Best Bargain Break £120 per person, 2 nights – full board
Children: a sliding scale depending on age
Facilities: plenty of cots and high chairs; and a baby patrol from 7.30pm to 11pm
80 rooms including 30 family suites
No credit cards accepted   Closed Nov-end Mar
No music except in leisure centre   **P** – own car park

Sturminster Newton, Dorset   map 2

STOURCASTLE LODGE GUEST HOUSE – ☎ Sturminster Newton (0258) 72320.

Just off the market square.
A delightful white-washed 18th century house which is set behind high stone walls in a narrow lane of the central square of this market town. The secluded

south-facing walled garden with its smooth lawn and colourful herbaceous borders completes a very attractive picture.

The various rooms, the number of which has been increased by two since last year, are most attractively furnished and very comfortable. One of the bedrooms is a family-sized room with a large sofa bed for children, and has its own bathroom. As well as two cots, there are two high chairs available; and the friendly owners will occasionally undertake baby-listening. They have their own small daughter and are consequently sympathetic to the needs of families.

Nearby: The River Stour is popular with anglers, and there is a 17th century working water mill on the river. Hambledon Hill, topped with an Iron Age fort, gives terrific views of the Stour Valley below. Other places to visit include Worldwide Butterflies near Sherborne, which has a splendid abbey and a ruined castle; Ham Hill Country Park; Montacute House; the motor museum at Sparkford; Stourhead; and a little further north Longleat Safari Park.

DINNER (7.30pm) £12
Children: half portions
£ medium
Children: £4 for cot; half price for extra bed
Facilities: 2 cots and 2 high chairs; baby listening system
5 rooms, 1 family   Open all year
Access/Visa   Unlicensed
P – ample

Sydling St Nicholas, Nr Dorchester, Dorset   map 2

LAMPERTS FARMHOUSE – ☎ *Cerne Abbas (0300) 341 790.*

Off the A37 and the A352 north of Dorchester.

The village of Sydling St Nicholas nestles in a beautiful and unspoilt valley, surrounded by fields and woods. The attractive farmhouse, built about 400 years ago of brick and flint under a thatched roof, stands hard by the approach road to the village, about three miles from the A37, the Dorchester to Yeovil road.

The bedrooms are nicely furnished; the family room has an antique brass double bed and an unusual old Swedish pine bed which can be adjusted to suit the size of the child. There is plenty of room for a cot or another bed.

The comfortable lounge has an inglenook fireplace with all the fittings for smoking bacon still in place. Board games, cards and toys are available. Meals are taken at the huge pine table in the farmhouse kitchen.

SYDLING ST NICHOLAS

The spacious garden is safely encircled by hedges and there is loads of room for children to play on the lawns. Mrs Bown is delighted to have families to stay, and the children can meet the farm's many animals – cows, chickens, ponies and dogs. There is much to do and see in the immediate vicinity.

Nearby: The attractive port of Weymouth is not far away, and it has an excellent sandy beach, from which dogs are banned. Lodmoor Country Park is close to the beach, as is the nature reserve at Radipole Lake. This is Thomas Hardy country, and his cottage is nearby; also within easy reach are the Tutankhamun Exhibition, Maiden Castle, Athelhampton and T.E. Lawrence's cottage, Clouds Hill. The children will no doubt make a bee-line for the Sea Life Centre at Weymouth.

DINNER (6.30–8pm) £7
Children: half portions
£ low
Children: cot £2; £8.50 up to 13 years
Facilities: 2 cots and 1 high chair; baby listening by arrangement
3 rooms, 1 family   Open March to November
No credit cards   Unlicensed
P – ample   No music

Please let us have reports – good or bad – on any establishments listed in the Guide as soon as possible after your visit.

Tarrant Monkton, Dorset   map 2
LANGTON ARMS – ☎ *Tarrant Hinton (025 889) 225.*

Just off the A354 east of Blandford Forum. The pub is by the lovely church.

This is a delightful village, and like many of the houses round about, the 17th century pub is thatched with a mixture of flint and brick underneath. The facade is festooned with climbing plants and flowers, and the lawned garden, with bench tables, looks away to the open country. A large paved terrace is also a pleasant place to settle on warmer days. There are swings for the children in the garden and plenty of space to play.

A few years ago the owners added six well-equipped double bedrooms, which have lovely views of the Dorset countryside. Two pairs of rooms have communicating doors and can therefore be used as family suites; there are two cots available and two high chairs. The pub has a good reputation for its food and offers an extensive bar menu and has a restaurant, which opens in the evening. The range of food is enlivened by special nights: pizzas on Tuesday and Friday, curries on Wednesday and Chinese on Thursday.

The pub also has a family room where you can sit with the children. It is actually the skittle alley, which also doubles as a function room and has plenty of tables and chairs, a pool table, darts and a piano. The adults will be pleased to know that there is always a good selection of real ales to be had. We have included the Langton Arms in the "Family Welcome Guide" since its very first edition.

Nearby: This is a very good base for a holiday or a short break. It is a delightful part of England with many places to see and enjoy: the remarkable house at Kingston Lacy with its superb collection of paintings; Wimborne Minster and Milton Abbey; and near Dorchester are Hardy's Cottage, the Tutankhamun Exhibition and Athelhampton House. There are excellent beaches along the coast from Weymouth to Swanage.

BAR SNACKS (11.30–2pm & 6–10.30pm) £1–8: lentil & onion soup, fisherman's pie, plaice, steaks, liver & bacon;
DINNER (6–10.30pm) £14: pasta with Parma ham, noisettes of lamb, pudding or cheese
Children: own menu, half portions
£ medium
Children: up to £12 depending on age
Facilities: 2 cots and 2 high chairs
6 rooms, 2 sets interconnecting   Open all year
Access/AmEx/Diners/Visa   • Ale – Flowers, Wadworth's
P – own car park

Also recommended in the Family Welcome Pub & Restaurant Guide.

Tetbury, Glos   map 2

FOLLY FARM COTTAGES – ☎ *Tetbury (0666) 502 475.*

SC   *On the B4014 on the Malmesbury side of Tetbury.*

There is an immediate appeal to these cottages, grouped around the farmyard and all constructed from the original farm buildings. The old tythe barn, of mid-17th century vintage, is an imposing sight on one side.

We had a good look at several of the cottages and were very impressed with the care which has gone into the conversion. As far as possible the original features have been retained and there is a wealth of original elm beams, for example.

Kiln Cottage is a luxury cottage for two people and the sitting room has a high vaulted ceiling on top of its thick stone walls. A huge stone fireplace, built from the cobblestones of the farm buildings, is a notable feature. There is a well-equipped kitchen and the little patio looks out to a large lawn.

Wheelwrights and the Weigh House are similar in design and sleep four adults and two children (sofa beds). The ceilings are crossed with wooden beams and there is plenty of space. As in all the cottages, the furniture is comfortable and varied, with a nice selection of old tables and good wooden doors.

We also saw one of the biggest properties, the Bull Pen, which is situated on one end of the courtyard and can sleep ten people. It is a splendid place, with a huge vaulted roof above the sitting room. There is a four poster in the ground floor bedroom, and the gallery above contains a double bedroom and two triples.

All linen and towels are provided and there is a communal laundry, a barbecue *and a children's play area. The only extra charge is a nominal one for heating (from £10 to £20 a week).*

Other cottages can accommodate from two to ten people and include the detached Folly Cottage. In addition, the owner, Julian Benton, has just made available some bed and breakfast accommodation in the farmhouse. There are four bedrooms available in what was once the loft and they share a comfortable sitting room. The rooms have their own entrance and have superb views of the surrounding countryside. The going rate is around £15 per person per night.

There are nearly a dozen acres of garden in which to relax and where the children can play. It's a delightful spot with top class accommodation for families of all sizes.

Nearby: Tetbury is an agreeable little town and it has an array of antique shops, as have so many of the Cotswold towns which are within easy reach. Westonbirt Arboretum is just down the road and there are many other attractions within a short drive: Slimbridge Wildfowl Trust, Berkeley Castle, the Cotswold Water Park, Sheldon Manor, Bowood House and Corsham Court. Bath and Bristol are pretty close, too.

Units: 11
Rent: £80 to £480 a week
Other costs: from £10 to £20 a week for heating
Central heating: provided
4 cots and 4 high chairs available
Open all year

Nr Thirsk, North Yorks — map 10

DOXFORD HOUSE, 73 Front St, Sowerby – ☎ *Thirsk (0845) 523 238.*

Off the A19 just south of Thirsk.

This Georgian house sits in a lovely tree-lined street in the attractive village of Sowerby on the outskirts of Thirsk. The rooms, with their good proportions and high ceilings, have a spacious look to them, especially the dining room and the comfortable lounge, with its piano. These are both at the front of the house with large bay windows and up above are the two family rooms. These are both sizeable and cheerfully furnished and have double beds and bunk beds for the children.

A large walled garden stretches away at the back of the house. There is plenty of lawn where the adults can relax and the children can play and there is also a paddock. A great bonus is the games room at the end of the garden, with a half-size snooker table, table tennis and darts. The owners also have a two-bedroomed self-catering cottage for rent.

Nearby: You are in the heart of the Dales, with marvellous countryside to tour, either by car, on foot, on horseback or by bicycle. Thirsk itself was "Darrowby"

THURLESTONE

in James Herriot's novels and there are many other interesting sights to see; Rievaulx Abbey, Sutton Bank with its white horse, Nunnington Hall, Flamingo Land, Eden Camp, Castle Howard, Fountains Abbey and Aldborough Roman Town.

✗ DINNER (6.30pm) £7: soup, lamb steaks, sherry trifle
Children: small portions
£ low
Children: £1 per year of age to a maximum of £7
Facilities: 2 cots and a high chair; baby sitting by arrangement
4 rooms, 2 family   Open all year except Xmas
No smoking in bedrooms   Unlicensed
P – at front and rear   No music

Thurlestone, Devon   map 1
THURLESTONE HOTEL – ☎ *Kingsbridge (0548) 560 382.*

In the centre of the village.
This has long been a favourite hotel of ours and on our various visits we have always found that the Grose family, who have owned and run this hotel since before the turn of the century, get most things right. Last year we had a

delightful room which overlooked the gardens and the sweep of Bigbury Bay, and we found the staff as friendly and efficient as always. The food was of excellent quality and cooked with skill.

That's a pretty good starting point for a family holiday. But, in addition, the hotel, in one of the loveliest spots in South Devon, has wonderful facilities including two hard tennis courts, two squash courts, a badminton court, a swimming pool and a play area with a climbing frame, swings and a slide. The well-designed indoor pool has a paddling pool for very young children, and there is also a fitness room. With table tennis and snooker, an excellent par-three course at the hotel and golf at Thurlestone and Bigbury all aspiring and perspiring superstars are wonderfully well catered for.

Good news for real ale fans: the listening service extends to the hotel's pub next door.

Nearby: There are plenty of sandy beaches all along this stretch of coast, including one at Thurlestone. Inland, you can visit the National Shire Horse Centre and the Dartmoor Wildlife Centre, Buckfast Abbey and the adjacent Dart Valley Railway, and the castles at Compton and Totnes.

BAR SNACKS (12.30–2pm & 6.30–9pm)) £1–7: Danish open sandwiches, smoked salmon, Torbay crab & prawns & salad;
LUNCH (12.30–2pm) £8: soup, halibut steak, fresh fruit salad;
DINNER (7.30–9pm) £22: salmon mousse, soup, roast turkey, pudding and cheese
Children: own menu
£ high
Best Bargain Break £65 per person per night – dinner, b & b
Children: free up to 2 years; £10 thereafter to 12 (includes breakfast and high tea)
Facilities: 6 cots and 6 high chairs; baby listening lines to all rooms
68 rooms, 13 family   Access/Visa
• Ale – Bass, Palmer's, Wadworth's   P – own car park

Tintern, Gwent   map 2

OLD RECTORY – ☎ Tintern (0291) 689 519.

On the A466 between Monmouth and Chepstow.

The house has an unrivalled position above the main road and with a sweeping view of the River Wye and its valley below. It is a white painted building with a Victorian front with a central gable, but behind the building is older and dates back to the 18th century. There is a comfortable sitting room, which includes a handsome stone fire-place with a log burning stove, and a separate dining room alongside. The bedrooms are bright and cosy and include a twin bedded room with a single room alongside and these could be combined to form a family suite. All the rooms are double-glazed.

TORQUAY

The garden at the rear is not really suitable for young children or elderly people because most of it is terraced, but there are vantage points for guests to get superb views of the valley.

Nearby: There are many attractions for the holiday maker, beginning with Tintern itself. The ruins of the Cistercian Abbey are justly famous, and you can imagine why its beautiful setting inspired one of Wordsworth's best known poems. It is wonderful walking and fishing country, and golfers are well cared for with several courses nearby including the championship course at St Pierre. Tintern is on the borders, and there are several fine castles to see: at Chepstow, Caldicot, Raglan and Penhow for example, and there is a Roman fort at Caerleon.

DINNER (6.30pm) £7
Children: half portions
£ low
Children: free up to 2 years; £6.50 thereafter up to 12
Facilities: 1 cot
5 rooms, 1 family Open all year
No credit cards Unlicensed
No smoking in bedrooms No music
P – in the drive

Torquay, Devon   map 1
CRAIG COURT HOTEL, 10 Ash Hill Road – ☎ *Torquay (0803) 294 400.*

Not far from the town centre and close to Castle Circus.

The hotel is smartly maintained and is a handsome building with a conservatory on one side and attractive shuttered windows. A pleasant and secluded lawned garden with sheltering trees stretches at the back of the building.

The hotel faces south and is in a reasonably quiet road, and yet it is within walking distance of the beaches, the main shopping centre and most of the attractions of the town. This comfortable hotel is a good base for a holiday in this part of the world, which has so much to offer to families.

Nearby: There is a host of things to do and see in this popular resort, with a wide selection of beaches – Blackpool Sands, Paignton, Anstey's Cove, Oddicombe Beach, Ness Cove, and Dawlish Warren, to name but a few. There are so many other attractions for the holiday maker: museums at Brixham, Torbay and Dartmouth; the Dart Valley railway, castles at Totnes and Compton; Buckfast Abbey; and the Dartmoor Wildlife Park and the National Shire Horse Centre are near Plymouth.

DINNER (6pm) £8
Children: half portions
£ low

Best Bargain Break £59 per person, 3 days – dinner, b & b
Children: half price to 11 years; 25% off from 11 to 14
Facilities: 1 cot and 1 high chair
10 rooms, 2 family   Open Easter to October
P – own car park   No credit cards

PALACE HOTEL, Babbacombe Road – ☎ *Torquay (0803) 200 200.*

On the coast road to the north-east of the town centre. Take the Babbacombe road from the harbour.

Originally built in 1841 for the Bishop of Exeter, this imposing hotel is in the grand seaside tradition with twenty-five acres of magnificent gardens which lead down to the sea. A terrace overlooks an excellent swimming pool, a nine-hole short golf course, and four tennis courts. Indoors is an equally good pool, two snooker tables and table tennis, two squash courts and, unusual for Britain, two indoor tennis courts.

For younger children there is an outdoor play area with swings, slides and a sandpit and an indoor playroom. To help the parents' relaxation a resident nanny is on hand every day from 11am to 7pm during the summer, and for five days of the week during winter. So, parents have a chance for some relaxation too.

The hotel has its own vegetable gardens and an excellent vegetarian menu is available.

With all these facilities, this is a splendid hotel for a family holiday and offers real value for money.

Nearby: Torquay is a thriving resort with many attractions, not least the many excellent beaches – Torre Abbey Sands, Meadfoot, Anstey's Cove and Oddicombe Beach, for example. If you have sightseeing in mind you can reach the Dart Valley Railway and Buckfast Abbey (which adjoin each other), Compton Castle, the National Shire Horse Centre, and, a little further away, the Dartmoor Wildlife Park.

LUNCH (1–2.15pm) £12: ravioli Milanese, Torbay plaice, pudding or cheese;
DINNER (7.30–9pm) £19: French onion soup, poached fillet of dab Mornay, roast sirloin of beef, pudding or cheese
Children: own menu, half portions
£ high
Best Bargain Break £60 per person per night – dinner, b & b
Children: free to age 12
Facilities: a dozen cots and high chairs; and a dozen lines for baby listening
140 rooms, 10 family   Access/Diners/Visa
Open all year   **P** – own car park

Trebarwith Strand, Tintagel, Cornwall map 1
OLD MILLFLOOR – ☎ Camelford (0840) 770 234.

Off the B3263, south of Tintagel. Take the road to Trebarwith Strand.

Idyllic is the adjective which immediately springs to mind as, from the road above, you gaze down at this delightful 16th century house with its leaded windows. It is set in ten acres in a little valley and the garden is so appealing and peaceful. You can sit at the bench tables and look around you at the wooded slopes with their profusion of ferns and flowers, trees and trailing greenery. A small stream meanders through the garden, and occasionally rushes through when the rain comes, so you must keep an eagle eye on your offspring.

Keep a wary eye on them too, and where you place your own feet, when you approach the house because the entrance can only be reached down a steepish gravel path and some steps. You must park your car in the spaces provided on the roadside.

The inside of the house lives up to its surroundings. The living room has four wooden dining tables and the sitting area is furnished with comfort and style; there are deep armchairs and a sofa on which to relax and a beautiful old padded wooden settle. The three bedrooms, one of which is a family room, are lovely high-ceilinged rooms and are quiet and peaceful.

This is definitely the place to "get away from it all", and for a very reasonable price too.

Nearby: Down the road is the little beach of Trebarwith Strand, with Gull Rock rising impressively from the sea. You must exercise care on this beach as the rising tide can cut off the unwary. There are many alternatives nearby: for example Crackington Haven, Harlyn Bay and Constantine Bay. There are superb walks along the coastal path. There are many attractions within easy reach, especially around Newquay: the zoo, the Lappa Valley Railway, Dairyland farm park and the lovely house at Trerice. The Tropical Bird Gardens at Padstow, Tintagel Castle, Pencarrow and Bodmin Moor are not too far away.

DINNER (7–8pm) £11
Children: high teas
£ low
Children: free if sharing with parents
Facilities: 2 cots and a high chair
3 rooms, 1 family   Open March to October
P – spaces on the road above   Unlicensed

Hotels were asked to quote 1992 prices, but not all were able to give an accurate forecast. Make sure that you check tariffs when you book.

Trewetha, Port Isaac, Cornwall   map 1
ARCHER FARM HOTEL – ☎ Bodmin (0208) 880 522.

Off the B3267 just south of Port Isaac.

Smartly painted signs will lead you to the Archer Farm hotel and that will in itself give you a clue to the care which the Weltons take of their guests. You will receive a warm and very friendly welcome to this quiet and relaxing place. You are well away from any main roads and all around are delightful views of the countryside. You might sit on the patio or in the large garden, which is encircled by hedges and boasts a large and shady horse chestnut tree.

The bedrooms are all nicely furnished and three of them have terraces overlooking the garden – a lovely place from which to gaze at the view and sip a glass of something or other. There is a small bar, a couple of lounges and a very pleasant dining room.

One of the family rooms has a double and a single bed, and another has a double and a single bed plus another single in an adjoining room. Four of the other rooms can accommodate a cot or an extra bed, and baby sitting can be arranged.

Nearby: There are sandy beaches all along the coast and the little villages of Port Isaac and Port Gaverne are within walking distance. Bodmin Moor is a great attraction where you can walk or go riding, or simply admire the views. In addition there are tropical bird gardens at Padstow; a zoo, the Dairyland Farm Park, the Lappa Valley Railway near Newquay, and the delightful Elizabethan house of Trerice.

✕ DINNER (7.30pm) £14: whitebait, boeuf Bourgignonne, pudding and cheese
Children: half portions
£ medium
Children: babies free; 20% discount from 3 to 10
Facilities: 2 cots; and a baby listening system
8 rooms, 2 family   Open April to October
No credit cards   No music
🅿 – own car park

Tunstead, Nr Norwich, Norfolk   map 8
OLD FARM COTTAGES – ☎ Tunstead (0692) 536 548.

SC   *Off the A149 east of Tunstead.*

The Old Farm is set in secluded and attractive countryside in the heart of the Norfolk Broads with all its attractions.

The five cottages have been converted from various original farm buildings,

Nr ULEY

the coach house, the granary and the stables, and a great effort has been made to retain as many of the original features as possible within their red brick walls.

The interiors of the cottages have been done out with style and comfort in mind. You will feel at home in the easy chairs and generous sofas; the kitchens are equipped with everything a cook needs; and every cottage has its own enclosed patio where you can sit at your ease and enjoy the peaceful surroundings. A barbecue is provided.

There are many attractive features, such as the arched windows in the Coach House, the original partitions and beams in the Stables and the ship's mast which runs across the eaves of the Mast Cottage.

Old Farm has some excellent facilities including a games room with a pool table and table tennis, a heated indoor swimming pool, a jacuzzi and a multi-gym and a play area with a sandpit, slide and swings. A walled farm pond, with attendant ducks, adds to the fun.

There is plenty of space here for children (and adults) to enjoy themselves. It all adds up to a most attractive and welcoming place for families in a lovely part of England, which is quieter than many other holiday areas.

Nearby: The unspoiled sandy beaches of Sea Palling and Happisburgh are just a few miles away, with a good choice of water sports. Sheringham, Blakeney and Brancaster are twenty or so miles away and are renowned bird watching areas. There are also excellent golf courses at Sheringham and Brancaster. Attractive places to visit include Blickling Hall, Norfolk Wildlife Park, Norfolk Shire Horse Centre, Felbrigg Hall, the North Norfolk Railway and the Thursford Collection of steam engines.

Units: 5
Rent: £150 to £500 a week (short breaks available)
Other costs: none
Heating: night storage
6 cots and 6 high chairs
Open all year

Nr Uley, Glos   map 2

OWLPEN MANOR COTTAGES – ☎ *Dursley (0453) 860 261.*

SC *Owlpen is signposted in Uley (turn by the Old Crown Inn). The brochure has clear directions.*

The Owlpen estate covers over 200 acres and sits in a secluded valley of meadows and trees. Gentle hills encircle the estate, whose core is the manor house, parts of which date from the 16th century, and its beautiful church.

The nine self-catering properties have all been converted from various buildings on the estate, and it is noticeable that nothing has been done to alter the basic structures or to harm the ambience of these delightful buildings.

Nr ULEY

We had a long look at the Grist Mill, a listed building of medieval origin which has been restored on occasion over the centuries. It would be difficult to exaggerate the charm and appeal of such a place, built from warm stone, with the mill pond and the massive wheel alongside, and with many of the original features still in place; huge wooden beams, machinery, shutes and traps and lifting gear. The Grist Mill is on three floors and a series of glass panels, let into the ceilings and floors, allow you to see right up to the cupola which crowns the roof. The house is beautifully furnished and very well-equipped and can sleep eight or nine people. It has its own garden.

The other properties can house between two and six people. They include Woodwells, a 19th century farmhouse; the Court House, a 17th century house on three floors (no children under five years); Marlings End, with its wonderful views; and Manor Farm and Over Court, two adjoining cottages which can be let together for a large family.

Peace and seclusion is here in abundance at Owlpen and you can wander about the estate at will; it is a wonderful spot for adults to relax and for children to play. There are over five miles of footpaths on the estate, beech woods

WALWYN'S CASTLE

and much more to explore in the surrounding countryside. Owlpen is a working farm and the children can see the feeding of the animals.

The rent includes electricity, linen and towels; but central heating is extra and is paid either by a £1 meter or by a meter reading at the end of the visit.

Nearby: You can fish for trout in the mill pond and there is other fishing to be had in the vicinity. There are several golf courses, riding schools, and leisure centres at Stroud and Cirencester. The Wildfowl Trust at Slimbridge, the Westonbirt Arboretum and Berkeley Castle are all close; Gloucester Docks, the Cotswold Water park, Sheldon Manor, Corsham Court and Bowood House can all be reached with ease, as can the cities of Bath and Bristol.

Units: 9
Rent: £140 to £600 a week
Other costs: heating
Central heating: provided
Cots and high chairs available
Open all year

Walwyn's Castle, Nr Haverfordwest, Dyfed map 1
ROSEMOOR – ☎ *Broad Haven (0437) 781 326.*

SC *Off the B4327 south west of Haverfordwest.*

It would be a difficult task, even in lovely Pembrokeshire, to find a more attractive spot for a holiday than Rosemoor, which is situated in the Pembrokeshire Coast National Park, with its scenic variations from sandy beaches and lakes to the Preseli Mountains.

Mr and Mrs Lloyd moved here in the mid-seventies and have eight cottages and two flats. The cottages, with their thick sandstone walls and slate roofs, form an open square and offer a variety of accommodation from one bedroom to three, to sleep from four to seven or eight people. The two flats can sleep four people (Holly Tree) or up to nine (Rosemoor House). Cots and high chairs are available in every property plus other essentials such as baby baths, potties and safety gates for the chairs. Even a playpen can be supplied.

The kitchens are equipped to a very high standard with fridge-freezers, microwave ovens and crockpots, and the only items you need to take with you are towels and bedding for cots. As well as a television, you will find games (scrabble, jigsaws, and chess sets) in your cottage, books, guide books, maps and the Radio Times. There is a laundry in Rosemoor House.

The gardens surrounding Rosemoor are delightful. The cottages back on to an enclosed lawned garden with plenty of bright flowers. There is loads of space for children to play and the parents can keep an eye on them from the patios, which most of the cottages have. The views of the encircling countryside will delight the eye and, from another stretch of garden alongside the house, you see the lake below. This is part of a nature reserve, which was created by Mr and Mrs Lloyd and covers around twenty acres. There is a great variety of bird life to watch and a family of otters has occasionally been seen.

We were struck by the peaceful atmosphere of Rosemoor and also by the great care (and efficiency) which the Lloyd family apply to the running of it. Their prices, as they rightly point out in their informative brochure, offer excellent comparative value, especially in the off-peak periods.

Nearby: You can have a very active holiday here, if you wish, since there are so many amenities within easy reach. You can tackle the Pembrokeshire Coastal Path; go riding; play golf; and fishing is available on sea, lake or river. All sorts of water sports can be arranged and there are plenty of safe and sandy beaches in the vicinity: at Broad Haven and Marloes Sands for instance. Sightseers can have their fill of ancient castles, at Pembroke, Carew, Manorbier and Tenby; and St David's Cathedral should also be seen. There is a Marine Life Centre at St David's and a butterfly farm, and Manor House Wildlife Park is near Tenby. Oakwood Park, twenty minutes from Rosemoor by car, is an excellent amusement park and is recommended in the Family Welcome Leisure Guide.

Units: 10
Rent: £90 to £380 per week
Other costs: none
Plenty of cots and high chairs
Open all year

01749 677160

Nr Wells, Somerset   map 2

GLENCOT HOUSE, Glencot Lane, Wookey Hole – ☎ *Wells (0749) 77160.*

North west of Wells. Follow the signs for Wookey Hole. The hotel is signposted.

We were told about this hotel by a reader from Shropshire, Mrs Beattie of Little Wenlock, who recommended the excellent facilities and the friendly atmosphere.

Glencot House is a stylish Victorian mansion, in a splendid location in 18 acres of gardens and parkland alongside the River Axe. There is plenty of space for the children to play and for the adults to relax. It is a quiet and peaceful place.

The building has been faithfully restored during the last few years and the interior has been decorated and furnished with style. Antique pieces abound and some discretion must be exercised by younger children. The bedrooms have been done in different styles and have the benefit of marvellous views to the Mendip Hills.

The gardens are very relaxing and guests can fish for trout in the river.

WELSHPOOL

Indoors, there is snooker and pool, table tennis and a sauna.

Nearby: The charming city of Wells with its great cathedral is just over a mile away and the famous Wookey Hole Caves are just down the road. The Mendips offer superb walks and you can take in Cheddar Gorge and the less populated Ebbor Gorge. The nature reserve at the Chew Valley Lake is of great interest, as are the Tropical Bird Gardens north of Frome. Nunney Castle, the Fleet Air Arm Museum, Montacute House, Ham Hill Country Park, Cricket St Thomas Wildlife park and the cities of Bath and Bristol are all within easy reach.

✗ DINNER (7–9.30pm) £16: smoked salmon salad, soup, medallions of pork, pudding
Children: own menu, half portions
£ medium
Best Bargain Break 10% discount for stays of 5 nights or more (not during Bank Holidays)
Children: free up to 4 years: £10 from 4 to 10
Facilities: a cot and a high chair
11 rooms, 2 family, 1 set interconnecting
Open all year except Xmas   Access/Visa
No smoking in restaurant   No music
P – own car park

Welshpool, Powys   map 6

MOAT FARM – ☎ *Welshpool (0938) 553 179.*

On the A483 just south of Welshpool.

This is a very busy dairy farm of 250 acres, with 200 cows to be milked, morning and evening. There is, needless to say, plenty to interest visitors, especially children, who are welcome to watch all the farming activities. They must of course be in the care of an adult.

The farmhouse was built of brick in the 17th century and has had various additions over the years. The oak-beamed dining room has antique furniture including a Welsh dresser, and the lounge overlooks the large and grassy garden, which reaches down to the meadow. Beyond is the River Severn, which is quite narrow here.

You can play tennis and croquet in the garden, and the games room has a pool table. The river offers excellent fishing, and this is wonderful walking country, especially through the Severn Valley to the Breidden Hills and Long Mountain.

Nearby: There is Powis Castle, the Welshpool and Llanfair Light Railway, and market day in Welshpool is worth a look (Mondays). Further afield lies the

delightful countryside of South Shropshire where Clun, Ludlow and Church Stretton are well worth a visit. To the north of Welshpool you can reach Lake Vyrnwy and Pistyll Rhaeadr, "spout waterfall" in Welsh.

✗ DINNER (6pm) £7: soup, roast leg of lamb, pudding and cheese
Children: smaller portions
£ low
Children: one third up to 6 years; half rate from 6 to 12
Facilities: 1 cot and 1 high chair; baby sitting can be arranged
3 rooms, 1 family   Open March to October
No credit cards   Unlicensed
P – own car park

West Anstey, Yeo Mill Nr South Molton, Devon   map 1
PARTRIDGE ARMS FARM – ☎ Anstey Mills (039 84) 217.

Off the B3227 east of South Molton.
It was once a coaching inn, and has been in the same family since the early years of this century. It is now a working farm of 200 acres, and sits on the southern slopes of Exmoor. The house has rough cast walls, painted pink, with

WEST ANSTEY

honeysuckle climbing over them and the lawned gardens sport several apple trees and a lily pond.

The lounge has comfortable chairs and a sofa, a large oak-beamed fireplace, and paintings of wildlife and hunting scenes adorn the walls. There are no less than three charming dining rooms, one of which contains a small bar, which has been kept as it was in the 19th century.

The farmhouse has the great advantage of having a separate family suite in the grounds with a bathroom and a large bedroom which takes a double bed and bunk beds. Everything overlooks the encircling farm land, and guests are welcome to wander around among the cows, sheep, pigs, geese, hens, dogs, cats and ponies. The farm, by the way, has its own stretch of trout fishing. This is a delightful place for a family to stay.

Nearby: You are not too far from the North Devon and Somerset coastal resorts, including Woolacombe Sand and Croyde Bay. The whole of Exmoor is also at your feet – lovely for nature lovers, walkers, and pony trekkers. There is much else for the holiday maker within easy reach: the nature reserve at Braunton Burrows and the Exmoor Bird Gardens; the Maritime Museum at Appledore; Arlington Court; the Dartington Glass factory; Watermouth Castle and the Combat Vehicles Museum near South Molton.

DINNER (6.45pm) £8
Children: own menu, half portions
£ low
Children: nominal charge up to 5 years; then according to age
Facilities: 2 cots and 2 high chairs
7 rooms, 2 family   Open all year
No credit cards   No music
P – ample

West Bexington, Nr Dorchester, Dorset — map 2

MANOR HOTEL – ☎ *Burton Bradstock (0308) 897 785.*

Signposted off the B3157 coastal road between Bridport and Weymouth.

This 16th century stone manor house has a marvellous position in a small village in the lee of rolling downland overlooking Chesil Beach and Lyme Bay – popular for fishing but dangerous for swimming. But there is safe swimming to be had at Weymouth's sandy beach, which is also patrolled by lifeguards during the summer season. Rowing and motor boats can be hired, and there are traditional children's attractions such as Punch and Judy shows and a children's beach club.

The hotel has a good reputation for food and is very attractive, with its Jacobean panelling and flagstones. The dining room has a light, airy feel with large windows, large inglenook fireplace, freshly ironed peach tablecloths and old racing prints on the wall.

The cellar bar has white-washed stone walls, a beamed ceiling, and horse brasses and harness. A conservatory was added a couple of years ago to one end of the bar, and families are welcome to use this. Parents should note that there is always an excellent choice of real ale including such gems as Bishop's Tipple.

The gardens include a lawned area in front of the hotel with bench tables, and a bigger stretch, overlooking the sea in the distance, which has swings, a slide and a climbing frame.

WEST BUCKLAND

Nearby: You are on the verge of the lovely Dorset countryside, made famous by Thomas Hardy and his cottage can be seen near Dorchester. The Tutankhamun Exhibition is near there too, as is Athelhampton, the Tank Museum at Bovington Camp, T.E. Lawrence's cottage (Clouds Hill) and Maiden Castle. Nature lovers will head for Abbotsbury, with its famous swannery and the sea life centre at Weymouth.

✕ BAR SNACKS (12–2pm & 7–10pm) £2–6: West Bay scallops, liver & bacon, pork fricassée, courgette & tomato lasagne;
LUNCH (12–2pm) £13: fresh sardines, chicken supreme, pudding;
DINNER (7–10pm) £17: seafood hors d'oeuvres, noisettes of lamb, pudding & cheese
Children: own menu, half portions
£ medium
Best Bargain Break £90 per person 2 nights – dinner, b & b
Children: half price for under 10's
Facilities: 2 cots and 5 high chairs, and a baby listening system
13 rooms, 2 family   Access/AmEx/Diners
Open all year   No smoking in conservatory
• Ale – Wadworth's, Palmer's, Eldridge Pope
🅿 – own car park

West Buckland, Nr Barnstaple, Devon   map 1
HUXTABLE FARM – ☎ Filleigh (0598) 760 254.

Off the A361 east of Barnstaple.

This is a delightful listed building which dates back to the 16th century, a Devon long house built of stone and with climbing jasmine over the walls. The house has been restored with care by the owners, and antique furniture complements the low oak beamed ceilings, the screen panelling and open fireplaces with adjoining bread ovens. The rooms are comfortable and welcoming: the lounge looks over the garden, and guests can enjoy candle-lit dinners around the large oval table in the dining room. Children have their own dining room for breakfast and high teas, so that the adults can enjoy their meals in peace.

There is a games room in the garden, with table tennis and darts, and a quarter-size snooker table. There is loads of room for children to play, and swings, slides and a see-saw are set up in the garden. Sheep are reared on the 80 acres of farmland and children are welcome to help to feed the Shetland ponies and pygmy goats. The large fruit, vegetable and herb gardens provide most of the produce used in the house, and guests will be offered a glass of the farm's homemade wine. Mrs Payne is an excellent cook who has won several awards.

WEST BUCKLAND

There are two family rooms, and each has a double and two single beds and a bathroom. A washing machine and a drier are also available to guests.

This welcoming and well-equipped farmhouse offers an excellent base for a family holiday.

Nearby: The coastal resorts of North Devon are fairly close and there are some excellent beaches to visit, especially at Woolacombe and Croyde Bay. The natural splendours of Exmoor are close and the Exmoor Centre is near Dulverton, a good starting point for walks. The Tarka Trail runs past the entrance to the farm. There is much else to see: Braunton Burrows, one of the largest nature reserves in Britain; Arlington Court; Watermouth Castle; Exmoor Bird Gardens; the Maritime Museum at Appledore; Dunster Castle and Combe Sydenham Hall, and Rosemoor Royal Horticultural Garden.

DINNER (7.30pm) £11: herb & liver paté, lamb korma, pudding and cheese
Children: own menu
£ low
Children: cot £5; extra bed £8
Facilities: 2 cots and 2 high chairs; baby alarms provided
6 rooms, 3 family   Open all year except Xmas
AmEx only   No music
No smoking in dining room   Unlicensed
P – ample

Westonbirt, Nr Tetbury, Glos   map 2

HARE AND HOUNDS HOTEL (Best Western) – ☎ *Westonbirt (066 688) 233.*

On the A433 south of Tetbury.
The gardens of this attractive Cotswold stone building, part of which started off as a farmhouse in the early 19th century, are a major attraction: ten acres of delightful gardens, with wide and smooth lawns, beautifully kept flower beds and hedgerows, and grand, mature trees. There is also a shady, walled garden outside the bar, with several bench tables.

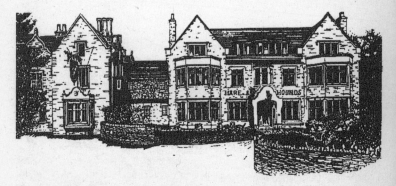

Other facilities include two hard tennis courts, a squash court, table tennis and snooker; and down the road is the famous Westonbirt Arboretum, which is open every day of the year.
A full range of meals can be found here, and there is a small area off the main bar where families can park themselves, as well as the lounge areas. The three course Sunday lunch offers pretty good value.
Nearby: The Arboretum is very close to the hotel and there is a variety of places to visit within a reasonable radius: Berkeley Castle, the Wildfowl Trust at Slimbridge, Lydeard Country Park, Corsham Court and Sheldon Manor. The Cotswold Water Park provides all sorts of water sports and has a nature reserve and an adventure playground.

BAR SNACKS (12–2.30pm & 7–10pm) £2–8: smoked Alderley trout, breast of chicken, steaks, pork chop;
LUNCH (12.30–2pm) £11: salami & orange salad, escalope of pork, pudding or cheese;
DINNER (7.30–9pm) £17: smoked halibut, soup, supreme of guinea fowl, pudding or cheese
Children: own menu, half portions
£ high

Best Bargain Break £88 per person, 2 nights – dinner, b & b
Children: free to age 16
Facilities: 3 cots and 2 high chairs; 5 baby listening lines
30 rooms, 5 family, 2 sets interconnecting
Access/AmEx/Visa   Open all year
• Ale – Wadworth's   **P** – own car park

Weymouth, Dorset   map 2

STREAMSIDE HOTEL, 29 Preston Road – ☎ *Weymouth (0305) 833 121.*

On the A354, just before the sea front.

The hotel was built in the 'thirties and the mock Tudor style was carried out rather successfully. The black and white facade, ablaze with flowers in tubs and window boxes and hanging baskets, is a cheerful sight. You will find a fresh and attractive interior and the Tudor theme is continued with beamed ceilings.

The garden has both lawned and terraced areas, with plenty of picnic tables and chairs and bench tables, and it overlooks a nature reserve. There is a swing in the garden. Indoors, there is a pool table, table tennis and darts.

Nearby: Weymouth has one of the safest beaches (it is patrolled by lifeguards throughout the summer), a broad sweep of sand which is overlooked by the fine Georgian houses on the esplanade. Dogs are rightly banned from the main beach areas. At the back of the beach is Lodmoor Country Park with its nature reserve. There is a Sea Life Centre in the town and many attractions within an easy drive: the Tutankhamun Exhibition, Hardy's Cottage, the Tank Museum at Bovington Camp, Athelhampton House, Corfe Castle and the Swanage Railway.

BAR SNACKS (12–2pm) £2–6: Cumberland sausage, spaghetti Napolitaine, grilled sardines, salade Nicoise, fillet of plaice;
DINNER (6.30–9pm) £10: smoked chicken, baked salmon in filo pastry, sherry trifle
Children: own menu, half portions
£ high
Best Bargain Break £230 per person, 7 nights – dinner, b & b
Children: cot £4; £6 from 4 to 7 years; £12 from 8 to 12
Facilities: 3 cots and 3 high chairs; baby listening to each room
15 rooms, 4 family   Open all year
Access/AmEx/Diners/Visa   **P** – own car park

Whimple, Devon   map 2

DOWN HOUSE – ☎ Whimple (0404) 822 860.

Off the A30, east of Exeter.

Down House is on the outskirts of the charming village, and sits in a quiet spot in the countryside, with views across to the Tiverton hills. It is a handsome Edwardian brick house, with large bay windows on all sides, and these contribute to the spacious and well-proportioned rooms. The main lounge, with its comfortable armchairs and fine marble fireplace, is an elegant room and its windows look out to the garden. Alongside is another large sitting room with a small billiard table, various games and a selection of books. Guests sit together around a large pine table in the dining room. The two family rooms have plenty of space: both accommodate a double bed and two singles with ease.

The house is surrounded by five acres of gardens, with spreading lawns and a fine display of flowers. There are some splendid mature trees, including a lovely red-leafed prunus. There is an orchard and a paddock – plenty of room for adults to relax and for children to play. The owners produce most of their fruit and vegetables organically in the garden, and also bake their own bread.

An extra facility offered to guests is temporary membership of a private swimming club; as well as the pool there is a sauna and a solarium.

Nearby: The coast is only a short drive away and there are many other places to interest all the family: the donkey sanctuary near Sidmouth and the Farway Countryside Park, Bicton Park, Killerton House, the castles at Bickleigh and

🍴 DINNER (6.30pm) £9: fruits de mer soup, chicken à la king, pudding & cheese
Children: half portions
£ low
Children: £2 linen charge per booking
Facilities: 2 cots and a high chair; a baby listening system
7 rooms, 2 family   Open March to October
No smoking in public rooms   Unlicensed
🅿 – own car park

Winchcombe, Glos   map 2
POSTLIP HOUSE – ☎ *Cheltenham (0242) 602 390.*

SC   *On the B4632, on the Cheltenham side.*

Postlip House was renovated a few years ago by Paul and Mary Sparks. You will now find an elegant Victorian manor house, built from honey-coloured Cotswold stone, and five very well-designed cottages which have been built in the outbuildings. There is also a ground floor flat in the main house.

The peace and beauty of the surroundings cannot fail to please, since the grounds are immaculately kept: smooth lawns, bright flowers and a fine collection of stately trees. There are lovely views of the neighbouring hills and the whole family can enjoy the spacious gardens. There is a wide expanse of lawn at the side of the house where the children can run and play freely. There is a slide and a climbing frame and a football net.

The cottages vary in size but, with the exception of Paddock Cottage which has one bedroom, they can accommodate 4 to 5 people. They are all equipped to the highest standards and you will not find any essential amenity lacking. They all have little patios or lawns, so that you can sit outside and enjoy the surroundings.

Mr and Mrs Sparks have in the past owned some highly-rated hotels and restaurants and one of the other bonuses of staying at Postlip House is the availability of freshly cooked dinners. A three course meal will cost you around £13 per person.

Nearby: The heart of the Cotswolds offers a great array of things to do and see. If you are interested in antiques this is a good area in which to browse; and Cheltenham, Stow-on-the-Wold, Broadway, Bibury and Bourton-on-the-Water are all within easy reach. Sudeley Castle is on the doorstep, as is Sezincote, Snowshill Manor, Batsford Arboretum and the Cotswold Farm Park. Bourton has a motor museum, a model village and Birdland, as well as several pubs and restaurants. Further afield you can visit the Cotswold Water Park and the Cotswold Wildlife Park.

WITHYPOOL

Units: 6
Rent: £160 to £440 a week. Two night breaks also available.
Other costs: none
Central heating: provided
2 cots and 2 high chairs
Open all year

Withypool, Somerset   map 1
WESTERCLOSE COUNTRY HOUSE HOTEL – ☎ Exford (064 383) 302.

Off the B3223, south west of Minehead. The hotel is signposted in the village.

The hotel sits just above the village in nine acres of gardens; there is plenty of space in which the children can roam. It is an agreeable, white-painted building, which began life as a hunting lodge in the 'twenties and has now assumed the mantle of a very comfortable and relaxing hotel.

If peace and quiet is what you seek this is an excellent place to be, surrounded by lovely countryside and with the whole of Exmoor, its moorland teeming with wildlife, to explore and enjoy.

We were impressed by the standard of the public rooms. There are two spacious lounges; one doubles as the reception area and the other has a good selection of books and a writing desk. They are nicely decorated and well furnished. The large conservatory is another agreeable place to sit; it is a comfortable spot and the bar is alongside. There is also a little terrace outside the windows.

We looked at several bedrooms, which have been decorated in a stylish and attractive way. They include a nice little single room which would suit an older child, and a splendid family room with a double bed built in an ingenious way against an old wooden pillar. This room also has a sofa-bed.

The gardens around the hotel are well maintained, with smooth lawns and mature trees. There are lots of animals in evidence – cats, chickens and donkeys – which should please the children; and the hotel has stables, so you can arrive on horseback, if you wish.

It is clear that the owners have put a great deal of care into this very appealing hotel, where families will be welcomed and where they will be very comfortable. There is, by the way, an excellent vegetarian menu.

Nearby: The hotel is right in the middle of Exmoor, a wonderful place to explore on foot or horseback. Birdwatching is a favourite pastime here and fishermen are very well catered for. The Exmoor Centre is just down the road at Dulverton. You can reach the coast to the north quite easily. If you like to see the sights there is plenty of choice: Combe Sydenham Hall, the West Somerset Railway, Dunster Castle, Fyne Court, Gaulden Manor, Knightshayes Court and Orchard Mill are all within easy reach. The restaurants at the two latter places are recommended in the Family Welcome Pub & Restaurant Guide.

BAR SNACKS (12.30–2.30pm) £2–8: smoked fish paté, beef & ale hot pot, Exe River trout, Somerset chicken, spicy bean casserole;
DINNER (7.30–9.30pm) £21: Exmoor smoked trout paté, roast leg of lamb, pudding & cheese
Children: own menu
£ medium
Best Bargain Break 10% discount, mid-week, for 3 nights or more (at certain times)
Children: free up to 3 years; half price from 3 to 14
Facilities: 2 cots and 2 high chairs; a baby alarm
10 rooms, 2 family   Open all year
Access/Visa   No music
No smoking in restaurant   P – own car park

Wix, Nr Manningtree, Essex   map 4

NEW FARM HOUSE, Spinnels Lane – ☎ *Wix (0255) 870 365.*

The village is off the A120 west of Harwich. In Wix take the road to Mistley and Bradfield and there is a sign to New Farm House.

This large modern farmhouse, at the hub of the fifty acres of arable farm, is very well equipped to welcome families. Of the twelve rooms, five are family sized;

there are several cots, a couple of high chairs, and there is also a baby alarm system. As well as a large and comfortable lounge with a television, there is a quiet lounge where guests can read or write. There are facilities to make tea and coffee in all the rooms, and a small kitchen which guests can use.

There is loads of room in the garden, which has a play area with swings and slides, and ample space for an impromptu game of cricket or football. If the weather is unkind the Mitchell family can provide board games to keep the children (and the adults) amused.

Nearby: Wix is surrounded by open farming country and there are delightful walks to be done, perhaps to the lovely Mistley, which has the largest population of mute swans in Britain. Castle House, the home of Alfred Munnings whose paintings are on show there, is at nearby Dedham, while Flatford was the home of John Constable, and children can feed the ducks at Flatford Mills. Other local attractions include Beth Chatto Gardens, St. Osyth's Priory, the wildlife sanctuary at Fingringhoe Wick, Abberton reservoir which is a great haven for birds of all varieties, and the zoo near Colchester.

 DINNER (6.30–7.30pm) £9
Children: half portions
£ low
Children: free up to 2 years; from £4 to £14 according to age
Facilities: 4 cots and 3 high chairs; baby listening system
12 rooms, 5 family   Open all year
Access/Visa   Unlicensed
P – own car park

Woolacombe, Devon   map 1
DEVON BEACH HOTEL, The Esplanade – ☎ *Woolacombe (0271) 870 449.*

H/SC   *On the coast road.*

The hotel's prices are inclusive of a six-course dinner and represent excellent value for families, but there are so many combinations of rates according to type of room and season that you must study the brochure and tariff to get an accurate idea. The hotel has plenty of family rooms, cots and high chairs, and a baby listening system.

The hotel is a modern-looking building with a sun terrace standing high above Woolacombe Bay with its sandy sheltered beaches. It has an indoor heated swimming pool and a games room with a pool table, table tennis and various machines. A washing machine and a drier are also made available to guests.

There are splendid views of the sea and the beach from all the lounges and the front bedrooms, and the hotel is well situated for all the holiday pursuits which are available: swimming, sailing and surfing; walking in the lovely countryside; or just lounging about.

WOOLACOMBE

Nearby: The beaches are wide and sandy and lifeguards patrol both Woolacombe and Croyde Bay beaches during the summer. There is a great range of other attractions within easy reach: Watermouth Castle and Arlington Court; the nature reserve at Braunton Burrows and Exmoor Bird Gardens; the Exmoor Park Centre; Dartington Glass; and the Combat Vehicles Museum near Barnstaple.

✗ BAR SNACKS (12.15–2pm) £1–3: ploughman's, jacket potatoes, salads, scampi & chips;
DINNER (7–8.30pm) £10: salmon ramekin, soup, roast turkey, pudding and cheese
Children: own menu, half portions
£ low
Best Bargain Break £24 per person per night – dinner, b & b
Children: from £4 to £23 per day (including meals)
Facilities: as many cots and high chairs as needed; baby listening system in every room
33 rooms, 17 family, 3 sets interconnecting
Closed end-Oct to Easter   Access/Visa
No smoking in one lounge   🅿 – car park

SELF-CATERING
The hotel has a penthouse apartment which can accommodate up to seven people. The lounge and one bedroom have sun terraces and every room has lovely views out to sea. The terms, which include linen, heating, etc, range from £150 to £400 per week for four people (an extra person is charged at £40 a week).

WOOLACOMBE BAY (Best Western) – ☎ *Woolacombe (0271) 870 388.*

H/SC *This resort has a magnificent stretch of beach and a lovely setting amid rolling hills. This large, traditional seaside hotel, smartly decorated inside, offers a great number of facilities for families. There is an indoor heated pool and an outdoor heated one with a flume slide; two hard tennis courts; three squash courts; a fitness room; a billiards room; and a pitch and putt course on a large stretch of grass at the front of the hotel. In addition there is a sauna, two solariums and a spa bath, and you can play short mat bowls. The hotel also has a motor yacht for charter.*

The bistro and coffee shop is open all day for meals and snacks, and also serves a three course carvery menu in the evening for well under £10. The full dinner menu in the restaurant is pretty good value, too.

Nearby: Woolacombe has a three mile stretch of sands and there are other excellent beaches nearby, including Croyde Bay and Saunton, where there is a superb golf course. If you are interested in the natural world you should visit Braunton Burrows, one of Britain's largest nature reserves and the Exmoor Bird Gardens should also appeal to the children. Watermouth Castle is great fun for youngsters, while the adults will perhaps favour a visit to Arlington Court. The beauties of Exmoor are not far away and the Exmoor Centre is near Dulverton and is a good starting point for walks.

✕ BISTRO (10am–10pm) £1–6: selection of hot & cold snacks;
DINNER (7.30–9pm) £16: 7 course menu
Children: own menu, half portions
£ high
Best Bargain Break £100 per person, 2 nights – dinner, b & b
Children: from free to £53 depending on age and season
Facilities: as many cots and high chairs as required; baby listening to every room
59 rooms, 13 family, 11 sets interconnecting
Closed January   Access/AmEx/Diners/Visa
• Ale – Bass   No music
P – own car park

SELF-CATERING

The hotel can also offer nearly forty self-catering apartments. They sleep from two to eight people and range in price from £195 to £1050 per week. All the facilities of the hotel can be used, and cots and high chairs and baby listening are made available.

Worfield, Nr Bridgnorth, Shropshire   map 6
OLD VICARAGE HOTEL – ☎ Worfield (07464) 497.

Off the A454 east of Bridgnorth.

This large red-brick house was built in 1905 and was bought from the Church Commissioners by Mr and Mrs Iles over a decade ago. It is a small and very comfortable hotel; there are some fine antique pieces, and the walls display watercolours and engravings. The small lounge bar is a relaxing place to have a drink, as is the spacious conservatory, full of plants and with excellent views of the countryside.

Hotels often claim that their bedrooms are individually designed, and this is certainly true at the Old Vicarage. The rooms in the coach house have a touch of luxury and those on the ground floor have a little private garden.

The hotel garden is safely enclosed and has spreading lawns and several mature trees. There is plenty of space for children to play and some swings have been installed for them.

Nearby: South Shropshire is a lovely part of the world with so many attractive villages and towns: Church Stretton and the Carding Mill Valley, Clun with its castle, Ludlow and Bridgnorth, which has a motor museum. Within an easy distance you can visit the Ironbridge Gorge Museum, the Severn Valley

Railway, Wilderhope Manor, the Safari Park at Bewdley, Wyre Forest and the Aerospace Museum at Cosford.

✕ DINNER (7–9pm) £18: curried leek & parsnip soup, fillet of pork, pudding or cheese
Children: half portions
£ high
Best Bargain Break £85 per person, 2 nights – dinner, b & b
Children: £13 up to 8 years; £25 from 8 to 14 (includes meals)
Facilities: 2 cots and 1 high chair; 1 baby listening line
14 rooms, 2 family   Open all year
Access/AmEx/Diners/Visa   No smoking in restaurant
🅿 – own car park

York, North Yorks   map 10
DISRAELIS HOTEL AND RESTAURANT, 140 Acomb Road – ☎ *York (0904) 781 181.*

On the B1224, one and a half miles from the city centre.

A Victorian building which stands in its own substantial grounds with a wide expanse of lawn at the front and the back of the hotel, and there is plenty of space for children to play and for adults to relax. It is a quiet hotel with welcoming and hospitable owners and staff and has the advantage of being quite close to the centre of the city. There are several cots and high chairs and, apart from the two permanent family rooms, at least three others can be made up to accommodate a family.

We had a very complimentary report about the hotel from Jane Green, over from New Zealand with her family. She commented on the "helpful, friendly staff ... good food and service" and thought the hotel good value for money. We stayed there for a weekend a couple of years ago and entirely agree with her assessment.

Nearby: York is a fascinating and very attractive city with many places to see; the Minster as a start, the Treasurer's House, the Railway Museum, the City Art Gallery and the Jorvik Viking Centre. There is a great deal more within an easy drive including Beningborough Hall, Aldborough Roman Town, Newby Hall, Fountains Abbey, Ripley Castle, Shandy Hall, Castle Howard, Eden Camp and Flamingo Land.

✕ DINNER (6.45–9.30pm) £12: seafood cocktail, beef Chasseur, pudding or cheese
Children: own menu, half portions
£ high

YORK

Best Bargain Break £37 per person per night – dinner, b & b
Children: free up to 3 years, £9 from 4 to 15 years
Facilities: 3 cots and 3 high chairs; and a baby listening system
12 rooms, 2 family   Access/AmEx/Visa
P – own car park

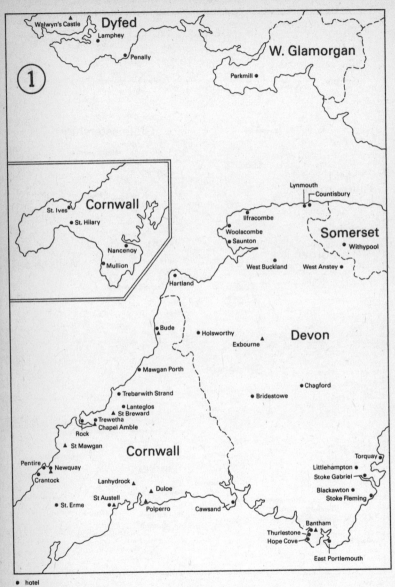

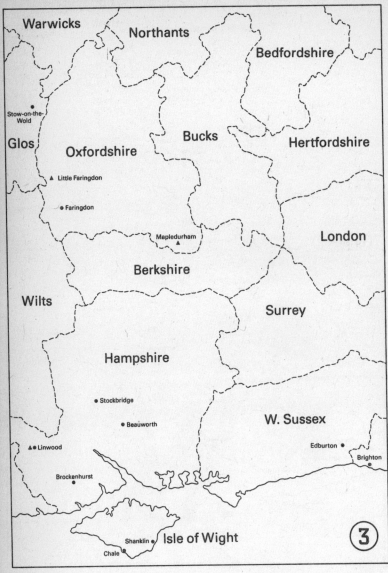

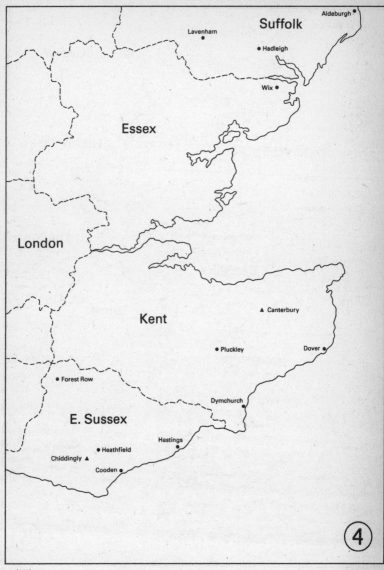

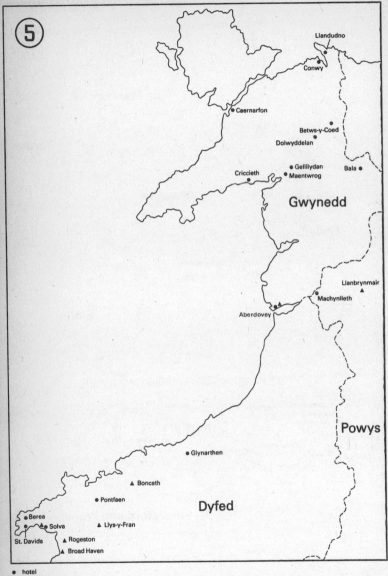

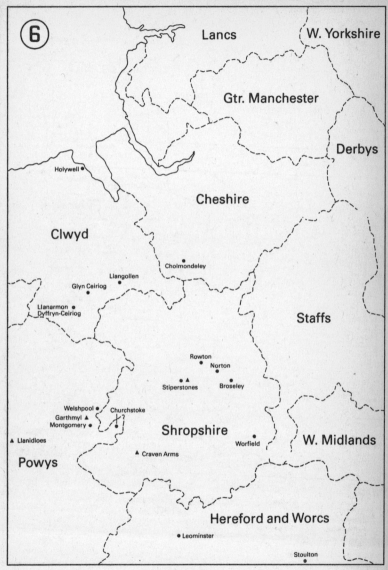

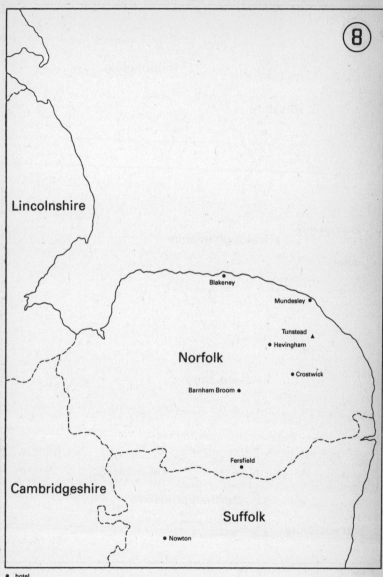

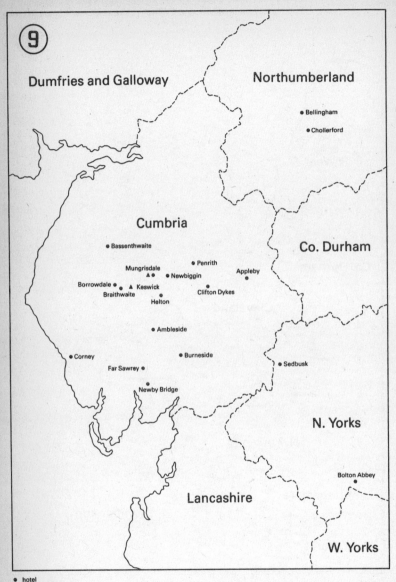

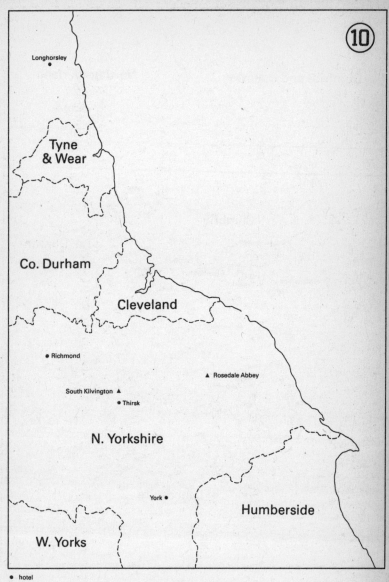

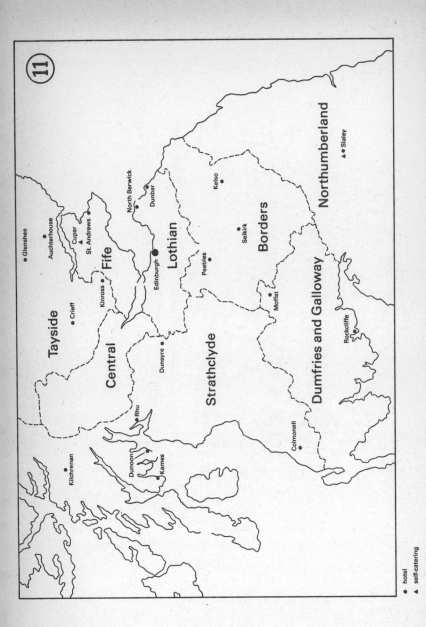

READERS' COMMENTS

Please use this sheet to recommend establishments which you think should be considered for the next edition of the Guide. The basic facilities we look for are:

    at least one cot and a high chair

    an evening meal (for hotel accommodation only, not self-catering)

Comments, adverse or otherwise, are welcome about any of the current *Guide's* entries.

To: The Editors, The Family Welcome Accommodation Guide 1992, c/o Hamer Books Ltd., Freepost, London SW13 9BR

Full name and address of establishment:

_____

_____

_____

_____

_____

Phone number:

_____

Comments

_____
_____
_____
_____
_____
_____
_____

Name and address of sender:

_____

_____

_____

_____

_____

We regret that we cannot acknowledge these forms, but they will be properly considered.

READERS' COMMENTS

Please use this sheet to recommend establishments which you think should be considered for the next edition of the Guide. The basic facilities we look for are:

at least one cot and a high chair

an evening meal (for hotel accommodation only, not self-catering)

Comments, adverse or otherwise, are welcome about any of the current *Guide's* entries.

To: The Editors, The Family Welcome Accommodation Guide 1992, c/o Hamer Books Ltd., Freepost, London SW13 9BR

Full name and address of establishment:

Phone number:

Comments

Name and address of sender:

We regret that we cannot acknowledge these forms, but they will be properly considered.

READERS' COMMENTS

Please use this sheet to recommend establishments which you think should be considered for the next edition of the Guide. The basic facilities we look for are:

at least one cot and a high chair

an evening meal (for hotel accommodation only, not self-catering)

Comments, adverse or otherwise, are welcome about any of the current *Guide's* entries.

To: The Editors, The Family Welcome Accommodation Guide 1992, c/o Hamer Books Ltd., Freepost, London SW13 9BR

Full name and address of establishment:

_____
_____
_____
_____
_____

Phone number:

_____

Comments

_____
_____
_____
_____
_____
_____
_____

Name and address of sender:

_____
_____
_____
_____
_____

We regret that we cannot acknowledge these forms, but they will be properly considered.

READERS' COMMENTS

Please use this sheet to recommend establishments which you think should be considered for the next edition of the Guide. The basic facilities we look for are:

    at least one cot and a high chair

    an evening meal (for hotel accommodation only, not self-catering)

Comments, adverse or otherwise, are welcome about any of the current *Guide's* entries.

To: The Editors, The Family Welcome Accommodation Guide 1992, c/o Hamer Books Ltd., Freepost, London SW13 9BR

Full name and address of establishment:

_____

_____

_____

_____

_____

Phone number:

_____

Comments

_____

_____

_____

_____

_____

_____

_____

Name and address of sender:

_____

_____

_____

_____

We regret that we cannot acknowledge these forms, but they will be properly considered.

READERS' COMMENTS

Please use this sheet to recommend establishments which you think should be considered for the next edition of the Guide. The basic facilities we look for are:

    at least one cot and a high chair
    an evening meal (for hotel accommodation only, not self-catering)

Comments, adverse or otherwise, are welcome about any of the current *Guide's* entries.

To: The Editors, The Family Welcome Accommodation Guide 1992, c/o Hamer Books Ltd., Freepost, London SW13 9BR

Full name and address of establishment:

_____
_____
_____
_____
_____

Phone number:

_____

Comments

_____
_____
_____
_____
_____
_____
_____

Name and address of sender:

_____
_____
_____
_____
_____

We regret that we cannot acknowledge these forms, but they will be properly considered.

THE FAMILY WELCOME PUB & RESTAURANT GUIDE 1992
Jill Foster and Malcolm Hamer £7.99

THE FAMILY WELCOME LEISURE GUIDE 1991 Jill Foster and
Malcolm Hamer £5.99

Queen Anne Press offers an exciting range of quality titles by both
established and new authors. All of the books in this series are available
from:

Queen Anne Press Paperbacks
Cash Sales Department,
P.O. Box 11,
Falmouth,
Cornwall TR10 9EN.

Alternatively you may fax your order to the above address. Fax No. 0326
76423.

Payments can be made as follows: Cheque, postal order (payable to
Macdonald & Co (Publishers) Ltd) or by credit cards, Visa/Access. Do not
send cash or currency. UK customers: please send a cheque or postal order
(no currency) and allow 80p for postage and packing for the first book plus
20p for each additional book up to a maximum charge of £2.00.

B.F.P.O. customers please allow 80p for the first book plus 20p for each
additional book.

Overseas customers including Ireland, please allow £1.50 for postage and
packing for the first book, £1.00 for the second book, and 30p for each
additional book.

NAME (Block Letters) _____

ADDRESS _____

_____

I enclose my remittance for _____

I wish to pay by Access/Visa Card

Number _____

Card Expiry Date _____